T0203314

Modeling and Optimization of Air Traffic

Modeling and Optimization of Air Traffic

Daniel Delahaye
Stéphane Puechmorel

Series Editor
Narendra Jussien

WILEY

First published 2013 in Great Britain and the United States by ISTE Ltd and John Wiley & Sons, Inc.

ISTE Ltd
27-37 St George's Road
London SW19 4EU
UK

www.iste.co.uk

John Wiley & Sons, Inc.
111 River Street
Hoboken, NJ 07030
USA

www.wiley.com

Library of Congress Control Number: 2013936316

British Library Cataloguing-in-Publication Data
A CIP record for this book is available from the British Library
ISBN: 978-1-84821-595-5

Printed and bound in Great Britain by CPI Group (UK) Ltd., Croydon, Surrey CR0 4YY

Table of Contents

Introduction

This book presents the main research topics that we have worked on over the last 15 years. Research is a fascinating occupation that allows permanent enrichment of knowledge and sustains rich intellectual activity. Moments of doubt do arise when a problem seems impossible to solve, but this is intrinsically linked to one of the great advantages of research: the feeling of satisfaction when a solution is finally found. As researchers at the *Ecole Nationale de l'Aviation Civile* (French Civil Aviation University), our research activity focuses on the theme of air transport and, specifically, on the domain of mathematical optimization. It is always fascinating to look at real problems taken from the operational domain as their characteristics are often complex, representing a significant challenge with applicable results. When observing real situations, we note that they are often considerably different from theoretical models, and our mathematical tools are of limited use when attempting to tackle a complex problem as a whole. These practical problems present a certain interest for researchers as they require the development of new tools.

Our research focuses on issues linked to reducing congestion in airspace. These types of problems are generally not only found in Western Europe and the United States, but also in Asia.

Our main research topics in recent years have been the following:

1) *Optimization through Artificial Evolution.* The complexity of the problems which we have considered generally leads us to study the possibilities of stochastic optimization, in particular artificial evolution. We were fortunate enough to work for a long period with Marc Schoenauer (CMAPX[1]), who introduced us to this groundbreaking technique that simulated genetic evolution, following the principles laid down by Darwin, to optimize mathematical functions. Since then, we have continued to work on this technique, in particular in the context of application to real world problems. We have also introduced a number of modifications to the genetic algorithms in order to improve their performances.

Finally, we also designed a new principle for genetic algorithms working on state space domains that are evaluated using order statistics within a continuous framework. This new algorithm presents improvements in performance compared to the standard version.

2) *Sectorization of airspace.* Using a set of airplane trajectories across a country or a continent that requires control of the airspace, sectorization consists of determining an optimal three-dimensional (3D) division of the airspace in order to balance the levels of control acrivity required for each sector and to minimize the number of times trajectories cross the sector borders, at the same time respecting a number of operational constraints.

---

1 Applied Mathematics Laboratory of Ecole Polytechnique.

We began working on this project using a two-dimensional (2D) modeling in the form of a Voronoi diagram[2]. Subsequently, we proposed a discrete model allowing direct division of the network of airways. This project was then extended to take account of a dynamic framework for which sectorization adapts to variations in air traffic flow (e.g. seasonal variations). Finally, we proposed a 3D extension to both approaches, allowing us to synthesize the cylindrical sectors with polygonal cross-sections corresponding to the characteristics of operational control sectors.

3) *Route distribution and take-off slots*. When it is not possible to increase the capacity of a transport network, we need to adapt demand to capacity in order to avoid the congestion phenomena in the network. In the case of air transport, this leads us to look for optimal routes and take-off slots for all the flights using a given airspace over a fixed period of time. A project for looking into these issues was launched by the *Centre d'Étude de la Navigation Aérienne* (Air Navigation Research Center) in 1992, and was then continued by the Aero-Astro department at MIT under the direction of Professor Amedeo Odoni. The project consisted of seeking the optimal bi-allocation (routes plus take-off slots) for all flight plans in the US airspace (around 50,000) while respecting the objectives of airlines. Taking 10 routes and 10 slots, the number of possibilities with this type of problem are of the order $100^{50,000}$ with non-separable criteria, which leads us to look immediately to stochastic optimization. This work was extended at the CMAPX within the framework of a research co-supervised by Marc Schoenauer and Daniel Delahaye (PhD thesis of Sofiane Oussedik and financed by

---

2 In mathematics, a Voronoi diagram is a particular decomposition of a metric space determined by the distances of a discrete set of objects in space, generally a discrete set of points.

Eurocontrol[3]). The results obtained during the course of this research demonstrated that it is possible, in a robust manner, to reduce the congestion by a factor of 2.5 across the entire French airspace by modifying the take-off times by ± 15 min with a maximum increase of 10% in the length of routes. Based on the target plan, which would create substantial reductions in congestion, we needed to find effective means for encouraging users to adopt this solution. This was the subject of another piece of research, carried out at ONERA, Toulouse (the PhD thesis entitled "Optimization of congestion pricing leading to system balancing, with user fairness" was written by Karine Deschinkel and co-supervized by Jean-Loup Farges).

4) *Modeling airspace congestion.* In the context of airspace sector design problems or traffic assignment problems, the measurements of operational congestion used to construct the objective function are not sufficient enough to correctly reflect the difficulty of managing traffic situations. The operational capacity of a control sector is measured by the maximum number of flights that may cross the sector in a given period of time. This measurement does not take into account the direction of the traffic, treating geometrically structured and disordered traffic in the same way. Thus, in certain situations, a controller may continue to accept traffic even though the operational capacity has been reached (structured traffic); in other cases, a controller may need to prevent the airplanes even though the operational capacity has not been reached (disordered traffic). Thus, the measurement using the number of airplanes per unit of time is insufficient to reflect the levels of difficulty involved in a traffic situation. To refine this congestion measurement, we propose the following three approaches:

---

3 European organization for the management of air traffic control.

– flow-based metrics;

– metrics based on the geometric distribution of speed vectors in the airspace;

– metrics obtained by modeling the air traffic using a dynamic system (linear or nonlinear).

The structure of this book broadly reflects the four main topics of our research:

1) optimization by artificial evolution;

2) sectorization of airspace;

3) route distribution and take-off slots;

4) modeling airspace congestion.

The main focus of our current research activity is on functional optimization using artificial evolution. The aim of this research is to synthesize a set of airplane trajectories (four-dimensional) allowing us to maximize or minimize a criterion. When dealing with a functional optimization problem (in a space of infinite dimensions), it is naive to attempt to discretize the trajectory in order to replace it in a state space of finite dimensions. This approach produces moderate results and it is preferable to search for a decomposition basis adapted to the problem in question. In the case of air traffic, for example, an airplane trajectory is a succession of segments of constant curve and torsion. For this specific case, we have developed a decomposition principle which allows effective and efficient synthesis of this type of trajectory using a limited set of coefficients. We may then simply run these coefficients using artificial evolution in order to synthesize the optimal trajectory. Other more traditional bases, such as wavelets and splines, may also be envisaged.

PART 1

Optimization and Artificial Evolution

Chapter 1

Optimization: State of the Art

In this chapter, we present the methodological principles involved in optimization, before introducing the main optimization methods used in an industrial context.

1.1. Methodological principles in optimization

This section presents the main characteristics of modeling of industrial optimization problems.

1.1.1. *Introduction*

When faced with a real optimization problem, we must analyze the problem in a precise manner in order to choose the best method to use. Real optimization problems correspond to needs observed in industrial or operational contexts, and aim to improve the performance of an economic process connected with an operational company or management organization. In practice, these problems are identified by domain experts who wish to develop an optimization principle in order to improve the performance of a system.

1.1.2. *Modeling*

The first stage in the optimization process consists of modeling the real problem using a mathematical abstraction that is as efficient as possible (see Figure 1.1). Using this abstraction, it is possible to develop solution algorithms that can be executed on a computer. This optimization process produces a set of solution points, which can then be implemented in the real world. In the past, there were few choices of optimization algorithms and it was necessary to use models that were somewhat different from reality but for which solution methods existed. Therefore, the solutions produced could be different from the true solution in the real world. A classic example involves linear programming (LP) for which we have efficient solution algorithms, but which requires linear modeling of the problem.

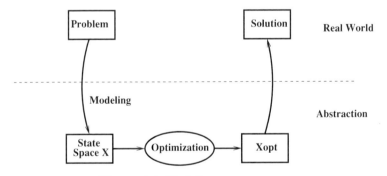

Figure 1.1. *Modeling process*

The modeling stage, then, consists of characterizing the state space and the objective space.

1.1.2.1. *State space*

The state space represents the set of parameters of the system upon which we may act in order to optimize one (or more) objective(s). Examination of the properties of the state space then helps us in choosing a suitable optimization method.

In most industrial optimization problems, the variables of the state space must remain within a subdomain defined by a set of constraints. We obtain the following general model:

$$\begin{cases} \min y = f(\vec{x}) \\ \vec{x}_{opt} \in \mathcal{A} \subset \mathcal{X} \end{cases}$$

where $\mathcal{X}$ is the state space and $\mathcal{A}$ is the feasible space bounded by the constraints. By studying the properties of $\mathcal{X}$ and $\mathcal{A}$, we can determine certain characteristics of the solution algorithm. Thus, the properties of connectivity and convexity of the admissible domain $\mathcal{A}$ are extremely important in the right choice of an optimization method. Within the group of convex state spaces, there is an extremely interesting subclass for which the admissible domain is bounded by a set of hyperplanes making up a polytope. If, moreover, the criterion is linear, then we have a linear optimization problem for which we may use the Danzig simplex method, for example. In the same way, the properties of connectivity of the state space determine whether or not it will be necessary to allow the optimization method to violate constraints in order to transit from one component to another to finally reach the optimum solution.

Based on the nature of state variables, we may classify the industrial optimization problems into three categories:

1) *continuous problem*

$$\mathcal{X} = \mathcal{U}_1 \times \mathcal{U}_2 \times ... \times \mathcal{U}_m$$
$$\mathcal{U}_i \subset \mathbb{R} \, i = 1, 2, .., m$$

We talk of optimization in a functional space when m is infinite (as in the case of trajectory optimization).

2) *discrete problem*

$$\mathcal{X} = \mathcal{I}_1 \times \mathcal{I}_2 \times ... \times \mathcal{I}_n$$
$$\mathcal{I}_i \subset \mathbb{Z}\, i = 1, 2, .., n$$

3) *mixed problem*

$$\mathcal{X} = \mathcal{U}_1 \times \mathcal{U}_2 \times ... \times \mathcal{U}_m \times \mathcal{I}_1 \times \mathcal{I}_2 \times ... \times \mathcal{I}_n$$

Mixed problems are the most difficult of the three classes to work with.

For certain problems, it is possible to voluntarily limit the feasible space by eliminating *a priori* the subdomains which we know will not contain the optimum. This restriction may be more or less accurate based on the information available for the specific problem. If, for example, we wish to optimize a firing angle to maximize the distance achieved by a projectile, we clearly need only to look at angles between 0 and $\frac{\pi}{2}$ (initial firing angle in relation to the ground). This type of reasoning is extremely useful in optimization algorithms as it avoids unnecessary exploration of some areas of the state space. It arises from a more general concept, which may be summarized as follows: the more we can bring information to the solution algorithm, the better this algorithm will perform.

One very important point characterizing the state space is its dimension. Generally, the higher the dimension n of $\mathcal{X}$, the harder it will be to find the optimum.

Optimization algorithms are implemented in a programming language which runs on a computer. Computer memory is always limited, in spite of significant progress in the domain. Thus, if the memory representation of a point in the state space is large, certain methods will be hindered by this limitation, in particular those that use populations of points of the state space (e.g. genetic algorithms).

Finally, we may face problems for which the state space has an infinite dimension. This is the case for trajectory optimization problems, where simple sampling should be avoided as it produces moderate results. It is preferable to use suitable decomposition bases and return to an optimization principle in a finite space by controlling the decomposition coefficients. The major challenge with this type of approach is to find a base suited to the real problem under consideration.

1.1.2.2. *Objective space*

The objective space represents the set of criteria that we wish to optimize. Based on the dimension of this space, we can identify two classes of problems:

– Mono-objective problems: this is the simplest case, insofar as a single criterion needs to be optimized and enables a total order relationship between points of the state space in terms of the criterion. The objective function is thus a function of $\mathbb{R}^n$ in $\mathbb{R}$.

– Multi-objective problems: in this case, we need to optimize several criteria, associated with each point of the state space, simultaneously. The most critical aspect of such problems is linked to the loss of the total order relationship between the solutions. Effectively, the objective function is now a function of $\mathbb{R}^n$ in $\mathbb{R}^m$, where m is the dimension of the objective space. Let $\vec{x}_a$ and $\vec{x}_b$ be two points of the state space, with which we associate the objective vectors $\vec{y}_a$ and $\vec{y}_b$ for which each component needs to be maximized (for example).

Finally, to simplify, let us consider $m = 2$ and the following three cases:

Case 1	Case 2	Case 3
$\vec{y}_a = (5,8)^T$	$\vec{y}_a = (5,8)^T$	$\vec{y}_a = (5,8)^T$
$\vec{y}_b = (3,4)^T$	$\vec{y}_b = (7,9)^T$	$\vec{y}_b = (6,3)^T$

In the first case, the two objectives of the solution "a" are better than those of solution "b"; we may say that solution "a" dominates solution "b". The second case corresponds to the opposite situation: "b" dominates "a". In the third case, however, it is impossible to identify a dominant solution as one of the objectives is better in each solution; we may say that "a" and "b" are mutually non-dominant. In the case of multi-objective optimization, we look for these non-dominant solutions which, are grouped into a set known as the Pareto front.

These solutions are then examined by an expert in the domain of application in order to identify the best solution for implementation in the real-world context.

In the case of mono-objective problems, we may also characterize the objective space in relation to the optima of the criterion. We can then distinguish between two types of optima:

1) *Global optimum:* $\vec{x}^*$

$$f(\vec{x}^*) \leq f(\vec{x}) \ \forall \vec{x} \in \mathcal{X}$$

$\mathcal{X}$ completes the state space.

2) *Local optimum:* $\tilde{x}$

$$f(\tilde{\vec{x}}) \leq f(\vec{x}) \ \forall \vec{x} \in \mathcal{V}(\tilde{\vec{x}})$$

$\mathcal{V}(\tilde{\vec{x}})$ vicinity of $\tilde{\vec{x}}$.

Within the context of industrial optimization problems, we seek to determine global optima and try to avoid being stuck on local optima.

The convexity of the criterion for optimization is thus a fundamental characteristic used for the right choice of an optimization method. When dealing with a (strictly) convex problem, there is only one optimum; it is therefore possible to use a local method to identify this optimum. In the opposite case, this local method would determine a local optimum (often that is closest to the initial starting point).

For certain non-convex problems, the function to optimize may present several quasi-equivalent optima which we need to identify. In this case, we speak of a multi-mode function. This type of problem requires a multi-mode optimization method to extract these equivalent optima. These multi-mode problems are generally more difficult to work with.

The continuity of the objective function is also a determining factor in the development of an optimization principle. For continuous problems, it is easy to approximate the slope of the criterion and thus orient the method used for resolution. When the criterion slope is bounded throughout the state space, the state space is said to be Lipschitz in terms of gradient, which allows us to guarantee the convergence of certain optimization methods. In the opposite case, these methods can diverge strongly in zones of discontinuity. In the same way, if large zones of the state space present plateaus, these methods, which use slope for orientation, tend to be ineffective for these regions.

More generally, all optimization methods require variation in the criterion across the state space in order to be directed toward the optima. This is the principle of locality in optimization. One case in which this principle is not followed is a criterion which takes the form of a plateau, for which only certain points of the state space present isolated peaks (see Figure 1.2). In this example, no optimization method will be able to find these optima.

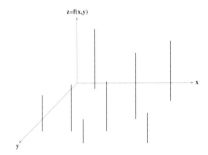

Figure 1.2. *Function for which the locality principle is not respected. Each vertical black line represents the peak of the function*

Another important point associated with an objective function is whether or not the function is bounded. This information allows us to define the termination criteria for certain stochastic optimization methods. These methods move through the state space in a random manner and do not ensure convergence to a global optimum for a given execution (proof of stochastic convergence is limited: the mathematical expectation of the set of solutions provided across multiple executions is equal to the global optimum of the function). Thus, if we know the value of the criterion at the optimum (and not its position in the state space), it is relatively easy to terminate a stochastic method by observing the value of the criterion for the current solution. If the value of the minima of a positive objective function is equal to zero, a stochastic method producing solutions with a value of the criterion close to zero is certain to be close to an optimum and may be terminated.

Consideration of the separability of the objective function also allows us to simplify the optimization algorithm. Let us take a function, $f(\vec{x})$, to minimize for the space $\mathcal{X}$. If $f(\vec{x}) = f\{g(\vec{x}), h(\vec{x})\}$ and if

$$\left\{ \begin{array}{l} min\ f(\vec{x}) \\ \vec{x} \in \mathcal{X} \end{array} \right. = f \left\{ \begin{array}{l} min\ g(\vec{x}) \\ \vec{x} \in \mathcal{X} \end{array} \right., \left. \begin{array}{l} min\ h(\vec{x}) \\ \vec{x} \in \mathcal{X} \end{array} \right\}$$

then the function f is separable. This property allows us to independently optimize functions g and h, which may be simpler to process. The most advantageous case is when g and h are functions for which the state spaces are orthogonal subspaces of $\mathcal{X}$ (state space of function f) with smaller dimensions. This reduction of the dimension allows the resolution principle to be accelerated.

The principles of evaluation of the criterion also enable us to select more or less suitable resolution algorithms. We may distinguish among three different types of cases:

1) Criterion accessible in analytical form: this is the most "comfortable" case, but is unfortunately rare in the context of real problems. By cancelling the associated gradient, it is sometimes possible to obtain an analytical form of the optimum (textbook case).

2) Criterion evaluated through numerical computations using real data: this is the most frequent of the three cases in which we attempt to extract additional information to guide the algorithm (gradient, Hessian, etc.).

3) Criterion evaluated using a complex simulation process: in this case, where evaluation of the criterion is often costly in terms of resources, it is not possible to obtain additional information and we use methods that do not need a criterion value in order to converge.

For certain problems, we also need to take into account the fact that the evaluation of the criterion is affected by noise and select a method that is not affected too much by such noise.

Finally, certain problems present dynamic criterion landscapes which require optimum tracking techniques. The timescale for the evolution of the criterion must be placed in a relationship with the time needed for the optimization algorithm to reach the optimum. If these two characteristics are of the same order of magnitude, we have an optimization problem with a dynamic criterion. Currently, only artificial evolution methods allow us to correctly solve this type of problem.

1.1.3. *Complexity*

The complexity of an optimization problem is linked to the number of operations needed to determine the optimum. In the case of combinatory optimization problems, we consider an instance of a problem of size n for which a resolution algorithm has been proposed. This algorithm will execute a number of operations K to process the problem. This number K is generally dependent on n. Based on the type of relationship between K and n, we can classify solution algorithms as follows:

Notation	Types of complexity
$O(1)$	constant complexity (independent of data size)
$O(\log(n))$	logarithmic complexity
$O(n)$	linear complexity
$O(n.\log(n))$	quasi-linear complexity
$O(n^2)$	quadratic complexity
$O(n^3)$	cubic complexity
$O(n^p)$	polynomial complexity
$O(n^p.\log(n))$	quasi-polynomial complexity
$O(2^n)$	exponential complexity
$O(n!)$	factorial complexity

In the same way, we classify optimization problems based on the best algorithms for their solution. Thus, we have a class of NP-hard problems, which cannot be solved using a known polynomial algorithm. An examination of the complexity associated with an optimization problem allows us to select an optimization method.

1.1.4. *Computation time*

Given that each optimization method requires a minimum computation time, it is important to be aware of the time we have available to produce a solution. As an example, in the context of an optimization problem concerning airspace sectorization, we have several months to produce a solution (6 months is needed before implementing a new sectorization). In the context of optimization of flight plans for a day, we have 24 h. To solve conflicts between aircraft, we have 3 min; finally, for a problem concerning satellite frequency allocations, we must produce a solution within 50 ms. In cases where this constraint is critical, we need to look for parallel methods. Two types of parallelism exist for methods using populations of points of the state space:

– Parallelization of criterion computation: this approach is advantageous in cases where the communication time between processors is low in relation to the time taken to compute the criterion.

– Islet parallelization: this allows effective parallel calculation, even in cases where criteria are computed rapidly.

1.1.5. *Conclusion*

When addressing an industrial optimization problem, we must respond to certain questions in order to create a suitable solution strategy:

– How can the problem be modeled?

- What objectives do we wish to optimize? (Mono-objective or multi-objective? Convex criterion? Linear? Quantified continuous? etc.)

- What parameters can (must) we act on? (Continuous or discrete state space? Large or infinite dimensions? etc.)

- What are the constraints? (Connected space? Convex space? Linear constraints? etc.)

– How much time do we have for the calculation?

– How much memory is needed for a point in the state space?

– How complex is the problem? (NP-hard?)

– Can we relate our problem to a known problem?

In the remainder of this chapter, we will discuss a number of solution principles used when dealing with industrial optimization problems.

1.2. Optimization algorithms

This section provides a concise overview of the main optimization methods by field of application.

1.2.1. *Introduction*

In what follows, the term "global optimization" will be used to refer to the search for global optima of the objective function. However, this term is somewhat ambiguous, as we often find the term "local search" in specialist literature, which refers to the search mechanism when it proceeds using successive neighbors. Thus, simulated annealing is a local search method (the tested solution is a neighbor of the current solution); from our perspective, this is a global optimization method (the method is, by principle, capable of determining the global optima of the objective function).

Optimization methods may be divided into two categories: local methods, which allow us to identify a local optimum, and global optimization methods, which are used to determine a global optimum.

Finally, depending on the mechanism used to move within the state space, we differentiate between deterministic and stochastic methods.

We will start with a description of local methods.

1.2.2. *Linear programming*

In the case of a linear problem, this method is able to determine a global optimum, but it cannot be applied to a general global optimization problem. For this reason, this method is classified as a local method.

LP is an extremely powerful operational research tool. A linear program is made up of a linear objective function and a set of constraints (equalities and/or inequalities) which are also linear. All linear programs may be written in the following canonical form:

$$
\begin{aligned}
\max z = \quad & \vec{c}^T . \vec{x} \\
s.c \quad A\vec{x} \leq \quad & \vec{b} \\
\vec{x} \geq \quad & \vec{0},
\end{aligned}
\qquad [1.1]
$$

where $\vec{c}$ and $\vec{x}$ are vectors of size n, $\vec{b}$ is a vector of size m and A is a matrix of size $m \times n$.

The feasible domain is then represented in the form of a polytope (simplex).

The simplex algorithm (presented for the first time by George Bernard Dantzig in 1947) allows us to solve LP problems by first creating a feasible solution, which is a vertex of a polytope, then moving along the edges of the polytope in order to reach vertices for which the value of the objective is increasingly high, until the optimum is reached (in the case of a maximization).

While this algorithm is effective in practice and guarantees that the optimum will be found, it does not always behave in a satisfactory manner in the worst cases. It is possible to create an LP for which the simplex method requires an exponential number of steps as a function of the size of the problem. Thus, the question of whether LP was an NP-complete or a polynomial problem remained unresolved for a number of years.

The first polynomial algorithm for LP was proposed by Leonid Khachiyan in 1979.

However, the practical effectiveness of Khachiyan's algorithm is disappointing, and the simplex algorithm nearly always performs better. Nevertheless, this result encouraged research into interior point methods. Unlike the simplex algorithm, which only considers the edges of the polytope defined by constraints, interior point methods operate inside the polytope.

In 1984, N. Karmarkar [KAR 84] developed the projective method. This was the first algorithm to be effective in both theory and practice. In the worst cases, its complexity is polynomial and experiments using practical problems have demonstrated that the method can reasonably be compared to the simplex algorithm.

1.2.3. *Nonlinear programming (NLP)*

1.2.3.1. *Methods of order zero*

The Nelder–Mead method is a local optimization algorithm developped by Nelder and Mead in 1965 [NEL 65]. This method uses the concept of the simplex, which is a polytope with $N + 1$ vertices in a space of N dimensions. Let N be the dimension of the state space. We therefore begin with a simplex of this space. In the case of a minimization, the method consists of replacing the point of the simplex with the highest objective value (the least satisfactory point) by testing several movements (reflection, expansion, contraction, etc.).

For application, this method only requires the value of the criterion at certain points in the state space, with no other information. It is therefore suited to the criteria that are non-derivable or for which the calculation of an approximation of a gradient would be very costly. Moreover, the method is not particularly sensitive to noise around this criterion, making it robust. See [CON 09] and [KAR 07] for more detail on this method.

1.2.3.2. First-order methods

To apply this type of local method, we require the gradient (or an approximation of the gradient) of each point of the state space. In the context of a minimization, the principle of these methods consists of moving in an iterative manner in the opposite direction to the gradient (or another descending direction) at the level of the current point. This is equivalent to replace the function f by its local linear model:

$$f(\vec{x} + \vec{h}) = f(\vec{x}) + \nabla_f(\vec{x}).\vec{h} + o(\|\vec{h}\|)$$

Supposing we start from point $\vec{x}_n$, the following point is given by:

$$\vec{x}_{n+1} = \vec{x}_n - \mu \nabla_f(\vec{x}_n)$$

with $\mu > 0$ as the parameter of the algorithm. We therefore verify:

$$f(\vec{x}_{n+1}) = f(\vec{x}_n) - \mu \|\nabla_f(\vec{x}_n)\|^2 + o(\mu \|\nabla_f(\vec{x}_n)\|)$$

which implies the reduction of f for a sufficiently small μ. This method is often modified by allowing μ to vary with each iteration

$$\vec{x}_{n+1} = \vec{x}_n - \mu_n \nabla_f(\vec{x}_n)$$

Variants of this algorithm differ in the choice of direction of descent and in the step size μ_n. These methods converge slowly on functions which are very different to the linear model [BER 99, NOC 06].

1.2.3.3. Second-order methods

Here, we suppose that f is of the class C^2 and that we are able to calculate its second derivatives. The principle of this method consists of constructing, locally, a quadratic model $q(\vec{x})$ of function f and seeking the minimum $(\vec{x}^*)$ associated with the model. The point $\vec{x}^*$ thus becomes the current point for the following iteration.

In the vicinity of a point, $\vec{x}_k$, we therefore approach f by the quadratic function given by the second-order Taylor formula:

$$\begin{aligned} q(\vec{x}) &= f(\vec{x}_k) \\ &+ (\vec{x} - \vec{x}_k)^T . \nabla_f(\vec{x}_k) \\ &+ \tfrac{1}{2}(\vec{x} - \vec{x}_k)^T . \nabla_f^2(\vec{x}_k).(\vec{x} - \vec{x}_k). \end{aligned}$$

We thus obtain the following recursion (in the case where the Hessian matrix $\left[\nabla_f^2(\vec{x}_k)\right]$ is invertible):

$$\vec{x}_{k+1} = \vec{x}_k - \left[\nabla_f^2(\vec{x}_k)\right]^{-1} . \nabla_f(\vec{x}_k).$$

The Newton method is generally more efficient than the gradient-based approach and converges in one iteration on positively defined quadratic forms. However, the global convergence[1] is not guaranteed as the Hessian may not be invertible for certain points. The complexity of the algorithm increases following the cube of the dimension of the problems under consideration due to the inversion of the Hessian in the recursion.

In practice, we generally solve the following system: $\left[\nabla_f^2(\vec{x}_k)\right].\vec{d}_k = -\nabla_f(\vec{x}_k)$.

Variable metric (quasi-Newton) methods are a robust alternative to the Newton method. Initially developed by Broyden, Fletcher, Goldfarb and Shanno, the BFGS method (the name uses the initials of the four authors who discovered it, independently, in 1970) [BRO 70, FLE 70, GOL 70, SHA 70], allows us to construct a positively defined approximation of the Hessian matrix at each point of the state space. Global convergence is therefore guaranteed and occurs considerably faster than when using the gradient algorithm. For large-scale problems, a limited memory variation exists: LM-BFGS [NOC 80].

1.2.4. *Local methods subject to constraints*

Let us consider the following problem:

$$\min f(\vec{x})$$
$$s.c \ g_i(\vec{x}) \leq 0$$

1.2.4.1. *Projection method*

In this case, the direction of descent $\vec{\delta}_x$ is calculated using a method without constraints. If the result is then found to fall outside the domain, we project the point onto the constraints. In practice, we may face the following difficulties:

---

1 Convergence for any initial point.

– calculation of the direction of projection;

– if several constraints are saturated, how should we choose the one on which to project?

– difficulties of projection onto nonlinear constraints.

1.2.4.2. *Linearization of the problem*

In this case, we linearize the criterion and the constraints.

$$\begin{cases} f(\vec{x} + \vec{\delta_x}) \simeq f(\vec{x}) + \left(\vec{\nabla}_{\vec{x}}f\right)^{T} \vec{\delta_x} \\ g_i(\vec{x} + \vec{\delta_x}) \simeq g_i(\vec{x}) + \left(\vec{\nabla}_{\vec{x}}g_i\right)^{T} \vec{\delta_x} \leq 0 \end{cases}$$

We then return to the following problem:

Minimization of $\left(\vec{\nabla}_{\vec{x}}f\right)^{T} \vec{\delta_x}$ in relation to $\vec{\delta_x}$ with constraints:

$$\vec{d}_{xmin} \leq \vec{\delta_x} \leq \vec{d}_{xmax}$$

1.2.4.3. *Penalizations*

The penalization method consists of optimizing a new function which takes into account the constraints:

$$\phi(\vec{x}) = f(\vec{x}) + \lambda(h(\vec{g}(\vec{x}))) \; \lambda > 0, \; h(.) \geq 0$$

Using the external penalization method, h is such that:

$h(\alpha) = 0$ if $\alpha \leq 0$
$h(\alpha)$ increases with α if $\alpha > 0$

$\Rightarrow$ if $\vec{g}(\vec{x}) \leq 0$ minimizing $f(\vec{x})$
$\Rightarrow$ if $\vec{g}(\vec{x}) > 0$, the added penalization term increases.

Using this method, it is possible that certain constraints may be slightly overstepped. If we wish to eliminate this possibility, it is better to use the interior penalization (see [BOU 68]).

1.2.5. *Deterministic global methods*

1.2.5.1. *Enumeration*

Enumeration offers an interesting alternative for discrete problems in state spaces of low dimension. This method consists of evaluating each point in the state space and identifying the point with the highest (or the lowest) criterion value. This is the only possible approach in cases where the locality principle is not respected (this principle indicates that it is possible to approximate (or calculate) a slope at each point in the state space). The use of this kind of algorithm is interesting when the number of points for evaluation is relatively small. In practice, however, many search spaces are too large for us to find all possible solutions.

1.2.5.2. *Branch and Bound*

This method was initially proposed by A.H. Land and A.G. Doigien in 1960 [LAN 60] in the context of solving linear problems using integers.

To apply this method, we need a lower bound (in the case of a minimization) of the criterion for any subspace of the state space $\mathcal{X}$ and a principle for dividing a subspace $\mathcal{X}_i$ into $K > 2$ subspaces $\mathcal{X}_{i1}, ..., \mathcal{X}_{iK}$.

If an optimal solution is found in subspace $\mathcal{X}_i$, it is not necessarily optimal for $\mathcal{X}$ as a better solution may be found later in the process when evaluating unexplored areas.

If the lower bound of a given subspace is greater than the best optimal solution found, the global solution will not be found in this subspace, and therefore exploration of this subspace may be stopped.

The Branch and Bound (B&B) principle is therefore as follows:

– Divide a problem into subproblems. We partition $\mathcal{X}$ into a finite collection of subsets $\mathcal{X}_1$, $\mathcal{X}_2$, ..., $\mathcal{X}_K$.

– Use bounds for the optimal cost in order to avoid exploring certain parts of the set of admissible solutions.

– The subproblems may be as difficult as the original problem. In such cases, the subproblems themselves are divided.

The success of this method largely depends on the precision of the bound associated with a subspace $\mathcal{X}_i$. Thus, the closer the lower bound $b(\mathcal{X}_i)$ is to the true minimum of $\mathcal{X}_i$, the more effective the method will be. The main field of application of this method is integer LP, which uses a bound based on the relaxation of the problem in real numbers computed using classic LP.

Interval arithmetic may be used to produce effective bounds for continuous state spaces. This particular form of B&B is known as "interval programming" [KEA 01].

B&B allows us to treat large-scale problems on the condition that we have a reliable boundary. In other cases, it is better to look to stochastic approaches. See Jaulin *et al.* [JAU 88] for more information on B&B method.

1.2.5.3. *The "Tunneling" method*

Alfufi-Pentini *et al.* and Levy and Montalvo [ALF 85, LEV 85] describe the foundations of this method, and Cetin *et al.* [CET 93] discuss the most advanced concepts in this domain.

Principle: the two following steps are carried out in an iterative manner:

1) Seek a local optimum $\vec{x}_{loc}$.

2) Eliminate $\vec{x}_{loc}$. To do this, we construct a tunneling function T *maximal* in $\vec{x}_{loc}$ and we carry out a local search on the new function T.

Drawbacks of the method:

– The tunneling function is difficult to create.

– Local minimization of the tunneling function is difficult.

– The method does not always produce the global optimum.

1.2.5.4. *Covering methods*

Principle: If f is *Lipschitz* with constant L, then:

$$\forall (\vec{x}, \vec{z}) \in \mathbb{R}^n \times \mathbb{R}^n | f(\vec{x}) - f(\vec{z})| \leq L||\vec{x} - \vec{z}||$$

thus, if we know the value of f at N points $\vec{x}_1, \vec{x}_2, ..., \vec{x}_N$ of $\mathcal{X}$ (search space), we can determine sets $\mathcal{X}_i$ ($i = 1...N$) such that:

$$\mathcal{X}_i \subset \{x \in \mathcal{X} | f(\vec{x}) \geq f(\vec{x}_i) - \delta\}$$

where $\delta > 0$ is fixed. Thus, if the points $\vec{x}_1, \vec{x}_2, ..., \vec{x}_N$ are chosen so that $(\mathcal{X}_1, \mathcal{X}_2, ..., \mathcal{X}_N)$ covers $\mathcal{X}$, so:

$$\mathcal{X} \subset \left(\cup_{i=1}^N \mathcal{X}_i \right)$$

then the global optimum $\vec{x}_{opt}$ is known with precision δ, that is:

$$\left(\min_{1 \leq i \leq N} f(\vec{x}_i) \right) - \delta \leq f(\vec{x}_{opt})$$

An important specific case:

$$\mathcal{X}_i = B(\vec{x}_i, \varepsilon) = \{\vec{x} \in \mathcal{X} / \|\vec{x} - \vec{x}_i\| \leq \varepsilon\} \; i = 1...N$$

($B(\vec{x}_i, \varepsilon)$ closed ball of center $\vec{x}_i$ and radius ε) then the problem is solved with precision $\delta = L\varepsilon$. Constant L, *a priori* unknown, is estimated by the algorithm. If we know the value of f at k points $\vec{x}_1, \vec{x}_2, ..., \vec{x}_k$, we may use:

$$L_k = \max_{1 \leq j \leq k} \frac{|f(\vec{x}_i) - f(\vec{x}_j)|}{\|\vec{x}_i - \vec{x}_j\|}$$

Advantages of the method:

– simple to implement;

– theoretically interesting;

– parallelizable method.

Drawback of the method:

– inefficient for large-scale problems.

1.2.5.5. *Continuous deformation methods*

The principle of continuous deformation methods consists of gradually deforming a function for optimization, f_0, toward the desired objective function f_1:

$$H(t, \vec{x}), \; t \in [0, 1]$$

$$\begin{array}{ccc} \min_{\vec{x} \in E} f_0(\vec{x}) & & \min_{\vec{x} \in E} f_1(\vec{x}) \\ f_0(\vec{x}) = H(0, \vec{x}) & \rightarrow & f_1(\vec{x}) = H(1, \vec{x}) \end{array}$$

Function H in the schema above is, mathematically speaking, a *homotopy*, i.e. a continuous function in the domain $[0, 1] \times E$. Intuitively, f_0 is continuously deformed into f_1 when t varies from 0 to 1. In practice, we ensure that f_0 only possesses a single optimum, which may be sought using an efficient local method. The difficulty therefore consists of finding a path $(t, \gamma(t))$ of $[0,1] \times E$ so that the following property verifies:

$$\forall t \in [0,1] \,, \forall \vec{x} \in E \,, \, H(t, \gamma(t)) \leq H(t, \vec{x})$$

Intuitively, we know that all points of the path $(t, \gamma(t))$ are optimal for E. The starting point $(0, \gamma(0))$ is obtained by local optimization of f_0. The path $(t, \gamma(t))$ is constructed step by step.

It is not possible to construct the path $(t, \gamma(t))$ without additional hypotheses: we will presume that the homotopy H is such that $\frac{\partial H}{\partial x}$ is continually differentiable for $[0,1] \times E$. Using this hypothesis and a condition stating that the path must start at a minimum of f_0, we obtain:

$$\frac{\partial^2 H}{\partial t \partial x}(t, \gamma(t)) + \dot{\gamma}(t)\frac{\partial^2 H}{\partial x^2}(t, \gamma(t)) = 0.$$

The differential equation above allows us to construct the optimal path. The classic algorithms for solving ordinary differential equations may be used to obtain a numerical solution to the problem.

These methods are efficient for continuous state spaces and are most effective for molecular conformation problems in the pharmaceutical industry. For more information on these methods, see [DUN 05].

1.2.6. Stochastic global methods

1.2.6.1. Tabu search

Tabu search is a metaheuristic initially developed by Glover [GLO 86] and, independently, by Hansen [HAN 86], under the name *steepest ascent mildest descent*. This method is based on simple principles but is nevertheless extremely effective, combining a local search procedure with a certain number of mechanisms which prevent it from becoming blocked at local optima or from returning to zones which have already been explored [CHA 96, REE 95]. It has been successfully applied to a number of difficult combinatory optimization problems, including vehicle routing problems [GEN 94], quadratic affectation problems [SKO 90], sequencing problems [WID 89], graph coloration problems [HER 87], etc.

Basic principle: during the first phase, the tabu search method may be seen as a generalization of local improvement methods. Starting with any given solution $\vec{x}$ belonging to the set of solutions $\mathcal{X}$, we move towards a solution $s(\vec{x})$ located in the vicinity $\mathcal{V}(\vec{x})$ of $\vec{x}$. To choose the best neighbor $s(\vec{x})$ in $\mathcal{V}(\vec{x})$, the algorithm evaluates the objective function f at each point of $\mathcal{V}(\vec{x})$, and retains the neighbor which improves the value of the objective function f, or, in the worst cases, which degrades it the least.

The originality of the tabu method when compared to local methods, which stop when no more neighbors $s(\vec{x})$ exist which improve the value of the objective function f, lies in the fact that we retain the best neighbor solution even if this result is worse than the initial solution. This criterion authorizing degradation of the objective function, prevents the algorithm from becoming blocked at local minima, but it does introduce a risk of cycling. Effectively, when the algorithm has left any given minimum by accepting the degradation of the objective function, it may turn back on itself at the following iteration.

To solve this problem, the algorithm requires a memory in order to temporarily retain the trace of the last best solutions found. These solutions are declared *tabu*; hence, the name of the method. They are stored in a list of given length L known as the *tabu list* $\mathcal{T}$. A new solution will only be accepted if it does not feature on the tabu list. This criterion for the acceptance of new solutions prevents the algorithm from cycling during visits to a number of solutions, which is at least equal to the length of the tabu list, and directs exploration of the method toward unexplored regions of the state space.

The tabu list is generally generated as a *circular* list: at each iteration, we eliminate the oldest tabu solution, replacing it with the new retained solution. However, the coding involved in a list of this type is bulky as we must retain all the elements which define a solution. To counteract this constraint, the tabu list of forbidden solutions is replaced by a list of *forbidden transformations* preventing all transformations which are the inverse of a recent transformation. We thus obtain the following pseudocode:

1) calculate an initial configuration $\vec{x}$

2) $\vec{x}_{best} \leftarrow \vec{x}$

3) $f_{min} \leftarrow f(\vec{x}_{best})$

4) $\mathcal{T} \leftarrow \phi$

5) $k \leftarrow 0$

6) as long as $k < k_{max}$ then

    i) $k \leftarrow k + 1$

    ii) $\mathcal{C} \leftarrow \mathcal{V}(\vec{x}) - \{m(\vec{x}); \forall m \in \mathcal{T}\}$ (set of candidate configurations)

    iii) determine the element $\vec{y} = m_{\vec{x}\vec{y}}(\vec{x})$, which minimizes f for $\mathcal{C}$ ($\vec{y}$ is one of the non-prohibited neighbors of $\vec{x}$);

    iv) if $f(\vec{y}) \geq f(\vec{x})$ then add $m_{\vec{x}\vec{y}}^{-1}$ to list $\mathcal{T}$ (eliminating the oldest element of $\mathcal{T}$ if necessary)

    v) if $f(\vec{y}) < f(\vec{x})$ then
    - $\vec{x}_{best} \leftarrow \vec{y}$
    - $f_{min} \leftarrow f(\vec{y})$

7) return $\vec{x}_{best}$

This basic version can be improved by adding an aspiration criterion (temporary removal of the ban on accepting an elementary transformation), intensification principles (deepening of the search in certain regions of the domain) and diversification principles (which encourage exploration) [GLO 88, GLO 91, GLO 92].

In practice, we use a stochastic implementation of this method, which consists of using a stochastic neighborhood of the current solution (we randomly select a number $N < |\mathcal{V}(\vec{x})|$ of configurations in the vicinity of the current solution $\vec{x}$).

The tabu search is thus a simple method, which is easily adapted to all types of problems (discrete or continuous). It requires a list of past transformations, the management of which is the critical point of the method [GLO 88, GLO 91, GLO 92].

1.2.6.2. *Simulated annealing*

Simulated annealing [CER 85, KIR 83] originated in the domain of thermodynamics. This method arose from an analogy with the physical phenomenon of slow cooling found in metals in a state of fusion which leads to a solid, low-energy state. The temperature must be reduced slowly with steps which are sufficiently long for thermodynamic equilibrium to be reached at each temperature increment. For materials, this low energy results in a regular, crystal-like atomic structure.

The annealing process thus consists of bringing a solid into a low energy state after raising its temperature, a process which may be summarized in the following two steps:

– raise the solid to a very high temperature in order to reach the point of fusion;

– cool the solid, following a specific temperature reduction plan in order to reach a solid state with minimal energy.

During the liquid phase, particles are distributed in a random manner. The state of minimal energy is attained if the initial temperature is sufficiently high and the cooling time sufficiently long; if either of these conditions is not respected, the solid enters a metastable state of non-minimal energy (the opposite process to annealing is tempering, which consists of cooling a solid extremely quickly).

Algorithm

In 1953, Metropolis [MET 53] developed an algorithm to simulate the physical process of annealing on a computer. Given a current state i of energy E_i, a state is generated by applying a disturbance which transforms the current state into a new state.

– If $E_j - E_i \leq 0$, the state j is accepted as the new current state.

– If $E_j - E_i > 0$, the state j is accepted as the new current state with probability P_a:

$$P_a = e^{\left(\frac{E_i - E_j}{k_b T}\right)}$$

where T is the temperature and k_b is Boltzmann's constant.

The temperature influences the probability of acceptance of a higher energy state. For a high temperature, the probability of acceptance at any given movement tends toward 1: all changes will be accepted. If the cooling process is sufficiently slow, the solid assumes the state of equilibrium at each temperature increment. In the Metropolis algorithm, this equilibrium is reached by generating a large number of transitions at each temperature. Thermic equilibrium is characterized by the Boltzmann statistical distribution. This distribution gives the probability that the solid will be in a state i of energy E_i at temperature T:

$$P_r\{X = i\} = \frac{1}{Z(T)} e^{-\left(\frac{E_i}{k_b T}\right)}$$

where X is the random variable associated with the current state of the solid and $Z(T)$ is the distribution function of X allowing normalization:

$$Z(T) = \sum_{j \in S} e^{-\left(\frac{E_j}{k_b T}\right)}$$

In the simulated annealing algorithm, we can apply the Metropolis algorithm to generate a sequence of solutions in the state space S. To do this, we create an analogy between a multi-particular system and our optimization problem using the following equivalences:

– The admissible solutions represent the possible states of the solid.

– The function to optimize represents the energy of the solid.

We then introduce a control parameter C, which plays the role of the temperature.

Let C_k be the value of this parameter and L_k the number of transitions generated at iteration k. Using this notation, we can summarize the principle of simulated annealing in the following manner.

At the beginning of the process, the values of C_k are high, allowing us to accept transitions with major degradation of the criterion, thus exploring the state space in a homogeneous manner. As C_k decreases, only transitions which improve or barely damage the criterion are accepted. Finally, as C_k tends toward zero, no deterioration of the criterion will be accepted, and the simulated annealing algorithm behaves in the same way as a local search algorithm.

Algorithm 1.1. Simulated annealing

Require: $\vec{x}_i, C_0, L_0, k = 0$

    repeat

        for $l = 0 \to L_k$ **do**

            Generate a solution $\vec{x}_j$ from the neighborhood $S_{\vec{x}_i}$ of the current solution $\vec{x}_i$;

            If $f(\vec{x}_j) < f(\vec{x}_i)$, then $\vec{x}_j$ becomes the current solution;

            Otherwise, $\vec{x}_j$ becomes the current solution with probability $p = e^{\left(\frac{f(\vec{x}_i) - f(\vec{x}_j)}{C_k}\right)}$

        end for

        k=k+1

        Calculate (L_k, C_k)

    until $C_k \simeq 0$

The simulated annealing algorithm may be used to solve a large number of combinatory optimization problems with properties of stochastic convergence to an optimal solution, but presents the drawback of only working on a single point of the state space (something which is problematic in cases with several quasi-optimal solutions) and is not suitable for multi-objective optimization. See [AAR 89, ING 89, ING 96] for additional information on this technique.

1.2.6.3. *Stochastic Branch and Bound*

Principle: the principle of Stochastic Branch and Bound method is the same as the deterministic branch and bound method, with the use of statistical results in order to eliminate parts of the search area which do not contain the global optimum.

Let us take the following problem:

$$\begin{cases} \min f(\vec{x}) \\ \vec{x} \in \mathcal{X} \end{cases}$$

Let η be the random variable for which realizations are the values of f and of which the distribution function is F. We wish to find an estimator of the theoretical minimum M of the random variable η defined by:

$$\begin{cases} P(\eta \geq M) = 1 \text{ and} \\ \forall \varepsilon > 0 \ P(\eta \geq M + \varepsilon) < 1 \end{cases}$$

Under certain hypotheses on the function F, we can determine an optimal linear estimator of M, denoted M_N, using the N values of f in the sample $\kappa = \{\vec{x}_1, \vec{x}_2, ..., \vec{x}_N\}$.

We are also able to calculate the confidence interval of asymptotic level $1 - \gamma$ associated with M of the form:

$$l_{N,\gamma} = [\inf_{N,\gamma}(f), \sup_{N,\gamma}(f)]$$

where $\gamma > 0$ is fixed.

We thus obtain:

$$\lim_{N \to \infty} P[M \in l_{N,\gamma}] = 1 - \gamma$$

Advantages of the method:

– Robustness.

– The parameters N, γ, etc. are easily controlled by the user.

– Tests have shown a linear evolution of the number of points generated with the size of the problem.

This is widely recognized as one of the most effective methods.

Drawback of the method: there are currently no demonstrations of stochastic convergence associated with this method.

1.2.7. *Genetic algorithms*

Genetic algorithms are inspired by the theory of evolution proposed by Charles Darwin in the 19th Century.

According to Darwin's theory, a population of individuals evolves through the mechanisms of sexual reproduction. Those individuals who are best suited to their environment reproduce more than other individuals, thus promoting the most appropriate characteristics. For example, a giraffe with a longer neck than others of its species will have access to more food, and consequently has an improved chance of survival and reproduction. The descendants of this giraffe will also have particularly long neck, and the average neck length in the giraffe population will increase. An algorithm based on this theory was first proposed by John Holland in the early 1970s [HOL 75]. From a set of approximate solutions (the population), we select two good solutions and recombine them to produce a new solution. At the same time, we generate new genes using a mutation operator in order to promote exploration of the state space. In parallel with this process, we eliminate the least suitable solutions using a selection process. By repeating this process, the adaptation of the population increases and converges to a solution to the problem.

These algorithms will be discussed in greater detail in Chapter 2.

1.2.8. *Conclusion*

As we have seen, a wide variety of optimization algorithms exist, each suited to a certain category of problems. These algorithms may be classified into the following:

– Deterministic:

- local: LP and NLP;

- global: enumeration, B&B, continuous deformation methods.

– Stochastic:

- Global: tabu search, simulated annealing, evolutionary algorithms, stochastic branch and bound.

The associated performances are shown in table represented in Figure 1.3.

	Lin	N Lin	Cont	Disc	G Di	GLO	Mu M	Mu O
PL	●		●		●			
PNL	●	●	●		●			
BB	●	●	●	●		●		
TAB	●	●	●	●	●	●		
RS	●	●	●	●	●	●		
BBS	●	●	●	●	●	●		
HOM	●	●	●	●	●	●		
EA	●	●	●	●	●	●	●	●

Figure 1.3. *Comparison of performances of optimization. When a method can be used for a class of problems, a dot is shown where the line and column meet. The size of the point reflects how suitable the method is for the class of problems: the larger the point, the better suitable the method is for the specified problem type*

The top row of the figure represents the classes of problems:

– Lin: linear problem;

– N Lin: nonlinear problem;

– Cont: continuous state space;

– Disc: discrete state space;

– L Di: large dimension;

– GLO: global optimum search;

– Mu M: multi-mode search (problem with several quasi-equivalent optima);

– Mu O: multi-objective problem.

The column lists the main classes of optimization algorithms:

– LP: linear programming;

– NLP: nonlinear programming;

– BB: branch and bound;

– TAB: tabu method;

– SA: simulated annealing;

– SBB: sotchastic branch and bound;

– HOM: homotopic approach;

– AE: artificial evolution.

Chapter 2

Genetic Algorithms and Improvements

This chapter introduces genetic algorithms along with certain extensions we have developed.

2.1. General points

In this section, we present the basic principles of these algorithms.

2.1.1. *Introduction*

Work on genetic algorithms began in the 1950s when a number of American biologists generated computer simulations of biological structures. Later, between 1960 and 1970, J. Holland [HOL 75], using previous work as a starting point, developed the fundamental principles of genetic algorithms in the context of mathematical optimization. Unfortunately, the computers of that time were insufficiently powerful for genetic algorithms to be used for large-scale real problems. A seminal work by Goldberg [GOL 89], describing the use of these algorithms in solving concrete problems, increased knowledge of genetic algorithms in the general scientific community and marked the beginning of a new wave of interest in this optimization technique. At the same time, a number of similar techniques were developed. Notable examples include:

– Evolution strategy [SCH 95];

– Evolutionary programming [FOG 94];

– Genetic programming [KOZ 92].

The mathematical theory associated with genetic algorithms developed concurrently, but remained limited when faced with the theoretical complexity resulting from these algorithms. A demonstration of stochastic convergence was finally established in 1993 [CER 94, FRE 83].

Genetic algorithms simulate the process of natural selection in a hostile environment linked to the problem under consideration [DAV 91]. They use a vocabulary similar to that found in natural genetics, without neglecting the fact that the underlying principles involved in the two domains are considerably more complex in their natural context. We thus refer to individuals in a population, and often individuals will be reduced to a single chromosome. These chromosomes themselves are made up of genes that contain the hereditary characteristics of the individual. We also use principles of selection, crossing (crossover), mutation, etc.

In the context of optimization, each individual represents a point in the state space to which we associate the value of the criterion to optimize. We then randomly generate a population of individuals from which the genetic algorithm aims to select the best specimens while ensuring efficient exploration of the state space.

Genetic algorithms may be applied in a wide variety of situations. They have produced strong results in problems associated with scheduling [KHU 94], adaptive control [FLO 93], business travel [HOM 93], transportation [YIN 91], shape synthesis [WAT 93], neuron networks [SCH 93b], molecular synthesis [UNG 93], the medical field [FOR 93], filtering   [SCH 93a,   BAL 93],   air   traffic   control [ALL 93, DEL 94a, DEL 94c, DEL 95b, DUR 94a], etc.

2.1.2. *Principle of genetic algorithms*

The steps of operations used in genetic algorithms are shown in Figure 2.1.

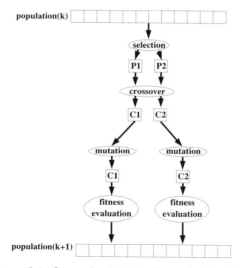

Figure 2.1. *General principle of genetic algorithms*

1) We begin by generating a population of individuals in a random fashion.

2) Two parents are then selected (P_1 and P_2) based on their fitness (performance). We then randomly apply the crossover

operator[1] with a probability P_c, which generates two children C_1 and C_2. We then modify some genes of C_1 and C_2 by applying the mutation operator[2] with the probability P_m, producing two new individuals C_1' and C_2'. We evaluate the fitness of these new individuals before inserting them into the new population. In the following, we reiterate the selection, crossover and mutation operations in order to complete the new population, thus creating a new generation.

We then repeat the loop N times for step 2 (where N is a parameter representing the total number of generations).

A different form, which is also used, includes an intermediary population. In this case, we begin by carrying out selection at global level, then apply recombination operators to the selected individuals (see Figure 2.2).

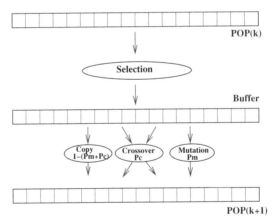

Figure 2.2. *Other equivalent form*

To use a genetic algorithm for a specific problem, we require the following six elements:

---

1 The purpose of the crossover operator is to randomly recompose the genes of the parents to generate children.

2 The mutation operator allows the creation of new genes in the population.

1) A chromosome coding principle. This step connects each point of the state space with a data structure synthesizing all the information associated with these points; it must therefore take place after the mathematical modeling phase (see Figure 2.3).

2) A mechanism for generating the initial population. This mechanism must be capable of producing a uniformly distributed population of individuals, which will act as a basis for future generations.

3) A criterion used to determine the suitability of an individual in relation to its environment in order to differentiate between individuals. In the context of genetic algorithms, the criterion to optimize is referred to as *fitness*.

4) A selection principle allowing statistical identification of the best individuals. This principle must regulate the selective pressure that promotes the fittest individuals to a variable degree in an effective manner.

5) Operators used to diversify a population over generations by exploring the state space. In general, two operators are used: crossover and mutation. Crossover is used to mix the genes of individuals in the population, whereas mutation is used to generate new genes. The suitability of the coding principle and of these operators in relation to a specific problem will determine the success or failure of a genetic algorithm, and we have to be careful of their design.

6) Dimension parameters (population size, number of generations to simulate and probability of application of operators).

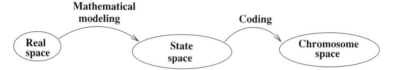

Figure 2.3. *Coding constitutes an additional step in relation to the mathematical modeling phase. Several codings may be envisaged for the same state space*

2.1.3. *Coding principles*

Initially, the coding used by genetic algorithms was represented in the form of chains of bits, which needed to contain all the information required to describe a point in the state space.

For optimization problems in spaces of higher dimensions, components are coded as chains of bits, which are then concatenated end-to-end. For example, for a function with two variables $z = f(x, y)$, we code x and y in their respective domains, then concatenate x, y. This type of coding works well, but has certain drawbacks; the structure of the problem is lost when fusing x and y into a single chain. Genetic algorithms using real vectors [GOL 91a, MIC 91a, WRI 91a] avoid this problem by directly coding the variables of the problem in the chromosome without having to use intermediary binary coding.

Finally, we may envisage all sorts of coding types, on the condition that these methods sufficiently reflect the structure of the problem and they are sufficiently easy to manipulate. The closer the coding is to the structure of the state space, the more the genetic algorithm will be effective in solving the problem. For example, if we consider a state space made up of matrices, it would be advantageous to use a tabular representation in the case of full matrices and lists in the case of sparse matrices.

Once the question of coding has been considered, we need to generate an initial population of individuals.

2.1.4. *Random generation of the initial population*

In cases where we have no idea of the position of the optimum in the state space, we may randomly generate individuals by uniform distribution for each component of the state space, checking that the individuals produced satisfy the constraints [MIC 91b]. Furthermore, in cases where we possess prior information indicating a subdomain containing the optimum, we generate individuals in this subdomain in order to accelerate convergence.

In cases where it is too difficult to randomly produce individuals respecting the known constraints, it is possible to include the constraints in the criteria in the form of penalties. An individual who does not meet a constraint has a penalty, reducing its fitness so that it will be eliminated by the selection process. We must be very careful while using this type of penalty system as the genetic algorithm risks spending its time eliminating those individuals who violate constraints without optimizing those who respect them, as the latter group is too small. In such cases, there is a risk of generating a solution that is only feasible as a result of the optimization, but is not the optimum. The violation of constraints must be a rare event in order for selection to operate successfully.

Once we have obtained a randomly distributed population of individuals, we need to maintain the diversity of the population through different generations in order to maintain exploration of the state space. This is the role of crossover and mutation operators.

2.1.5. *Crossover operators*

The purpose of crossovers is to enrich the diversity of the population by manipulating the structure of chromosomes [ESH 89, ESH 93, SYS 89, QI 93]. Traditionally, crossovers involve two parents and generate two children, but we may envisage crossovers with N parents and K children.

Initially, the type of crossover used with chains of bits involved chromosome slicing (slicing crossover). To carry out this type of crossover using chromosomes containing M genes, we randomly select an inter-gene position in each of the parents. We then exchange the two terminal sub-chains of each of the parents, producing two children C_1 and C_2 (one-point crossover (Holland)). This principle may be extended by slicing into three, four, or more sub-chains [BRI 91] (k-point crossover (DeJong)). Finally, it is possible to randomly inject genes from the parents into the children [SYS 89] (uniform crossover (Syswerda)). These crossovers are illustrated in Figure 2.4).

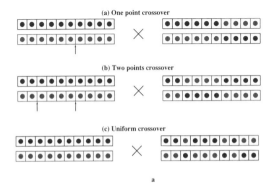

Figure 2.4. *Slicing crossover*

This type of slicing crossover is very effective for discrete problems, but for continuous problems it is better to use barycentric crossovers. The latter type of crossover is carried out by selecting two genes, $P_1(i)$ and $P_2(i)$, in each of the parents at the same position i, which are associated by weighting, in order to create two new points on the line between the two, thus creating $C_1(i)$ and $C_2(i)$:

$$\begin{cases} C_1(i) = \alpha P_1(i) + (1 - \alpha) P_2(i) \\ C_2(i) = (1 - \alpha) P_1(i) + \alpha P_2(i) \end{cases}$$

where α is a random weighting coefficient suited to the domain of extension of the genes (minimum and maximum values of each gene).

In a particular case of a matrix chromosome created by the concatenation of vectors (see Figure 2.5), we can extend the crossover principle to the vectors making up the genes:

$$\begin{cases} \vec{C}_1(i) = \alpha \vec{P}_1(i) + (1 - \alpha)\vec{P}_2(i) \\ \vec{C}_2(i) = (1 - \alpha)\vec{P}_1(i) + \alpha \vec{P}_2(i) \end{cases}$$

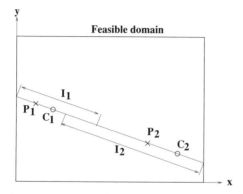

Figure 2.5. *Extension of the principle to matrix chromosomes*

It is possible to develop and test more or less complex crossover operators for a given problem, but we must remember that the effectiveness of the operator is intrinsically linked with the problem [SEB 94].

2.1.6. *Mutation operators*

The mutation operator gives genetic algorithms the property of ergodicity over the space by enriching the population gene space. This property indicates that the genetic algorithm will be capable of reaching all points in the state space, without needing to consider all of these points during the resolution process [TAT 93]. Thus, strictly speaking, the algorithm would be able to converge without crossovers, and certain variations actually function in this way [BAC 91b, FOG 94, FOG 66, HOF 90]. The convergence properties of genetic algorithms are therefore highly dependent on this operator.

For discrete problems, the mutation operator generally consists of randomly selecting a gene in the chromosome and replacing it with a new value, also selected at random within the space belonging to that particular gene.

In the case of continuous problems, we proceed in the same manner, selecting a gene at random in the chromosome, to which we add a random noise, while ensuring that the resultant gene remains within its own domain of extension, possibly by bouncing off the constraint.

REMARK 2.1.–

1) As in the case of crossovers, we may focus mutations on *weak* genes when the problem presents a fitness constructed with the help of a set of sub-fitnesses associated with each gene (as in the case of quasi-separable problems)

2) In the case of optimization problems with constraints, we need to take account of the constraints during the mutation operation [DUR 94b].

Adaptive mutation operators exist, which allow us to optimize the mutation rate by coding it in the chromosome structure [BAC 92a, BAC 92b, BAC 93, FOG 89, GRE 86].

Evolution strategies [BAC 91b] allow us to go further by coding the standard deviation applied in mutation (even the covariance matrix) directly into the chromosome. This principle is highly efficient, but its use is limited to spaces of low dimension.

Once we have all the tools necessary to explore the state space, we use the fitness of individuals to direct our search for the next generation. This task is known as selection.

2.1.7. Selection principles

Unlike other continuous optimization techniques, genetic algorithms do not require us to know or estimate the derivative of the objective function, a fact that extends their domain of application (in the same way as the taboo method, the annealing method, etc.). Algorithms of this type may also be used on systems themselves and not just on models, on the condition that we are able to retrieve a computed or simulated "fitness" for each evaluation of the chromosome and that the proposed individuals do not take the system out of its domain of operation (see Figure 2.6). To apply selection, we simply require access to a criterion value for each individual.

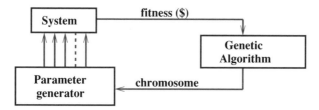

Figure 2.6. *Example of the use of genetic algorithm for a real system*

As its name indicates, selection is used to identify the best individuals in a population and eliminate the worst individuals in a statistical manner. A significant number of selection principles are discussed in specialist literature, which are more or less suited to different types of problems. Examples include

– Roulette wheel selection [GOL 89];

– Stochastic remainder without replacement selection [GOL 89];

– Selection by rank [GOL 89];

– Stochastic tournament [BAC 91a, OEI 91, MAH 91a];

– Adaptive selection [BAK 85, GOL 91b, KUO 93].

Stochastic tournament selection is currently the most widely used method and operates using the following principles (see Figure 2.7).

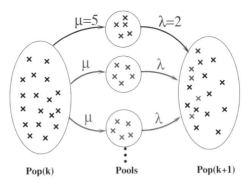

Figure 2.7. *Stochastic tournament selection. The initial population is shown on the left. Each of the circles located in the center of the diagram represents an elementary tournament used to construct the new population, represented on the right*

We begin by randomly selecting λ individuals in the current population. We retain the best individuals $\mu(\mu < \lambda)$, which we insert into the intermediary population. This process is repeated to complete the intermediary population. This technique allows efficient regulation of selection pressure by modifying the relationship λ/μ.

2.2. Classic improvements

In this section, we discuss classic improvements to genetic algorithms, which allow us, among other things, to avoid problems of premature convergence (loss of diversity in the population), to discover multiple optima and to address multi-objective problems.

2.2.1. *Scaling*

The aim of scaling [GOL 89] is to avoid premature convergence[3]. The principle of scaling consists of artificially deforming the individual criterion in order to reduce the differences in fitness between individuals at the beginning of the evolution process (leading to broader exploration of the search space) and accentuating these differences at the end (using the best individuals). To this end, initial fitness values are replaced by scaled fitness values, which are used in the selection process.

Several scaling methods exist using different deformations of criteria. Examples include

– linear scaling;

– exponential scaling.

In the case of linear scaling, the scaling function is defined as [MIC 91a]:

$$f_s = af_r + b$$

where f_r is the initial fitness, f_s the fitness after scaling, which will be considered by the selection process, and a and b the parameters to be adjusted by the user. The effect of scaling is shown in Figure 2.8.

As a rule, the slope of the scaling line is inferior to 1 at the beginning of the evolution process in order to reduce differences in the criterion, then gradually increases to accentuate differences toward the end of the evolution process.

---

3 In cases of premature convergence, an individual is reproduced in an abusive manner in the following generation, something which can even provoke the complete elimination of its peers.

In the case of multi-mode objective functions presenting quasi-equivalent optima, this scaling technique favors the dominant mode by amplifying differences of fitness toward the end of the convergence project. However, it also masks suboptimal modes, which may still be interesting. Scaling thus allows a thorough exploration of the state space, but does not favor the distribution of individuals over the different modes of the objective function. For this reason, we use sharing while identifying multiple optima.

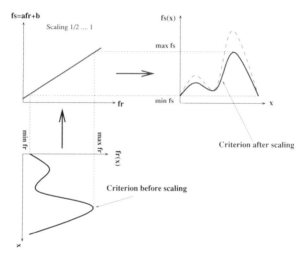

Figure 2.8. *Selection is carried out on the dotted curve and not on the plain, real curve. In this particular case, the scaling line is lower than 1 and so reduces differences*

2.2.2. *Sharing*

The aim of sharing is to distribute a number of individuals proportional to their fitness across each mode.

In the same way as scaling, the sharing consists of modifying the fitness used in the selection process. To avoid grouping of individuals around a dominant mode, we penalize fitness based on the level of aggregation of the population in the neighborhood of an individual. To do this, we require a method to allow us to estimate aggregation levels. In Figure 2.9, close individuals tend to modify the fitness used in selection at local level.

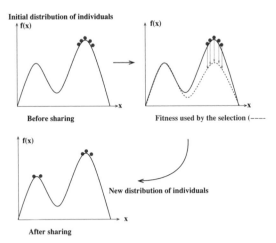

Figure 2.9. *Aim of sharing. The effect of sharing may be understood by considering that each individual has a weight that deforms the criterion at local level. Individuals will, therefore, look to move to less "busy" modes to increase their chances of survival*

In practice, we "open" a domain around each individual, then calculate the distances from the individual to other individuals in the neighborhood (see Figure 2.10).

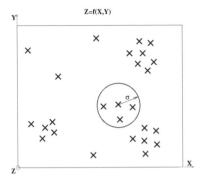

Figure 2.10. *Opening a neighborhood around each individual*

We therefore need a distance indicating the dissimilarity between individuals. These distances are then used to calculate the new fitness, penalizing herding individuals.

In practice, this type of sharing does give good results, but it requires N^2 inter-chromosome distance calculations for each generation, where N is the dimension of the population. To reduce this number, we used "clustered" sharing (which we will discuss later). Further details on sharing may be found in [DEB 89a, DEB 89b, GOL 91c, GOL 87, GOL 92, MAH 93b, MAH 94].

2.2.3. *Crowding*

In the same way as sharing, the purpose of crowding is to distribute the individuals of a population across the modes of the function. Initially proposed by DeJong [DEJ 75], crowding is based on the natural analogy of competition for resources between individuals [MAH 93a, MAH 93b]. Thus, dissimilar individuals occupying different domains of the state space are not in competition for resources (fitness). In this case, the strongest individuals will push out the weaker individuals, on the condition that the two groups are in competition. In the context of genetic algorithms, we simulate this principle as follows: we begin by selecting two parents in the population (P_1 and P_2). We then generate two children (C_1' and C_2') by crossover and mutation, which we then put into competition with the parents in a tournament. To organize this tournament, we first seek the parent–child pairings, which are closest in the state space, then apply the law of survival of the fittest. The individuals selected in this way are then placed into the new population, which corresponds to the next generation. Thus, when a child is better than the parents, it replaces the closest parent in order to produce descendents in its spatial zone. This procedure is iterated $N/2$ times to complete the new generation.

Note that $2N$ distance calculations are required for each generation (instead of N^2 for classic sharing). However, after evaluation, the results of this method have been seen to be weaker than those produced by sharing.

2.2.4. *Memetic algorithms*

Memetic algorithms are a hybrid between local search algorithms and genetic algorithms. The basic principle is the same as the case of genetic algorithms, with the addition of a local search operator after the mutation operator. The genetic part of these algorithms may be seen as a high degree of diversification, while the local search aspect constitutes an intensification. Memetic algorithms make full use of the search power of local methods and the recombination properties of evolutive algorithms using a population of solutions. More details on these algorithms may be found in [MOS 89, MOS 03].

2.2.5. *Multi-objective genetic algorithms*

2.2.5.1. *Introduction*

The genetic algorithms presented above focus on optimizing a scalar fitness, which represents the level of suitability of an individual. In reality, however, many problems involve the simultaneous optimization of several objectives, which may even be contradictory. These various objectives are often expressed using different units, making them difficult to compare. One method consists of weighting each criterion using a coefficient to harmonize units, bringing us back to a mono-objective optimization problem. As we will see, this method is far from ideal as the solution obtained is highly dependent on weightings and often focuses on simply determining a point on the Pareto front; moreover, certain points on the Pareto front cannot be found using this approach. The multi-objective genetic algorithm, in addition [KEE 76, SAW 85], allows the points of the population to be distributed across a large part of the Pareto surface in a uniform manner, thus giving a high level of diversity in the proposed solutions. These solutions are "equivalent" from the perspective of multi-objective criteria.

2.2.5.2. *Multi-objective genetic algorithms*

The key difference between classic genetic algorithms and multi-objective genetic algorithms is encountered in the selection process, which now needs to deal with vector fitness. The crossover and mutation operators remain unchanged as they operate within the state space.

In 1985, Shaffer [SHA 85] proposed a first method for multi-objective artificial evolution (VEGA), using the following principle:

– We divide the population into M subpopulations of the same size M (dimension of the objective space).

– Each subpopulation is reproduced by carrying out selection using a single objective ($\Rightarrow M$ selections).

– Application of crossover and mutation operators to the whole population.

This method distributes the population to the extremities of the Pareto front, but is limited by the mono-objective evolution of the subpopulations, which does not allow comparison of the various multi-objective solutions available at each iteration in order to exploit their characteristics.

Another more effective approach was put forward by Horn (NPGA: Niched Pareto GA [HOR 93, HOR 94]) in 1995. To select an individual, we begin by randomly selecting two chromosomes (I_1, I_2) then a subpopulation SP that contains neither I_1 nor I_2, of which the size is specified in the parameters.

– If I_1 is dominant in relation to SP, that is if it dominates all the individuals of SP and if I_2 is not dominant in relation to SP, then I_1 is selected.

– If I_2 is dominant in relation to SP and if I_1 is not dominant in relation to SP, then I_2 is selected.

– In the two other cases, no individual may be chosen above another. We could then randomly choose between I_1 and I_2, but we would risk limiting the distribution of the population to one part of the Pareto surface. To avoid this, we practice sharing in the objective space, thus promoting diversity across the Pareto surface.

The sharing method used does not modify the criteria, but selects I_1 or I_2 on the basis of the levels of aggregation of the population in the respective neighborhoods of I_1 and I_2 (in the objective space). Thus, the most isolated individual is selected in order to ensure its survival on the Pareto front.

An extension to Horn's approach consists of calculating the Pareto rank of each individual in the population using an algorithm for classifying non-dominated solutions (see Figure 2.11). This algorithm examines each individual in the population and determines whether it is dominated (in the Pareto sense) by other individuals. If this is not the case, the individual belongs to the first Pareto front and is classed as front 1. The algorithm proceeds in the same fashion using the remaining individuals, extracting individuals of rank 2 and so on until each individual has been classified.

The effect of this algorithm on the objective space is shown in Figure 2.12 in the context of a problem with two objectives to minimize.

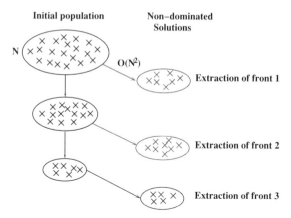

Figure 2.11. *Classification algorithm for non-dominated solutions*

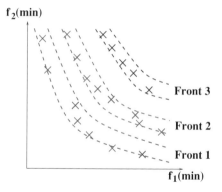

Figure 2.12. *Effect of the classification algorithm for non-dominated solutions on the objective space*

As each individual is associated with a Pareto front, multi-objective artificial evolution algorithms associate a fitness with each individual based on its Pareto ranking. Differences between methods are apparent in the way in which fitness is associated with a rank and in the distribution of solutions across the Pareto surface. These different algorithms include:

– Srinivas and Deb: NSGA (non-dominated sorting genetic algorithms) [SRI 95];

– Fonseca and Fleming: MOGA (multi-objective genetic algorithms) [FON 93];

– Zitzler and Thiele: SPGA (strength Pareto genetic algorithms) [ZIT 99].

The NSGA approach begins by associating the fitness $F^1(I) = N$ with individuals of rank 1 (where N is the number of individuals in the population). We then apply sharing (in the objective space) along the first front to ensure diversity. In the following, the fitness of the second front is calculated from the smallest fitness on the first front: $F^2(I) = \min F_s^1 - \epsilon_1$ before applying the sharing principle on the second front, and so on until all fronts have been processed.

The MOGA approach is as follows: for each individual I, we calculate the number of individuals it dominates (e.g. if $Dom(I) = k$, the fitness is $f(I) = k + 1$). Selection is carried out using ranks and sharing in the objective space.

The SPGA algorithm maintains two subsets of individuals corresponding to the dominated and non-dominated solutions (front 1). To reduce the size of the set of individuals making up front 1, clustering is carried out. The representatives of these clusters are then used in the selection process. Crossover and mutation operators are applied to create the new population (the next generation); this new population is then subjected to the same process to identify non-dominated individuals and enrich the Pareto set.

This last algorithm (SPGA) is currently seen to present the best performances.

2.3. Our contributions

This section presents the three improvements we have developed for genetic algorithms:

– Adaptive clustered sharing;

– Association of genetic algorithms and simulated annealing;

– Parallel genetic algorithms (islet technique).

2.3.1. *Adaptive clustered sharing*

This work was carried out in association with J-M. Alliot and N. Durand [DEL 95a]. To perform this type of sharing, we first identify the different clusters of individuals in the population using a MacQueen's K means clustering algorithm. This algorithm uses two parameters, d_{min} and d_{max}, to respectively fuse clusters and create new clusters. Initially, each individual in a population is considered as the centroid of a cluster. We then apply the two following principles one after the other:

– If two centroids are at a distance lower than d_{min}, we fuse them into a single cluster, of which the resulting centroid is the barycenter of the two initial centroids.

– A new individual is aggregated to a cluster if its distance from the closest centroid is lower than d_{max}, and in this case we recalculate the global centroid. Otherwise, we create a new cluster containing the single individual.

This fusion-aggregation principle produces a number of clusters, which fluctuate with the distribution of individuals in the state space (see Figure 2.13).

We then apply the principle of sharing, modifying fitnesses as follows:

$$f_i' = \frac{f_i}{m_i'}; \ m_i' = n_c \left(1 - \left(\frac{d_{ic}}{2d_{max}} \right)^\alpha \right);$$

with

– n_c: number of individuals contained in the cluster to which individual i belongs;

– α: sensitivity coefficient;

– d_{ic}: distance between individual i and the centroid of cluster c;

– $d_{\max}$: maximum distance of individuals from a centroid, allowing the individuals to be associated with the same cluster;

– m'_i: fitness penalization coefficient for each individual i belonging to the same cluster.

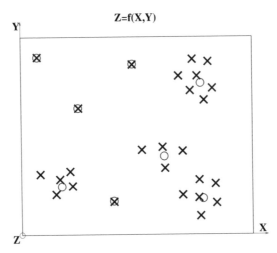

Figure 2.13. *Clustered sharing. Once individuals have been classified, they are then compared to the centers of clusters (circles)*

For a population of size N, we can show that this type of sharing involves a complexity in $O(N \log N)$ [YIN 93] for results that are comparable with those produced by traditional sharing. In practice, we note that the setting of the coefficients $d_{\min}$ and $d_{\max}$ is tricky, as their effectiveness essentially depends on prior knowledge of inter-mode distances in the state space, and these values are particularly difficult to estimate.

We therefore extended this sharing principle, rendering it adaptive. To do this, we observe the best fitnesses of each of the clusters, and if these are higher than S_1 percent of the best global fitness, we increase the number of clusters by reducing d_{min} and d_{max}. In the same way, if these fitnesses are less than S_2 ($S_2 < S_1$) percent of the global optimum, we reduce the number of clusters by increasing d_{min} and d_{max}. This procedure is summarized in algorithm 2.1.

2.3.2. *Association of genetic algorithms with simulated annealing*

As genetic algorithms and simulated annealing are both used for the same types of problems, it might be interesting to combine them in order to profit from their respective advantages. After multiple evaluations of these two techniques using the same test problems, we noted that simulated annealing, on the one hand, converges more rapidly to an optimal solution, but only produces one solution, confirming the results given in [ING 92]. Genetic algorithms, on the other hand, produce several quasi-optimal solutions, but with a longer convergence time. It thus seems natural to associate the two techniques in order to improve convergence in genetic algorithms.

Several attempts have been made to fuse genetic algorithms and simulated annealing; details of these attempts may be found in [ADL 93, ING 92, LIN 91, MAH 92a, SIR 87]).

Our approach consists of introducing an annealing principle into the crossover operator.

Algorithm 2.1. Adaptive clustered sharing

Require: $d_{moy} = 0$; $\Delta = 2$

    STEP 1

$$d_{\max} = \frac{d_{moy}}{\Delta} \; ; \; d_{\min} = \frac{d_{\max}}{3} \; ;$$

Calculate the average distance of individuals from the barycenters of clusters:

$$d_{moy} = \left(\frac{1}{N.C}\right) \cdot \sum_i \sum_c d_{ic}$$

where N represents the size of the population and C the number of clusters.

STEP 2 We then calculate the number of clusters for which the best element is above a threshold fixed in the parameters; let this number be C_{Opt}:

$$C_{Opt} = \eta f_{\max} \; ;$$

where η represents a coefficient close to 1 (but lower than 1) and $f_{\max}$ the best fitness.

STEP 3

$$\text{if } \left\{\frac{C_{Opt}}{C} > S_1\right\} \text{ and } \{\Delta < 100\}, \text{ then } \Delta = \Delta.(1.05)$$

(We will therefore reduce $d_{\min}$ and $d_{\max}$ in 2.)

STEP 4

$$\text{if } \left\{\frac{C_{Opt}}{C} < S_2\right\} \text{ and } \{\Delta > 1\}, \text{ then } \Delta = \Delta.(0.95)$$

(We will then increase $d_{\min}$ and $d_{\max}$).

return to **STEP 1**;

To apply this new crossover principle, we begin by selecting two parents P_1 and P_2 in the population (see Figure 2.14). We apply the traditional crossover operator, generating two children C_1 and C_2. In the following, we implement a tournament between the parents and the children; the two winners are then selected using the following annealing principle. In our example, we consider the individual C_1, then one of the parents (P_i) is selected at random:

– If C_1 is better than P_i, then C_1 is selected.

– Otherwise, C_1 is selected with the probability:

$$P = e^{-\left(\frac{f_{P_i} - f_{C_1}}{c(n)}\right)}$$

where $c(n)$ is a function that decreases based on the current generation (n) (this formula applies to cases of maximization). When C_1 is not selected by this process, we retain the parent P_i.

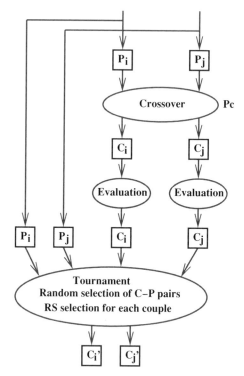

Figure 2.14. *Crossover principle with simulated annealing*

We complete the same process for C_2 with the remaining parent, thus identifying two individuals C_1' and C_2'.

REMARK 2.2.–

1) In the case of continuous optimization problems, for which we can use barycentric crossovers, the convergence of the algorithm is considerably improved by rendering the extension of domains of movement dependent on the generation, triggering major movements at the beginning of the process and small movements toward the end of convergence.

2) The variable $c(n)$ evolves in the following manner. We use a standard geometric annealing pattern with a tipping point. In practical terms, we calculate three "temperatures" for which the values depend on knowledge of the minimum and maximum differences of fitness in the initial population:

$$
\begin{cases}
C_s = -\dfrac{\Delta f_{\max}}{\ln\left(\frac{1}{k-1}\right)} & k = 0.75 \quad \text{"Initial temperature"} \\[2mm]
C_x = -\dfrac{\Delta f_{\max}}{\ln\left(\frac{1}{k-1}\right)} & k = 0.99 \quad \text{"Tipping temperature"} \\[2mm]
C_f = -\dfrac{\Delta f_{\min}}{\ln\left(\frac{1}{k-1}\right)} & k = 0.99 \quad \text{"Final temperature"}
\end{cases}
$$

where $\Delta f_{\min}$ and $\Delta f_{\max}$ represent the minimum and maximum differences of fitness in the initial population. In the geometric cooling scheme, the current temperature evolves as follows:

$$
\begin{cases}
C_0 = C_s \\
C_{n+1} = \alpha_1 C_n \text{ for } C_s > C_n > C_x \\
C_{n+1} = \alpha_2 C_n \text{ for } C_x > C_n > C_f
\end{cases}
$$

with $0 < \alpha_1 < \alpha_2 < 1$.

For each level, we calculate the number of stabilization iterations using the following formulas:

$$
N_1 = \frac{\ln\left(\frac{C_x}{C_s}\right)}{\ln \alpha_1}, \quad N_2 = \frac{\ln\left(\frac{C_f}{C_x}\right)}{\ln \alpha_2}
$$

These two formulas allow us to calculate the total number of generations for a given problem.

3) We have tried applying the same annealing principle to the mutation operator, creating an annealing stage between the mutated individual and the original individual, but this did not produce the desired effect. In this case, simulated annealing seems to considerably reduce the mixing of the population through mutation, limiting the explored space to zones, which statistically improve the criterion by "forbidding" subdomains that degrade it (this boils down to a local pseudo-search: Monte Carlo).

4) Possible improvement: in the case of multi-modal optimization problems to promote sharing, which remains essential, it would be preferable to introduce an annealing stage between those parents and children who are closest in terms of the state space rather than selecting them at random, thus ensuring a certain level of stability at cluster level. This would have the same effect as crowding on the crossover operator.

This crossover principle effectively improves the convergence of our algorithms for all of the problems we have seen.

A complementary approach to reduce the execution time of genetic algorithms consists of using several machines in a process involving islet parallelism.

2.3.3. Parallel genetic algorithms

This work was carried out jointly with J-M. Alliot and N. Durand.

Two methods were considered for the parallelization of genetic algorithms, but only the second produced good results for our problems. The first approach consisted of implanting the population on a machine and using several CPUs to evolve the population. The interest of this principle is clear when the time taken to evaluate a fitness is very high in relation to the communication time between machines; if this is not the case, parallelism slows down the solution process instead of speeding it up. To avoid this problem, an islet parallelism method has been developed, which is suited to all cases (whatever the fitness evaluation speed). To apply this type of parallelism, we begin by distributing the population across n machines on which n genetic algorithms optimize a subpopulation. For every k generations, a master machine, selected from the n, randomly selects a subpopulation for which a proportion α of good individuals are selected statistically (α and k are parameters with values selected by the user). In the following, another (different) subpopulation is chosen at random, in which we replace the same proportion of bad individuals with the good individuals selected from the first population (see Figure 2.15).

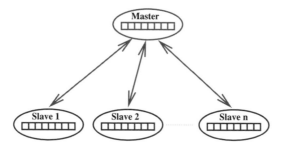

Figure 2.15. *Parallelization of the population*

This type of parallelism has produced a quasi-linear *speed up*[4] with high-quality solutions for the problems we have dealt with in this manner.

---

4 We speak of a linear speed up if, for a given problem P, with one machine, P is solved in time T and with N machines, P is solved in time $T' = T/(\alpha N)$ where α is close to 1 but $\alpha < 1$.

Parallelism may be considered when tackling real problems of large dimensions and high complexity levels. Further information on the use of these methods with genetic algorithms may be found in [COL 91, MUH 89, PET 87, SMI 93b, BER 93b].

2.4. Conclusion

Evolutionary methods allow us to efficiently process real problems and produce quasi-optimal solutions for a variety of criteria (non-continuous, non-convex, multi-mode, multi-objective, etc.) in spaces of large dimensions. The basic principle is simple, and these methods require relatively little information relating to the process we wish to optimize; only the value of the criterion is required. It is thus possible to use evolutionary methods for optimization processes where the value of the objective function is supplied by a real simulation process. However, it is important to remember that these algorithms should not be used in the absence of a deterministic method allowing the problem to be treated in an efficient manner.

In the following (Chapter 3), we will consider an extension of artificial evolution based on order statistics, which allows us to obtain very good results for continuous state spaces.

Chapter 3

A New Concept for Genetic Algorithms Based on Order Statistics

3.1. Introduction

To accelerate the evolution process, we have developed a genetic algorithm which works on individuals representing domains of the state space instead of points. This approach is based on the stochastic extension of branch and bound (branch and probability bound) developed by Zhigljavsky [ZHI 91], for which the bounds are evaluated using order statistics.

Our new genetic algorithm works in the same way, coding each individual in the population as a hypercube for which the exploration and exploitation phases are guided by the probability of including the global optimum.

Currently, this new method only applies to continuous state spaces.

The first part of this chapter discusses important notions of order statistics. The second part describes the principle used to evaluate individuals and the crossover and mutation operators associated with this new algorithm. The final part of the chapter compares this new algorithm with classic genetic algorithms.

3.2. Order statistics

Let $y_1, \ldots y_N$ be a sample of N independent random variables of the same law, with the distribution function F. The order statistic of this sample is given by $\epsilon_1, \ldots, \epsilon_N$, which represents the classification, in descending order, of $y_1, \ldots, y_N$, with ϵ_i the ith highest value in the sample. A classic result in the theory of order statistics [GUM 58] indicates that the random variable associated with the maximum of a set of N independent random variables produced using the same law converges, when $N \to \infty$, to one of the three distributions: Frechet, Weibull or Gumbell. More precisely, it is always possible to find sequences $(a_n)_{n \in \mathbb{N}}$, $a_n > 0$ and $(b_n)_{n \in \mathbb{N}}$ such that:

$$\forall x \in \mathbb{R} \ \lim_{n \to +\infty} F^n(a_n x + b_n) = G(x)$$

with $G_\alpha = G_{1\alpha}, G_{2\alpha}$ or $G_{3\alpha}$:

$$
\begin{array}{lll}
G_{1\alpha} : & x \mapsto \exp(-x^{-\alpha}) & \text{Frechet} \\
G_{2\alpha} : & x \mapsto \exp(-(-x)^{-\alpha}) & \text{Weibull} \\
G_{3\alpha} : & x \mapsto \exp(-\exp(-x)) & \text{Gumbell}
\end{array}
$$

and α a real positive number known as the "Tail index".

In most cases, α must be estimated using a relatively large number of samples in order to obtain a sufficiently precise value. In the context of optimization applications, this value may be fixed beforehand.

Moreover, taking $M(F) = \sup\{x | F(x) < 1\}$, we obtain the following result [REI 89]:

– If $M(F) = +\infty$

$$\lim_{t \to +\infty} [1 - F(tx)]/[1 - F(t)] = x^{-\alpha}$$

for $x > 0$.

– If $M(F) < +\infty$:

$$\lim_{t \to 0} [1 - F(M(F) - tx)]/[1 - F(M(F) - t)] = (-x)^{\alpha}$$

for $x < 0$.

– In the asymptotic case:

$$\lim_{t \to M(F)} [1 + F(T + g(t)x)]/[1 - F(t)] = e^{-x}$$

for $x \in \mathbb{R}$ and:

$$g(t) = \int_t^{M(F)} \frac{(1 - F(u))}{(1 - F(t))} du$$

This result provides a necessary and sufficient condition for weak convergence of distributions associated with the lower boundary of the sample.

In the case of a problem requiring maximization of a function $f : \mathbb{R}^n \to \mathbb{R}$ and taking the hypothesis that f may be locally approximated by a positively defined quadratic form on a ball centered on each point in the state space, the distribution associated with the maxima of a set of samples taken randomly from the domains of the state space follows a Weibull law with $\alpha = 2/n$ (n dimension of the state space).

If function f is an exact negatively defined form:

$$f : x \mapsto \langle x, Hx \rangle$$

and if the samples are taken following a probability measurement μ, we obtain:

$$F : t \mapsto 1 - \mu({}^t Q \Lambda^{-1/2} B(0, t^{1/2}))$$

where Q and Λ are, respectively, the orthogonal matrix and the diagonal associated with the decomposition:

$$H = {}^tQ\Lambda Q$$

and $B(0, t)$ represents the open ball with center 0 and radius t. By linearity, we deduce the Haan condition [DET 70]:

$$(1 - F(ut))/(1 - F(t)) = u^{n/2}$$

for $u > 0$. This result can be adapted to the case of a non-zero maximum $M(F)$ associated with a function f for which we also obtain an asymptotic Weibull distribution:

$$\lim_{N \to +\infty} F^N(M(F) + a_N x) = exp(-(-x)^{2/n})$$

with:

$$a_N = M(F) - inf\{t | 1 - F(t) \le N^{-1}\} + o(1)$$

If function f possesses several equivalent maxima, each of which locally respects the Haan condition, then the asymptotic distribution of the maximum is once again a Weibull distribution with $\alpha = 2/n$.

For the rest of this chapter, we will work using the hypothesis that at each point in the state space, a quadratic model approaching function f exists, locally. We are thus able to take $\alpha = 2/n$.

Note that after a sufficient number of draws in the context of an optimization process, it is possible to improve the estimation of α in order to accelerate the algorithm. This improvement has not been implemented in the version of the algorithm presented in this chapter. Several estimators of α have been developed and are discussed in detail in [ZHI 91].

3.3. Estimating the probability that the global optimum belongs to a given domain

Let us consider a hyper-rectangle D (parallel to the coordinate axes) of the state space defined using the two extreme points of the main diagonal: $(\vec{P_1}, \vec{P_2})$ with $\vec{P_1}, \vec{P_2} \in \mathbb{R}^n$. A sample $(\vec{x}_1, \ldots, \vec{x}_N)$ of N points is then randomly drawn from the domain D following a uniform law. Let $\epsilon_1, \ldots, \epsilon_N$ be the order statistic associated with the sample $(f(\vec{x}_1), \ldots, f(\vec{x}_N))$.

The probability that the global optimum will be found in D (denoted $c(D)$) can be estimated using the first order statistic (ϵ_1):

$$c(D) = \left(1 - \left(\frac{M - \epsilon_1}{M - \epsilon_k} \right)^{2/n} \right)^k$$

with $k = min(5, N/10)$ (this value is determined experimentally [ZHI 91]) and where M represents the observed maximum of function f from the start of the optimization process (in the context of our genetic algorithm, this value is updated after each generation).

Using the calculation of $c(D)$, it is possible to qualify and compare domains. A high value of $c(D)$ indicates that the domain (D) is promising and should therefore be used; inversely, a low value of $c(D)$ indicates that the domain is of limited value and should be either eliminated or extended.

3.4. Genetic algorithms and order statistics

3.4.1. *Introduction*

The general structure of this new genetic algorithm follows a classic pattern: we randomly generate an initial population for which we reproduce the fittest individuals using a selection operator. We then diversify the genetic pool of individuals by using crossover and mutation operators. The originality of the new method is essentially contained in the coding used to represent real-state spaces and in the calculation of individual fitness.

This algorithm works using domains of the state space rather than points; these domains are evaluated using an estimation of the probability that they include the global optimum. Thus, if the estimated probability is weak (close to zero), then the domain is considered to be bad. The strength of order statistics is that they enable the evaluation of large domains of the state space using a reduced number of samples, thus directing evolution toward the most promising domains. We thus avoid wasting time on large zones of the state space where the optimum is clearly unlikely to be found. Note that this improvement may be adapted for use with any genetic algorithm operating on continuous spaces.

3.4.2. *Coding*

The chromosomes used in this genetic algorithm are represented by hypercubes that are parallel to the coordinate axes in a dimension n state space which we code using the two extreme points located on the principal diagonal (P_1, P_2) (see Figure 3.1).

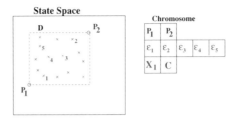

Figure 3.1. *Domain coding using the two extremities of the diagonal of the hypercube*

Only the points P_1 and P_2 will be manipulated by the crossover and mutation operators.

The other fields are updated during the evaluation phase associating a fitness value with the chromosome. These additional fields allow us to improve the exploitation and exploration. During the evaluation of the chromosome, a sample of points is taken from the associated hypercube, and the first five order statistics are computed (ϵ_1–ϵ_5). Value X_1 represents the position of the maximum in the sample and C is the trust associated with the first order statistic.

3.4.3. Recombination operators

3.4.3.1. Crossover

Several different crossover operators have been described for this type of coding, but the one that gives the best results is based on the geometric properties of the parent hypercubes (see Figure 3.2).

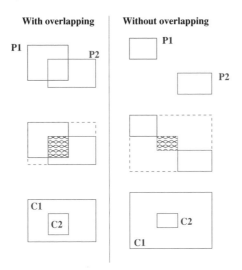

Figure 3.2. *Crossover operator*

To carry out the crossover, we begin by randomly selecting two parents P_A and P_B. Following the selection, there are two possible cases:

1) The parent hypercubes have a non-empty intersection (left-hand side of Figure 3.2). The first child C_A is made up of the intersection subdomain (shaded section) and the second child C_B is made from the smallest domain covering the two parent domains (dotted).

2) The parent hypercubes have an empty intersection (right-hand side of Figure 3.2). A central subdomain is created in order to create the first child C_A (shaded section) and the second child is made from the smallest domain covering the two parents, as in the first case.

Depending on the parents, this operator may improve the exploitation and (or) exploration.

3.4.3.2. *Mutation*

Mutations are divided into two categories. In 20% of cases, this operator carries out a new random selection of a domain in the state space; in the remaining 80% of cases, the mutation is guided by the probability that the global optimum is associated with the domain ($c(D)$). When $c(D)$ is close to 1 (>0.9), we need to reinforce exploitation; we thus center the domain on the position of the maximum (X_1) followed by a contraction of the associated hypercube. In the other extreme case, where $c(D)$ is close to 0 (<0.20), we need to increase exploration by selecting another domain. Finally, when $c(D)$ is not close to the boundaries (0,1), we mix exploration and exploitation. The position of the new domain is first centered on X_1 then the size of the associated hypercube is increased. An example of these three operators is shown in Figure 3.3.

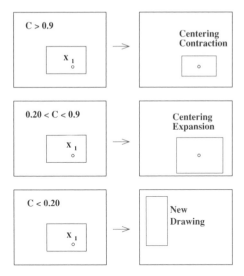

Figure 3.3. *Mutation operators*

3.4.4. *Evaluation of fitness*

Before applying the selection operator, we need to obtain information on a quality known as fitness for each individual. To evaluate a domain, we begin by carrying out random (uniform) sampling across the domain and calculate the value of the objective function for each sample. We then calculate the associated order statistics in order to estimate the probability that the optimum belongs to the domain.

3.5. Application to test functions

We have used a number of different test functions in order to compare this new algorithm with a classic genetic algorithm. All these functions have a minimum at zero, except for the Lennard-Jones functions for which only an experimental minimum value is known: min $= -128.287$ for 30 atoms. For the two algorithms, we use the same selection operator ("stochastic remainder" which is not necessarily the best option), with no scaling or sharing heuristics (from this point of view, the algorithm has scope for improvement). As our aim is to compare the influence of domains and order statistics, the two algorithms had to operate in the same way in terms of selection.

As the number of criterion evaluations per generation is different from one algorithm to another (more evaluations are used in the new algorithm), the number of generations has been adapted in each algorithm in order to obtain the same total number of criterion evaluations.

Note that the curves of the results presented below have been adapted to produce abscissae in order to visualize the results of the two algorithms on the same graph.

The x-axis represents the number of generations for the new algorithm and the number of generations multiplied by 20 for the standard algorithm. The y-axis represents the fitness for both algorithms. As the results for the two algorithms were very different, a logarithmic scale was used to allow visualization of the two graphs.

The parameters used for the two algorithms are shown below.

| Number of individuals : 100 |
| Number of generations : 500 |
| Probability of crossover : 0.4 |
| Probability of mutation : 0.3 |

For the Rosenbrook and Lennard-Jones functions, the number of generations was extended to 1,500 and 2,500, respectively.

The algorithms were executed using a Pentium 300 MHz processor and lasted 7 min for a state space of dimensions $n = 200$ and 14 min for $n = 2,000$.

To avoid symmetry effects, the position of the optimum was modified when testing the other functions; this had no impact on the obtained performances.

We will present the results of this algorithm for three functions (Griewank, Rosenbrook and Lennard-Jones). Details of all the tests carried out may be found in [DEL 00] including the Sphere, Step and Ackley functions, for which the new algorithm presents significantly better results than the classic algorithm.

3.5.1. *Results for the Griewank function*

Griewank function:

$$f_1(\vec{x}) = \frac{1}{400*N} \sum_{i=1}^{N} x_i^2 - \prod_{i=1}^{N} \cos\left(\frac{x_i}{\sqrt{i}}\right) + 1$$
$$\vec{x}^* = (0, ..., 0)^T$$
$$f_1(\vec{x}^*) = 0$$
$$N \in \{200; 2,000\}$$
$$-600.0 \le x_i \le 600.0$$

$n = 200$

- Standard GA: final value $= 20.11$.

- Domain GA: final value $= 0.96$.

$n = 2000$

- Standard GA: final value $= 165.79$.

- Domain GA: final value $= 1.11$.

3.5.2. *Results for the Rosenbrook function*

Rosenbrook function:

$$f_2(\vec{x}) = \sum_{i=0}^{N-1} 100 * \left(x_i^2 - x_{i+1}\right)^2 + \left(1 - x_i\right)^2$$
$$\vec{x}^* = (0, ..., 0)^T$$
$$f_2(\vec{x}^*) = 0$$
$$N \in \{200\}$$
$$-30.0 \le x_i \le 30.0$$

$n = 200$

- Standard GA: final value $= 15{,}663{,}259.86$.

- Domain GA: final value $= 254.13$.

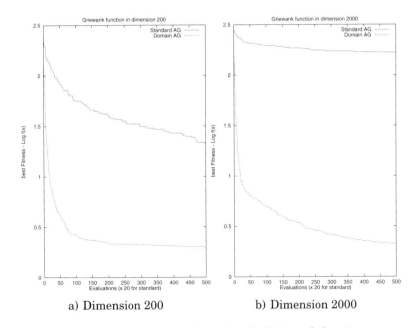

a) Dimension 200   b) Dimension 2000

Figure 3.4. *Evolution of fitness for the Griewank function*

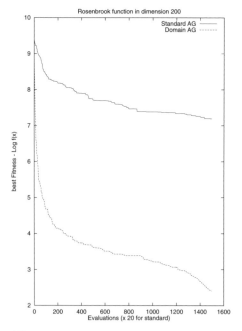

Figure 3.5. *Rosenbrook dimension 200*

3.5.3. *Results for the Lennard-Jones function*

This function comes from a real industrial optimization problem concerning molecular conformation known as the Lennard-Jones problem. The problem consists of determining the geometric structure of a set of atoms to minimize the potential energy of the resulting structure. For this problem, we consider that the potential energy is the sum of the interactions between pairs of atoms. As the atoms have three geometric coordinates (x, y, z), a problem with K atoms involves $3 \times K$ variables.

The potential energy of an atomic structure is given by the following function:

$$f_3(\vec{x}) = \sum_{i=0}^{N/3} \sum_{j=0}^{i-1} \left[\frac{1}{d_{ij}^6} - 2 \cdot \frac{1}{d_{ij}^3} \right]$$

$$d_{ij} = x_i * x_j + x_{i+1} * x_{j+1} + x_{i+2} * x_{j+2}$$
$$\min f_5(\vec{x}) = -128.287$$
$$N = 90 \ (30 \ atoms)$$
$$-2.0 \le x_i \le 2.0$$

N = 90

– Standard GA: final value $= -77.21$.

– Domain GA: final value $= -125.09$ (a local approach based on the Hooke method [HOO 61] further improves this result, with an objective value of -128.18 (very close to the best-known result, -128.28)).

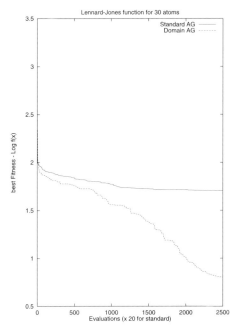

Figure 3.6. *Lennard-Jones with 30 atoms*

3.6. Conclusion

This new algorithm presents clear improvements in the performance of the standard genetic algorithm. The strongest point of this new approach is the use of order statistics on a small number of criterion samples in order to rapidly qualify large zones of the state space. This qualification of domains of the state space allows us to guide the evaluation process and avoids time being wasted on zones where the global optimum is unlikely to be found. The level of improvement is significant, leading us to conclude that this new approach is an important step in the improvement of genetic algorithms. We should remember that it is possible to improve the performance of the algorithm still further by using a better selection principle ((λ, μ) tournement, for example). Instead of carrying out uniform selection across domains, we could also consider directing future selections using the order statistics of previous random selections in order to guide exploration. It would also be possible to use a large set of state space samples from which domains could be selected at random. This method would allow the use of samples in several domains in order to reduce the number of evaluations of the objective function. The sample set would be updated every K generations.

PART 2

Applications to Air Traffic Control

Chapter 4

Air Traffic Control

This chapter provides a brief overview of the air traffic control system to which we have applied the optimization principles presented in the previous chapters.

When an aircraft travels between airports, a flight plan must be registered in order to inform the relevant air navigation services. This plan contains all the indicative elements needed to describe the planned flight, notably:

– departure time;

– the first flight level[1] requested for the cruise;

– the planned route, described using a series of markers.

Airplanes usually use pre-established routes known as airways. These airways take the form of tubular corridors with rectangular cross sections, surrounding segments of

---

1 Flight level: altitude reading from an altimeter referred to an isobar surface 1,013 millibars (expressed in hundreds of feet); thus, a difference of 5,000 ft gives an FL of 50.

straight lines; markers are located at the intersections of these lines. Collision risks, known as conflicts, most often arise around these markers. At these points, we define a horizontal distance, expressed in nautical miles (NM)[2], the horizontal separation and a vertical distance, which is expressed in feet (ft)[3]: the vertical separation. We say that two aircraft are separated when the distance between their projections on a horizontal plane is higher than the standard horizontal separation, OR when the distance between their projections in a vertical plane is higher than the standard vertical separation.

Air traffic control consists of organizing the flow of traffic in order to ensure flight security (in terms of managing collision risks) and improve the capacity of the route network used by aircraft.

Three different types of control may be identified based on the nature of the traffic:

– airport control: management of the taxiing, take-off and landing phases;

– approach control: management of traffic in the stage before landing or after takeoff in the vicinity of an airport;

– en route control: essentially concerns traffic during the cruise phase between airports.

Currently, approximately 8,000 movements take place each day on French territory, representing a control workload which is too large for a single controller. The workload is distributed by dividing the airspace into several sectors, each managed by a control team. The number of sectors is thus

2 1 NM = 1,852 m or the length of a minute of an arc on a large terrestrial circle.
3 1 ft = 0.3048 m.

determined by the capacity of a controller to manage N aircraft simultaneously (in practice, the average appears to be from 10 to 15 aircraft; when this limit is reached, the sector is said to be saturated). A control center brings together a set of sectors across a given geographical zone.

Air control organizations are responsible for the flow of traffic in their allocated airspace. The service to users must provide not only perfect security but also the best possible flow rate. Within each sector, controllers keep each airplane separate from the rest of the traffic by issuing instructions to pilots. In a sector, one controller ensures coordination with neighboring sectors and is responsible for the predetection of conflicts. Another controller, the radar controller, monitors the traffic, ensures conflict resolution and communicates with pilots.

Controllers are not solely responsible for maintaining the traffic flow. En route control forms part of a chain of successive filters of which each element attempts to improve the traffic flow. Each filter has different objectives and manages distinct spaces and timeframes. Broadly speaking, we may identify five levels of elements:

1) Long-term organization: the crudest filter. Its aim is to organize traffic at a macrascopic level in the mid- and long-term (over 6 months). Examples of this include traffic orientation schemes, measures taken by the flight schedule committee, inter-center agreements or arrangements with the military allowing civil aviation to use their airspace in order to manage the Friday afternoon peak.

2) Short-term organization: this is often known as preregulation. It consists of organizing traffic for a day d, the day before $(d-1)$ or the day before that $(d-2)$. Relatively precise data are available in this case:

i) the known flight plans;

ii) the control capacity of each center based on the workforce available on day d;

iii) the maximum aircraft flow that may enter a sector in a given time, known as the sector capacity;

iv) data from previous weeks and years. Air traffic is relatively repetitive: traffic for any given Monday will be very similar to the previous Monday; the days before Christmas are similar to the same period the previous year, etc. This allows us to predict where congestion will occur, the capacity needed to respond to the demand or even more limiting measures, which need to be taken.

This filter does not only act at a macroscopic level, organizing traffic flow based on the available capacity, but also on each airplane, managing takeoff slots[4]. This filtering was carried out at a national level across Europe until 1995, when it was transferred to a European level in order to improve coordination. Short-term organization is now the responsibility of the CFMU[5].

3) Real-time regulation: this filter organizes different flows with regard to the day's events. It consists of adjustment measures that take account of events from the day before, which may not be fully understood. Thus, transatlantic traffic is not well known at $d - 1$, but much better information is available 3–6 h before the arrival time. The fraction of available capacity reserved for pre-regulation can then be adapted. Additional airplanes may be sent into other sectors, or the number of non-transatlantic flights dealt with by the center may be increased if there are fewer transatlantic flights than what is initially expected. In the same way,

---

4 A takeoff slot is a time window during which the aircraft is authorized to take off.
5 Central Flow Management Unit.

unused time slots (due to delays, technical incidents, etc.) may be reallocated, or changes may be made to take account of weather conditions (e.g. inaccessible terrain). This role is generally performed by the FMP[6] of each center.

4) Tactical: this is the last filter in the chain of air traffic control and consists of the action of a controller on their sector. The average time an airplane spends in a sector is approximately 15 min. The visibility of the controller is slightly higher, as flight plans become available a few minutes before the aircraft enters the sector.

Detection and, moreover, resolution of conflicts are not automated. Controllers are therefore trained to recognize types of conflicts and apply known maneuvers in such cases. The controller can only prevent conflicts by altering the airplane trajectories. To do this, four types of order may be given:

- change in direction (offset or turning point (see Figure 4.1));

- intermediary stages for ascending or descending aircraft;

- change in flight level;

- speed regulation measures (essentially for descending aircraft).

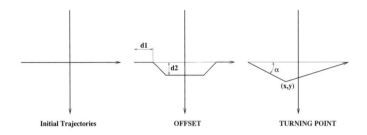

Figure 4.1. *Operational maneuvers: offset and turning point*

---

6 Flow Management Position.

5) Emergency: this filter is only supposed to operate when there is no control system or when it is defective. It consists of two complementary systems:

- The safety net predicts the trajectory of each airplane within a timeframe of a few minutes using past radar positions and pursuit algorithms. In cases of conflict, an alarm triggers. This system does not propose solutions to the conflicts it detects.

- The TCAS[7]: the aim of this filter is not to separate airplanes, but to avoid a presumed collision. The prediction timeframe is less than a minute and varies between 25 and 40 s. At this point, it is too late for a controller to act, as we consider that operatives require between 1 and 2 min to analyze a situation, find a solution and communicate with the aircraft. Currently, the TCAS detects nearby airplanes and gives a resolution order to the pilot (orders given concerning the vertical plane). This filter is used to resolve unpredictable conflicts caused, for example, by an aircraft moving outside of the flight level given by air traffic control, or a technical accident with significant effects on the performance of the aircraft.

More details on the methods used in air traffic control can be found in [TUA 76, ZAN 94, MAI 91, VIL 84, COL 92].

---

7 Traffic Alert and Collision Avoidance System: onboard system included in certain aircraft, made obligatory by the United States for all airplanes carrying more than 30 passengers.

Chapter 5

Contributions to Airspace Sectorization

In this chapter, we present the main principles of airspace sectorization which we have developed.

After a brief introduction, we will first present a continuous two-dimensional (2D) approach based on Voronoi diagrams, followed by a second, discrete 2D approach using connected graphs.

We will then present two three-dimensional (3D) extensions (continuous and discrete) followed by a number of methods used to synthesize dynamic sectorizations.

5.1. Introduction

Over the last few decades, with the increase in traffic, airspace has been divided into increasingly small sectors in order to avoid sectors becoming saturated. Unfortunately, this resectorization principle has its limits in that the controller needs sufficient time to manage his or her traffic (creation of conflict resolution strategies); for this reason, sectors cannot be smaller than the minimum size required by this constraint. Moreover, the controller is only aware of traffic linked to his sector, and when an aircraft moves from one sector to another, a communication between controllers and pilots is essential to ensure the safety of the flight entering the new sector (this dialog generates an additional workload for controllers, known as the *coordination workload*). Thus, an increase in the number of sectors results in an increase in coordination, and thus in the overall control charge.

In an operational context, the principle of resectorization of an airspace domain is as follows. When a sector is often close to saturation, a team of experts is assembled to propose a new sectorization of the problem zone. Two types of simulations are then used to validate the proposition: arithmetic simulation and real-time simulation. The first case consists of evaluating the sectorization using simulation software and recorded (or simulated) traffic. If the results of these first evaluations are satisfactory, the sectorization is then tested in real-time using a simulated control environment, involving controllers and pseudo-pilots (with a replica control panel on the ground (simplified version)). After this last step, the borders of the sectors are modified on-site, and we monitor these changes to see if they effectively solve the problem. The new sectorization is kept until new problems emerge, generally linked to increases in traffic.

This approach is essentially local and produces a global sectorization, which is a juxtaposition of individually optimized regions of control.

The aim of the research presented in this chapter is to supply a global method for the sectorization of European airspace based on a mathematical modeling of the space in question. The goal is not to provide a final sectorization which solves all control problems, but to propose an initial division of the airspace which will then be improved by experts using a graphic interface (only these experts will be able to effectively judge the performance of a proposed sectorization). One of the main objectives of sectorization is to provide sectors with a minimum of coordination and maximum balance in terms of control workload so that each control team works in the same way. The first work presented below is based on 2D modeling, which was then extended to 3D, before being enriched with a dynamic sectorization principle.

5.2. Modeling in 2D

5.2.1. *Model based on a transportation network*

This first model uses a graph, in which the nodes correspond to way points or airports and the links represent airways. As each node has two coordinates (x, y), the model is known as a 2D model. The flows of aircraft transiting through this network, which intersect at nodes, generate conflicts between aircraft. The controllers in charge of this traffic must then ensure that the aircraft are on the correct routes (monitoring) and solve conflicts which appear in the network nodes (conflict resolution). Finally, they are responsible for coordination when aircraft change sectors. In the case of this model, based on a transportation network, the monitoring workload is proportional to the flow along the links, the conflict resolution workload to flows crossing at nodes and the coordination workload depends on flows intersecting the edges of sectors. An example of a network is shown in Figure 5.1. The problem we wish to solve consists of determining the geometric form of sectors which optimizes a criterion while respecting a number of constraints. Our state space thus corresponds to the geometric edges of the sectorization. We thus aim to balance the workload for each sector and minimize the flows cut by sector boundaries. Let

$w(k)$ be the control workload associated with sector k. The balancing criterion is thus represented by the following formula, showing deviation from the average workload:

$$y_1 = \sum_{k=1}^{k=K} \frac{\|w(k) - \frac{W}{K}\|}{\frac{W}{K}}$$

where $W = \sum_{k=1}^{k=K} w(k)$ and K is the total number of sectors. This criterion needs to be minimized. The values of y_1 belong to an interval $[y_{1min}, y_{1max}]$, for which the values y_{1min}, y_{1max} represent the following extreme cases:

$-\, y_1 = y_{1min} = 0$: completely balanced sectorization.

$-\, y_1 = y_{1max} = 2(K - 2)$: completely unbalanced sectorization (one sector contains all of the workload (W) and all of the other sectors are empty).

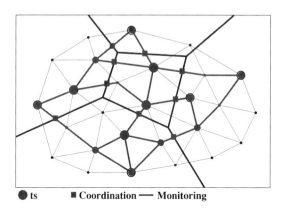

Figure 5.1. *Example of a 2D model. In this figure, the fine links represent the airways network. These airways carry flows (thick lines), for which the controller must verify that the aircraft are on the correct routes (monitoring). Potential conflicts are represented by large dots on the nodes. Finally, the coordination workload is shown as squares where a flow crosses over the edge of a sector*

The lower bound for the optimal value of the criterion y_1 ($y_1 = 0$) is important, and this information may be used to establish a termination condition for the optimization process. Effectively, when the solutions produced have a value of y_1 which is close to 0, we may conclude that the method is close to an optimum for this criterion.

The minimization of flows cut is represented by a second criterion, y_2:

$$y_2 = \sum_{k=1}^{k=K} \sum_{\substack{i \in \mathcal{N}_k \\ \oplus j \in \mathcal{N}_k}} \beta_{ij} f_{ij} + \sum_{\substack{i \notin \mathcal{N}_k \\ j \notin \mathcal{N}_k \\ (i,j) \in \mathcal{L}_k}} 2\beta_{ij} f_{ij}$$

where $\oplus$ represents the logic function XOR (exclusive or), f_{ij} is the flow between nodes i and j, β_{ij} is the weighting coefficient, $\mathcal{N}_k$ is the set of nodes located in the sector S_k and $\mathcal{L}_k$, is the set of links of which the extremities are not in sector S_k but have a non-empty intersection with this sector (these links are thus intersected twice by the sector). Figure 5.2 shows the three possible situations (links with zero, one or two coordinations). This property is only valid when the sectors are convex (in the geometrical sense). In the case of non-convex sectors, there may be more than two intersections (see Figure 5.3). As we will see later, our algorithm permits automatic generation of convex sectors.

These two criteria are then fused to give a global criterion $y = \alpha y_1 + (1 - \alpha)y_2$[1].

After describing our state space and objectives, we must describe the constraints associated with this problem. The sectorization synthesized by our algorithms must respect

---

1 This work is relatively old, and at the time there was no idea of using multi-objective artificial evolution, which only appeared in late 1995.

certain requirements originating in the operational field. When we examine the current sectorization and the associated network of routes, we note that for each actual origin-destination trajectory, we only cross each sector once. Thus, a pilot will only contact the controller in charge of the sector he or she is currently traversing. This property is known as route convexity and is described as follows:

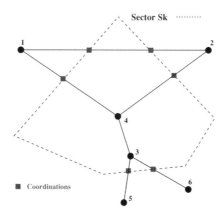

Figure 5.2. *Examples of coordination. The control sector S_k is represented by a dotted line and has four intersections with the route network, of which the nodes are shown as black circles. The links $(1, 4)$, $(4, 2)$, $(3, 6)$ and $(3, 5)$ each have a single intersection with an edge of the sector. Arc $(4, 3)$ has no intersections, whereas arc $(1, 2)$ crosses the edges of the sector twice*

"A sector is convex in the sense of airways if each of the routes, which traverse it, crosses the border two times or fewer".

Depending on the nature of the underlying route network, a sector may or may not be convex in the sense of airways (see Figure 5.3).

We thus obtain our first constraint:

⇒ *convexity constraint:* The synthesized sectors must be convex in relation to air routes.

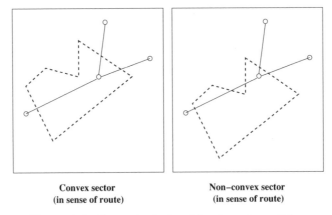

Convex sector
(in sense of route)

Non–convex sector
(in sense of route)

Figure 5.3. *Convexity induced by the nature of the
subjacent network*

When a controller detects a conflict between two aircraft, a sufficient timeframe is required to establish a feasible solution. As we have already seen, conflicts between aircraft occur where routes cross, and thus at the nodes of the transportation network. Moreover, the traffic managed by a controller is limited to their sector of responsibility, and he or she does not have information on the traffic present in neighboring sectors. If, at the moment of transfer, an aircraft is in conflict, the controller will not have enough time to create a feasible solution. To avoid this problem, sector borders must be sufficiently distant from crossing points to give controllers sufficient time to resolve conflicts. This time depends on individual controllers, but on average, seven minutes are required before a conflict is resolved. We translate this time into distance by considering the maximum speed of aircraft, 500 knots:

$$\Rightarrow d_{secu} = \frac{V T_{secu}}{60} \simeq 60 NM;$$

where d_{secu} in NM represents the minimum distance between sector borders and crossing points, V in kts is the maximum speed of the aircraft and T_{secu}, in minutes, is the security time.

This gives us our second constraint:

⇒ *security constraint:* the distance between a potential point of conflict, i.e. a node, and a sector border must be at least equal to the security distance.

Finally, for a controller to be able to act easily on the flights present in a sector, flight paths must spend sufficient time in the sector. This is expressed as a third constraint:

⇒ *minimum stay constraint:* an aircraft must remain in each sector it traverses for a sufficient period of time.

We can now summarize our problem as follows:

> *Airspace sectorization:* We consider a transportation network in a 2D space, for which a flow distribution produces a control workload distributed across the entire airspace. We wish to divide this space into K balanced sectors (in terms of control workload) while minimizing coordination requirements. This sectorization must respect constraints of route convexity, security at waypoints and minimum stay time.

5.2.2. *Associated complexity*

The sectorization problem may be divided into two subproblems, corresponding to our two objectives:

– balancing sector workloads;

– minimizing coordination.

The first subproblem is discrete-continuous NP-difficult (discrete: balancing conflict and coordination workloads; continuous: balancing monitoring workloads). If we only consider the discrete aspect linked to the conflict and coordination workload, the problem is equivalent to a K_partitioning of the graph into connected components, which is known to be NP-hard [CHE 92]. The coordination minimization subproblem is also a K_partitioning of a graph for the minimization of flows cut and is thus NP-hard. It would therefore be reasonable to assume that the combination of these two problems will also be NP-hard.

Two types of modeling have been considered for the solution of this problem:

1) continuous modeling;

2) discrete modeling.

5.3. Continuous modeling

5.3.1. *Principle*

This approach consists of dividing the underlying geometric space containing the transportation network. A simple method to obtain this type of K-partitioning consists of randomly drawing a set of K points (known as class centers) from the domain D and grouping each of the points contained in D with the nearest class center (aggregation principle leading to a Voronoi diagram).

As an example, Figure 5.4 shows a possible division of a rectangle into five sectors.

By construction, the sectors produced in this way are convex in the geometric sense of the term and even more so in the sense of airways (geometric convexity implies that a straight line intersecting with a sector will only cross the sector border twice, including all possible directions, including those of the airways).

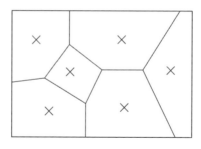

$\times$ class centers

Figure 5.4. *Example of sectorization generated by Voronoi diagram*

To take account of the security constraint, we modify the network by grouping a fraction of monitoring workload of the links connected to the crossing point in order to create an aggregated node. Thus, when these new nodes are assigned to a sector, the whole of the neighboring zone will also be associated with that sector S (see Figure 5.5).

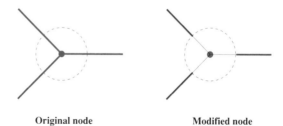

Original node   Modified node

Figure 5.5. *Grouping of monitoring workload at crossing nodes for a limited horizon*

Finally, the minimum stay constraint is enforced by the use of a penalty coefficient (δ_{ij}), which artificially increases the coordination load of links which violate this constraint. The new coordination workload is expressed as follows:

$$C_{co}(S_k) = \sum_{\substack{i \in N_k \\ \oplus j \in N_k}} \delta_{ij} \beta_{ij} f_{ij} + \sum_{\substack{i \notin N_k \\ j \notin N_k \\ (i,j) \in L_k}} 2\delta_{ij} \beta_{ij} f_{ij}$$

The penalty coefficient δ_{ij} models the constraint violation and is calculated in the following manner: Let p_{ij}^k be the relative length of the segment of the link (i,j) contained in the sector S_k and L_{ij} the total length of the link (i,j). If the length of the portion of the link contained in sector S_k is smaller than the minimum distance d_{secu}, we must increase the contribution of the associated coordination:

$$\begin{cases} \text{If } (p_{ij}^k.L_{ij}) < d_{secu} \text{ then } \delta_{ij} = e^{-[2(\frac{p_{ij}^k.L_{ij}}{d_{secu}}-1)]} \\ \text{Otherwise } \delta_{ij} = 1 \end{cases}$$

Using this formalization, we can then develop an optimization principle using genetic algorithms.

5.3.2. *Chromosome coding*

As we have already seen, knowledge of the position of class centers in the geographic space is sufficient to define a sectorization, and thus to evaluate its performances. This information is coded in the chromosome using a matrix (of dimensions $2.K$) containing the abscissa and the ordinates of the class centers. An example of chromosome coding is shown in Figure 5.6.

5.3.3. *Initial population generation principle*

The process used to generate the initial population is immediate. Effectively, for each individual contained in the population, we randomly generate, with a uniform distribution, K pairs of geographic coordinates representing the K class centers defining each sectorization.

5.3.4. *Crossover operator*

We have tested two types of crossovers for problems of this type:

– slicing crossover [BRI 91];

– barycentric crossover [WRI 91].

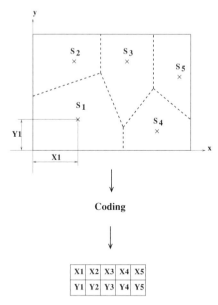

Coding

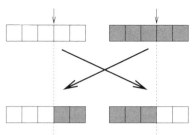

Figure 5.6. *Chromosome coding. The positions of the class centers are shown in a matrix*

The first method corresponds to the classic crossover used in binary genetic algorithms, but in this case, it is implanted using chains of real numbers. This crossover consists of randomly drawing a position in the chromosome and exchanging the two subchains produced in this manner (see Figure 5.7).

Figure 5.7. *Slicing crossover. In our application, a single slicing point has been used (other versions of this type of crossover use multiple slicing points)*

The second method consists of randomly selecting a class center in each of the parent chromosomes, and then artificially joining them by a straight line. We then randomly move centers (uniform distribution) along this line in order to generate two new individuals. The position of the new class centers is then given by:

$$C_1 = \alpha P_1 + (1 - \alpha) P_2$$
$$C_2 = (1 - \alpha) P_1 + \alpha P_2$$

(see Figure 5.8).

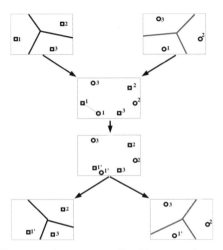

Figure 5.8. *Barycentric crossover. In this example, gene number 1 has been selected*

This latter type of crossover is better suited to continuous spaces and produces better results for our problem, which includes continuous components.

5.3.5. *Mutation operator*

To mutate a chromosome, we randomly select a position in the chromosome, and then move the associated class center by adding noise to each of its coordinates following a particular distribution law. An example of mutation is shown in Figure 5.9.

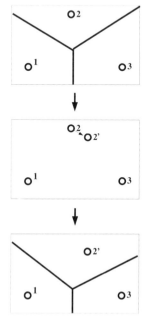

Figure 5.9. *Mutation operator. In the example shown here, class center number 2 has been randomly selected, then moved in 2′, thus producing a new sectorization*

5.3.6. *Calculation and normalization of the fitness function*

For each of the sectors synthesized by the chromosome, we evaluate the associated conflict, coordination and monitoring workloads. As the conflict workload at the nodes is independent of the sectorization, it is calculated once at the beginning of the resolution process; only the classification of nodes in different sectors needs to be carried out for each fitness evaluation. For the two other workloads, we need to determine, for each link:

– the sectoral distribution of flow along the link (i.e. the distribution of flow across different sectors);

– the number of sector borders which intersect with this link.

These two quantities are evaluated by dichotomy for each of the links making up the transportation network.

Using the conflict workload at the nodes and the sectoral distribution of flow, we deduce the three workloads associated with each sector; this then allows us to determine the balancing and coordination criteria used in the final evaluation of fitness. In this way, we are able to determine the criteria y_1 and y_2 and thus calculate the aggregated criterion y. As we saw previously, we wish to minimize y. However, the artificial evolution algorithms used are designed to maximize fitness. We thus use the following fitness:

$$\text{fitness} = e^{-\alpha y}$$

where α is a positive weighting coefficient. In this way, when y is minimum ($y = 0$), fitness will be maximum with a value of 1. In the same way, the minimum fitness value will be equal to zero.

For each fitness evaluation, we need to carry out some operations, the number of which depends on the size of the network. Remember that the calculation of the conflict workload at the nodes is carried out once during initialization, and does not, therefore, intervene in the fitness calculation[2]. The remaining tasks are:

---

2 The computation of the conflict workload at the nodes is in $O(N^3)$, where N is the number of nodes in the network.

– calculation of the conflict workload in sectors ⇒ $O((N.K))$;

– calculation of the coordination workload in sectors ⇒ $O((L+1)K)$;

– calculation of the monitoring workload in sectors ⇒ $O((L+1)K)$;

where N is the number of nodes in the network, L is the number of links and K is the number of sectors. Thus, the overall number of operations needed to compute a fitness value becomes:

$$O(NK + 2(L+1)K) = O(K(N+2L))$$

5.3.7. *Results*

To evaluate and compare different versions of algorithms, we use a test network for which an evident solution is known (see Figure 5.10).

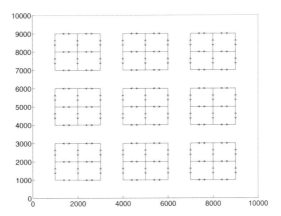

Figure 5.10. *Symmetrical test network*

Without impacting the general evaluation principle, we adopt the hypothesis that the flows on the network links are constant. For humans, the faculty of perception makes the optimal solution to this problem evident; we are easily able to identify the symmetries of the network and isolate a clear nine-sector solution.

The parameters used in dimensioning our algorithm were obtained experimentally. As a general rule, the probability of crossover is much higher than the probability of mutation. Initially, we used a population with a dimension of 50 individuals, which allowed us to reach an optimum after 150 generations. By using a population with 400 individuals, the algorithm converges to the optimum in less than 20 generations. The behavior of the algorithm (for this type of problem) is satisfactory using the following parameters:

Population dimension	400
Number of generations	200
Probability of crossover	0.6
Probability of mutation	0.06

To observe the convergence of the algorithm, the best fitness and the mean fitness across the whole population are memorized for each generation. In the present case, the algorithm works using a normalized fitness which is bounded at "1" when the balancing and coordination criteria cancel each other out. The evolution of these two parameters as a function of the generation is shown in Figure 5.11 (GA with simulated annealing in the crossover [EGA]).

An example of a solution produced by the algorithm is given in Figure 5.12.

After this first network, we tested the algorithm on a network without an obvious solution (see Figure 5.13).

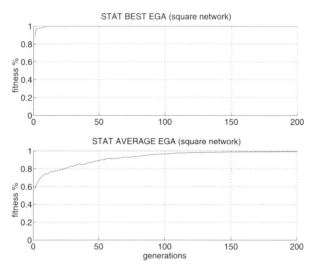

Figure 5.11. *Convergence of GA with SA on the symmetrical network. The top curve represents the evolution of the fitness of the best individual as a function of the number of generations. The lower curve corresponds to the average fitness of the population as a function of the number of generations*

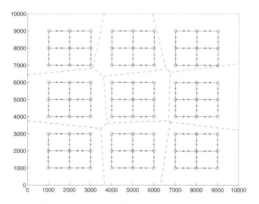

Figure 5.12. *Final sectorization represented by dotted lines*

We wanted to divide this network into five sectors. As we can see from the convergence curves, the algorithm behaves very well and provides a quasi-optimal solution in, less than 10 generations (see Figure 5.14; for this solution, the least balanced sector is within 0.7% of the exact balance).

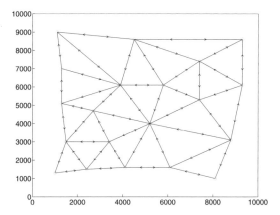

Figure 5.13. *Asymmetric test network*

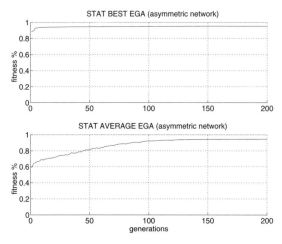

Figure 5.14. *Convergence of GA with SA in an asymmetric network. The top curve represents the evolution of the fitness of the best individual and the lower curve represents the evolution of the average fitness*

Unlike the previous case, the fitness cannot reach 1 in this situation as it is impossible to cancel out the coordination workload. The physical sectorization generated by the algorithm is shown in Figure 5.15.

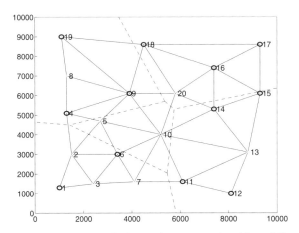

Figure 5.15. *Generated physical sectorization (dotted lines)*

As we can see, this sectorization respects the imposed constraints and appears entirely satisfactory.

5.3.8. *Conclusion*

This first study has produced encouraging results in the use of genetic algorithms in the sectorization of transportation networks. The coding of the chromosomes is very important in determining the effectiveness of the algorithms as it allows us to synthesize sectorization in a way which is simple to implement. This simplicity is also encountered in the crossover and mutation operators, improving the performance of the algorithm.

In the description given above, the value of K (number of sectors) was fixed, but it is possible to code it directly into the chromosome so that the genetic algorithm is able to adjust this value in an adaptive manner. In this case, we would need to modify the criterion to heavily penalize individuals in which sectors have a workload higher than the maximum acceptable for a controller.

This first approach has been improved by working directly on the transportation network (discrete approach).

5.4. Discrete modeling

5.4.1. *Principle*

This second approach consists of synthesizing a set of connected components in a graph which is itself connected. We can then apply this method directly to the transportation network representing the airways network, for which the links correspond to the main traffic flows. In this case, we obtain a crude sectorization suitable for use in macroscopic studies of the airspace. If we wish to refine this approach in a microscopic framework, we must construct the initial network in the following manner:

– Consider a day with relatively high traffic.

– Identify all crossing points.

– Calculate the conflict and monitoring workload for the network.

– Crossing points in close proximity to each other are grouped using a clustering algorithm. These clusters are then modeled by a single hyper-node, for which the control workload includes the monitoring and conflict workloads of the cluster.

– When a flow exists linking two hyper-nodes, we create a link for which the flow corresponds to the traffic between the two clusters.

– Isolated hyper-nodes are then linked to the final graph using a flowless link, connecting the isolated hyper-node to the closest connected hyper-node. This final step ensures connectivity in the final graph.

We wish to divide the resulting graph into K connected components. The classic formulation of the graph partitioning problem is as follows:

Let $G = (\mathcal{V}, \mathcal{E})$ be a non-oriented graph, where $\mathcal{V} = \{v_1, v_2, ..., v_n\}$ represents the set of nodes (with an associated weight) and $\mathcal{E} \in \mathcal{V} \times \mathcal{V}$ is the set of links carrying the traffic flow. The graph partitioning problem consists of seeking a set of K-connected components $P_1...P_k$ of equal weight which minimize the flow cuts.

Our problem is slightly more complex as when a link crosses a sector border, a new workload is created (the coordination charge which depends on the flow along the link) which is shared between the two components sharing the link. Thus, the total workload before and after division is not the same, indicating that a balanced situation before the division may be affected by the division. The value of the objective function is not known beforehand, but only once the decision to divide the network is made.

5.4.1.1. *Accounting for constraints*

– *Route convexity:* this constraint is satisfied by the principle used in the construction of components.

– *Security constraint:* this constraint is taken into account in the construction of the initial graph: the hyper-nodes include monitoring for a given vicinity (the same approach used in the continuous case).

– *Minimum stay time:* this constraint is also covered by the clustering algorithm, which groups links of insufficient length into the same cluster.

This discrete approach also allows us to take into account all constraints with no artificial penalization of the criterion.

The K partitioning problem is known to be NP-hard [GAR 79] and, for small networks, it is generally treated by recursive application of a bi-partitioning heuristic [CHE 92, HEN 95], generating a suboptimal solution which may be quite distant from the desired solution. Even in a simplified case of bi-partitioning, the best heuristic developed by Goemans and Williamson [GOE 94] produces a solution up to 13% distant from the optimum (worst-case scenario).

The characteristics of this problem naturally lead us toward artificial evolution.

5.4.2. *Coding*

The coding used for this problem consists of modeling connected components by partitioning the nodes into non-empty subsets. The construction method described below ensures that the nodes of the same subset are connected by at least one path. Each subset is associated with a power factor (Fp_1 and Fp_2 in Figure 5.16), which allows us to determine the position of the split in a link when this link is shared between two connected components. An example of coding is shown in Figure 5.16.

In order to create an initial population, we need to be able to randomly generate chromosomes. To do this, we use a greedy heuristic summarized in Figure 5.17, including the following steps:

1) We begin by randomly selecting K different nodes from the graph (where K represents the number of connected components (2, in this example)). These nodes represent the seeds of the connected components which will be generated by the greedy heuristic. Each of these nodes is given a label ("A" and "B" in our example).

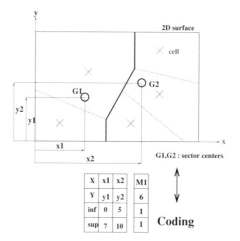

X	x1	x2	M1
Y	y1	y2	6
inf	0	5	1
sup	7	10	1

Coding

Figure 5.16. *Example of coding*

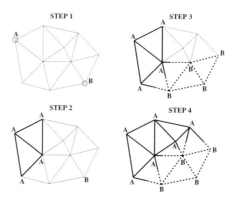

Figure 5.17. *Greedy heuristic for random chromosome generation*

2) The neighborhood of each component is then checked (a node is considered to be a neighbor of a connected component if there is a link joining this node to a node of the component). If a node is a neighbor of a component and does not carry a label, it is associated with this component and is given the same label. If the node is already labeled (and thus already belongs to another component), the link connecting the component to this node is cut. The position of the cut is calculated using the

respective power factors of the components which share the link. Let Fp_1 and Fp_2 be the respective power factors of two components sharing the link. The link portions (l_1 and l_2) in each component are then expressed in the following manner:

$$l_1 = \frac{Fp_1}{Fp_1 + Fp_2}L \quad l_2 = \frac{Fp_2}{Fp_1 + Fp_2}L$$

where L represents the length of the cut link.

3) The second step is repeated until all nodes are marked.

5.4.3. Recombination operators

For this problem, we only use mutation operators. A crossover operator was developed, but did not ensure connectivity of the generated components in the children. A repair operator was then implemented for the child chromosomes, but it proved too costly, and so the idea of crossovers was disregarded for this type of problem. Mutation operators can be classified into three categories (see Figure 5.18):

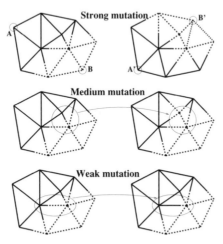

Figure 5.18. *Mutation operators*

1) *Strong mutation*. This operator modifies all connected components, randomly selecting K new seed nodes and propagating the connected components using the same greedy heuristic involved in initializing the population.

2) *Medium mutation*. This operator begins by statistically selecting the component with the heaviest workload, then seeks the neighboring component with the least load. This second step is also carried out statistically (introducing a bias into a random selection). We thus obtain a border link separating the two components. A node is then moved from one component to the other, while verifying that the component losing a node remains connected. As we see from Figure 5.19, this operator is capable of breaking connectivity to the least loaded component. In such cases, the operator is applied again. In practice, these events are extremely rare, and this operator generally works first time.

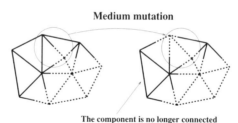

Figure 5.19. *Example of a connectivity breakdown*

3) *Weak mutation*. The initial principle of this operator is the same as for medium mutation, but only the power factors of the connected components sharing the cut link are modified. As there is no exchange of nodes, there is no risk of losing connectivity.

In practice, weak and medium mutation operators are applied several times in order to promote the balancing of connected components.

5.4.4. *Results*

Our algorithm has been successfully applied to networks containing several hundred nodes. In this section, we will present the results obtained for two test networks. The first network presents a set of symmetries, allowing us to identify a trivial solution with 81 independent sectors (see Figure 5.20). The second network (see Figure 5.21) also has a strictly balanced solution with 100 sectors but no symmetry, and this is much harder for a human operator to identify the solution. For the machine, these two problems are almost exactly equivalent in terms of difficulty of resolution.

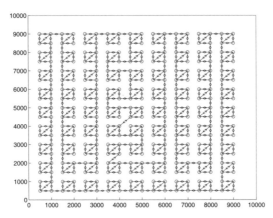

Figure 5.20. *A 324-node network with 81 balanced blocks. Between each block, a flowless link has been added in order to obtain connectivity in the initial graph*

The parameters of artificial evolution used to solve this problem are as follows:

Population size	100
Number of generations	100
Probability of mutation	0.7
Sharing (clustered)	yes
Elitism	yes

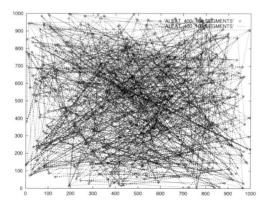

Figure 5.21. *A 400-node network with 100 balanced blocks*

The fitness evolutions (best individual and average) for these two test networks are shown in Figure 5.22 for the symmetrical network and in Figure 5.23 for the asymmetric network.

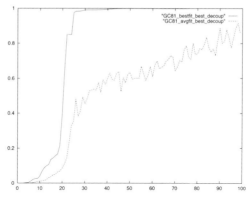

Figure 5.22. *Evolution of fitness of the best individual and average fitness as a function of the number of generations for the symmetrical network*

In both cases, the fitness of the best individual attains a value of "1", which represents the optimum for the two criteria (fully balanced sectorization and no split flows). The rapid progressions through different levels of fitness are linked to the balancing principle used in the medium and weak mutation operators.

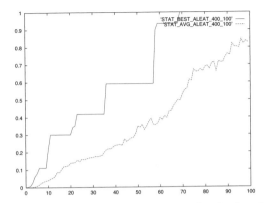

Figure 5.23. *Evolution of fitness of the best individual and average fitness as a function of the number of generations for the asymmetric network*

5.4.5. *Conclusion*

This new discrete approach produces very good results on instances of realistic problems. It presents the advantage of directly accounting for constraints within the structure of the chromosome without using fitness penalization techniques.

The two approaches discussed above cover spaces in two dimensions. In the rest of this chapter, we will extend these concepts into 3D spaces corresponding to the context of air transport.

5.5. 3D extension

This section presents two principles for extending the previous continuous and discrete approaches to spaces of 3D.

5.5.1. *Introduction*

Direct 3D extension of the two approaches described above does not present any obvious problems. For the continuous model, we simply need to work with 3D Voronoi diagrams, thus generating polyhedral sectors. For the discrete approach, the use of a 3D network does not hinder the operation of the algorithm. Problems arise in the operational domain, which imposes 3D sectors of which the elementary blocks are polygonal cylinders with an axis perpendicular to the ground. This constraint arises from the 2D representation used in control screens, where an aircraft is represented as a comet, with an associated label containing flight information, including the flight level of the aircraft (see Figure 5.24).

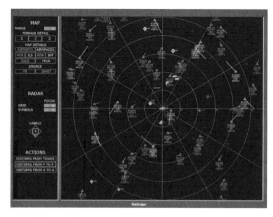

Figure 5.24. *Example of a radar image used in air traffic control*

This limitation of the user interface can create uncertainty in transfers between sectors when the vertical extension of these sectors is not perpendicular to the ground. Effectively, in the case of oblique borders (diamond-shaped sectors), for a transfer to a neighboring sector, the controller may have difficulty determining at what point the aircraft will move into the neighboring sector. This situation is represented in Figure 5.25. This figure shows an aircraft transiting from a sector S_1 to another sector S_2 in two different situations, based on the geometry of the sectors used. These situations are shown on the right and left hand sides of the figure, respectively. The upper section gives a top-down view of the two situations, and the lower section gives a side-on view.

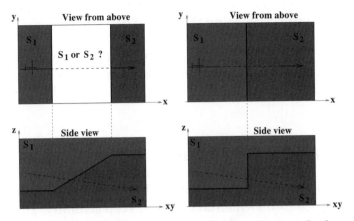

Figure 5.25. *Constraint on the lateral edges of sectors. In the situation on the right, it is easier for the controller to determine the moment when the aircraft moves into sector S_2*

For each of these situations, the trajectory taken by the aircraft is shown as a dotted line. This aircraft follows a downward trajectory in passing from sector S_1 to sector S_2. In the first situation (top left), the sector border is not perpendicular to the ground (xy). The controller in charge of the situation (sector S_1) only has a top-down view, and thus has trouble determining at what moment the aircraft leaves the first sector to enter into sector S_2. Effectively, to the left of line "a", the aircraft is in S_1. To the right of line "b" it is in S_2, but between the two lines it is difficult to determine the point of transfer, particularly in cases where the aircraft is descending of change with significant uncertainties concerning the rate of descent. At operational level, the method used to solve this problem consists of bringing lines "a" and "b" closer together and of creating a border perpendicular with the ground (situation shown on the right of Figure 5.25).

When the controller looks at the "corrected" sector with the new separation line (line "c" in Figure 5.25, top right), it is much clearer where the transfer occurs, even in the presence of uncertainties regarding the rate of descent.

In the horizontal plane (x, y), the sectors take the form of polygons; thus, the elementary form of an operational control sector is a polygonal cylinder with an axis perpendicular to the ground.

5.5.2. *Mathematical modeling*

The model used in this approach is based on a division of the airspace into elementary cells of responsibility. To obtain this initial division, we begin by identifying regular crossing points in the airspace, which we project onto a plane representing the ground. Using these projected points, we construct a Voronoi diagram, which is then modified by fusing cells with class centers which are too close together or cells which are too small. This procedure allows us to respect our security and minimum stay constraints. In this way, we obtain a set of Voronoi cells in 2D (see Figure 5.26).

We then consider a set of altitude layers for which each Voronoi cell is duplicated (see Figure 5.27).

Each cell and each altitude interval is associated with an elementary control workload made up of the conflict and monitoring workloads for all of the flight levels corresponding to this interval. The vertical localization of this elementary workload is equal to the average altitude of the layer in question. These workloads are represented as black circles in Figure 5.27. We then carry out a Delaunay triangulation [PRE 85] of the initial mosaic in the horizontal plane in order to create a 2D graph (see Figure 5.28).

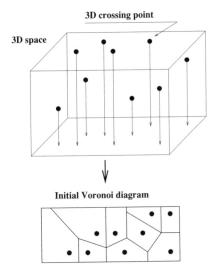

Figure 5.26. *Initial division. The lower illustration represents the Voronoi diagram of the 2D projection of elementary points in the air space*

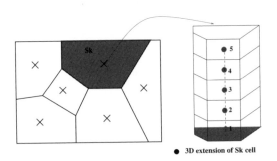

Figure 5.27. *Vertical duplication of each Voronoi cell. In this example, the Sk cell is duplicated into 5 layers*

The links of the graph represent the neighborhood relationship between two cells. This graph is then duplicated (see Figure 5.29) for each altitude interval for which the links are weighted by the number of flights transiting from one cell to another for the layer in question. This information is then used in minimizing the number of coordinations.

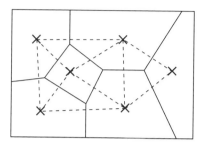

Associated Delaunay triangulation

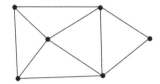

Figure 5.28. *Delaunay triangulation associated with the initial mosaic*

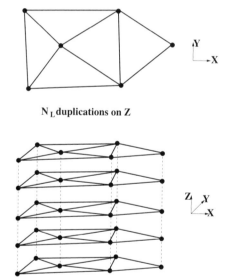

Figure 5.29. *Vertical extension of the Delaunay triangulation associated with the initial mosaic*

Using the initial mosaic and the associated Delaunay graph, we can develop an elementary sector construction principle, which respects all of the operational constraints. We begin by creating a set S of K *sector centers*. These sector centers are 2D points which we select randomly from the mosaic plane. We then associate each sector center with an interval from the altitude layer, ensuring that these intervals fully cover the altitude layers. For example, if we consider five altitude layers, they may be covered by three intervals: $I_1 = [1, 4]; I_2 = [3, 5]; I_3 = [2, 4]$. This property ensures that each layer is associated with at least one interval.

Next, we apply an aggregation principle, linking elementary cells to sectors based on the altitude layers they may attain (interval). For each cell and for each altitude layer, we begin by seeking the subset of sector centers for which the interval contains the considered layer. The altitude layer covering property ensures that the subset will not be empty. We then examine the subset to find the sector center which is closest to the current cell and associate the two. This process allows unique associations between each cell and a sector center.

To develop the associated mathematical model, we must introduce some notations. C represents the set of elementary cells. Each cell c_i is defined by its position $p_{c_i} = (x_{c_i}, y_{c_i}, l_{c_i})$ and its weight w_{c_i}, where (x_{c_i}, y_{c_i}) is the position in the plane (ground) and l_{c_i} is the altitude layer where the cell is located.

The number of elementary cells is given by $|C| = N_v.N_L$ where N_v is the number of cells in the plane and N_L is the number of altitude layers considered.

We then introduce K subsets of cells s_k, each representing a sector (K = number of sectors). This gives us the following property:

$$\bigcup_{i=1}^{K} s_i = C \quad s_i \cap s_j = \emptyset \; \forall i \neq j \tag{5.1}$$

The graph associated with the Delaunay triangulation is noted $\mathcal{A}$, of which link a_{ij} is weighted by the number of flights f_{ij} transiting from cell i toward cell j.

Using this notation, we can determine the workload for a sector and thus calculate y_1:

$$w_k = \sum_{c_i \in s_k} w_{c_i} + \beta \sum_{\substack{i,j| \\ c_i \in s_k \\ c_j \notin s_k}} f_{ij} \tag{5.2}$$

$$y_1 = \sum_{k=1}^{K} \frac{\left| m_k - \frac{M}{K} \right|}{\frac{M}{K}} \tag{5.3}$$

where $M = \sum_{k=1}^{K} w_k$.

In the same way, criterion y_2 is given by the following formula:

$$y_2 = \frac{1}{F} \sum_{\substack{i,j| \\ c_i \in s_k \\ c_j \notin s_k}} f_{ij} \tag{5.4}$$

where $F = \sum_i \sum_j f_{ij}$

5.5.3. *Application of artificial evolution to the problem*

To use artificial evolution, we need to develop an effective coding method which allows us to randomly generate a set of sector centers and a means for covering altitude layers.

The chromosome structure used is as follows:

x_1	x_2	$...$	x_i	$...$	x_K
y_1	y_2	$...$	y_i	$...$	y_K

$L(M_1)$	$L(M_2)$	$...$	$L(M_i)$	$...$	$L(M_{K-1})$
$Ext_{1_{inf}}$	$Ext_{2_{inf}}$	$...$	$Ext_{i_{inf}}$	$...$	$Ext_{K-1_{inf}}$
$Ext_{1_{sup}}$	$Ext_{2_{sup}}$	$...$	$Ext_{i_{sup}}$	$...$	$Ext_{K-1_{sup}}$

Each column in this table represents a gene made up of a position in the 2D space ((x_i, y_i)), an *altitude marker* $L(M_i)$ and two altitude extensions, one downward $Ext_{i_{inf}}$ and the other upward $Ext_{i_{sup}}$. These three parameters ($L(M_i)$, $Ext_{i_{inf}}$ and $Ext_{i_{sup}}$) will allow us to efficiently construct random coverings for our altitude layers.

For a given layer, the position of the sector centers involving this layer can be used to construct the polygonal borders of the sectors by aggregating the cells of the layer to the nearest center (see Figure 5.30).

The markers are used in the following manner: for K sectors, we must generate $(K - 1)$ markers, each of which has a position $L(M_i)$ and two extensions $(Ext_{i_{inf}}, Ext_{i_{sup}})$. Figure 5.31 presents an example where four intervals of altitude layers are constructed using three markers. To create the intervals, markers $M_1, M_2, ..., M_{K-1}$ are first arranged by increasing altitudes: $L(M_i)$ $(L(M_1) \geq L(M_2) \geq ... \geq L(M_{K-1}))$; here, the index represents the position in the ordered list, not the gene number.

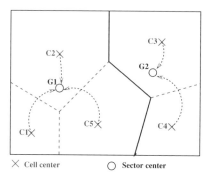

Figure 5.30. *Example of cell aggregation for a given altitude layer (the solid lines represent sector borders)*

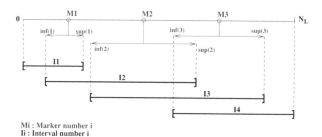

Figure 5.31. *Construction process covering altitude layers using a set of markers. The markers are ordered according to their altitudes. The altitude interval k is built by using marker (k − 1) and marker (k + 1) and their associated extensions (inf(k − 1) and sup(k + 1)*

The first interval is constructed taking the first altitude layer (0) and the layer defined by $L(M_1) + Ext_{1_{sup}}$. We obtain:

$$I_1 = [0, L(M_1) + Ext_{1_{sup}}]$$

The second interval begins at $L(M_1) - Ext_{1_{inf}}$ and ends at $L(M_2) + Ext_{2_{sup}}$:

$$I_2 = [L(M_1) - Ext_{1_{inf}}, L(M_2) + Ext_{2_{sup}}]$$

Generally, interval number i ($i = 2..(K-1)$) has the following structure:

$$I_i = [L(M_{i-1}) - Ext_{i-1_{inf}}, L(M_i) + Ext_{i_{sup}}]$$

Finally, the last interval is given by:

$$I_K[L(M_{K-1}) - Ext_{K-1_{inf}}, N_L]$$

Intervals with a negative lower boundary are cut off at zero, and those with a higher boundary above N_L are cut off at N_L.

Each chromosome is initialized by randomly selecting K positions in the 2D plane of the mosaic and drawing variables $L(M_i)$, $Ext_{i_{inf}}$ and $Ext_{i_{sup}}$ for each value of i ($i = 1, 2, ..., (K-1)$).

An example of a chromosome is shown in Figure 5.32.

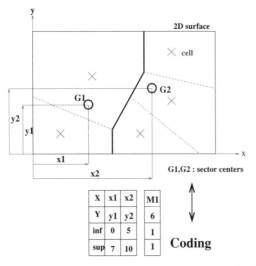

Figure 5.32. *In this coding example, two sectors are built in the horizontal dimension by using the positions of the two sector centers G_1 and G_2. Their extension in the vertical dimension is given by the position and the extensions of marker M_1*

This example shows an elementary mosaic with five Voronoi cells (dotted lines), from which we construct two sectors. In this example, we have ten altitude layers ($N_L = 10$). The first sector covers layers 0–7, the second layers 5–10. These intervals were produced using marker M_1, located in layer 6 and with the following extensions: $Ext_{1_{inf}} = 1$ and $Ext_{1_{sup}} = 1$. The sector centers are marked by the symbols G_1 and G_2. For layers 0–4, only the first sector covers these altitude levels, indicating that all these layers are associated with the first sector. In the same way, layers 8–10 are attributed to the second sector. Finally, layers 5–7 are shared between the two sectors depending on the position of the sector centers G_1 and G_2.

Based on this coding principle, it becomes possible to create crossover and mutation operators. The crossover operator works in two stages. The first step consists of modifying the position of the sector centers, randomly selecting a center in each parent, and then modifying their positions along the straight line connecting the two (Figure 5.33).

The second step mixes the markers of the two parents (see Figure 5.34).

To carry out this crossover, we begin by grouping and ordering the markers of the two parents (P_1, P_2) by altitude layer. Next, we take every second marker alternately to constitute the markers of the first (C_1) and second child (C_2), respectively.

The mutation operator begins by identifying the most unbalanced genes (in terms of the control workload) in the chromosome in order to introduce a bias in the selection of the gene for mutation. Two types of operators have been developed:

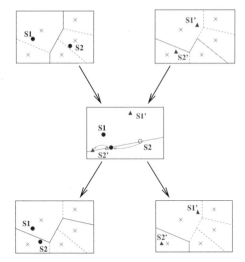

Figure 5.33. *Crossover of sector centers. This operator begins to randomly select two sector centers (S2 and S2' on the figure). Then, a straight line is built between those centers and two new positions are randomly generated on this line. Those new positions induce new sectors*

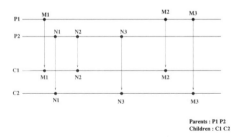

Figure 5.34. *Crossover of markers. First markers of both parents P1 and P2 are ordered by altitude layer. Next, we take every second marker alternatively to create children C1 and C2*

1) Strong mutation: this first operator modifies the structure of the chromosome by randomly selecting a gene (taking into account the bias), then modifying the position of the sector center, the value of the marker and its associated extensions.

2) Medium mutation: this operator affects vertical extensions based on the sign of the unbalanced value. If the sector has insufficient workload, one of the extensions, selected at random, defining its altitude interval is increased; in the opposite case, we reduce this extension.

These mutation operators are selected randomly with a bias determined by the current generation. The strong mutation operator is most often selected at the beginning of the evolution process, and medium mutation tends to be used toward the end of this process.

5.5.4. *Results*

As in previous situations, this algorithm has been tested using a symmetrical problem for which we have an optimal solution, then using an asymmetric problem. The first problem is made up of a set of 500 elementary Voronoi cells, selected at random from a 10×10 square (see Figure 5.35).

Figure 5.35. *Initial mosaic containing 500 Voronoi cells. The weightings of the first layer are randomly selected and duplicated across 10 levels*

The weightings of the first layer are randomly selected between 0 and 100. In the same way, we select a random set of flows between each cell and its neighbors. This layer is then duplicated across 10 levels, retaining the weightings and associated flows. Each layer therefore has the same total weight. We then propose to divide the cube into 10 balanced sectors. A trivial solution consists of dividing the 3D space into 10 altitude layers, each with the same workload. The parameters used by the genetic algorithm are shown in Table 5.1.

Number of generations	500
Population size	500
Probability of crossover	0.4
Probability of mutation	0.2
Elitism	yes
Selection (λ, μ)	(5,2)

Table 5.1. *Parameters of the genetic algorithm*

Figure 5.36 represents the evolution of fitness as a function of generations. The exact solution is obtained after 30 generations (here, the fitness is given as a percentage, with 100 representing a completely balanced solution with no divided flows).

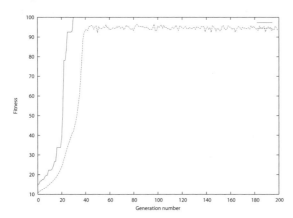

Figure 5.36. *Evolution of fitness in the case of the symmetrical problem. The full line represents the fitness of the best individual and the dotted line represents the average fitness of the population*

Figure 5.37 shows the evolution of the associated criteria for the best individual. The two objectives evolve rapidly toward zero, indicating that the sectorization produced is completely balanced and that the sector borders do not cut across any flows.

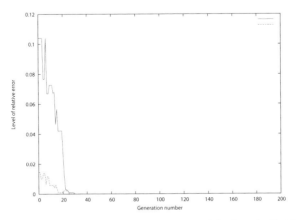

Figure 5.37. *Evolution of the two objectives of the best individual as a function of the generation. The full line corresponds to the balance criterion (y_1) and the dotted line to the criterion associated with divided flows (y_2)*

The algorithm was then tested on a larger instance of the asymmetric problem, with 1,000 elementary cells developed across 10 altitude layers. For each layer, the weights and the flows between cells were selected at random. The evolution of fitness for this test is shown in Figure 5.38. The evolution of the associated criteria is shown in Figure 5.39. In this case, fitness cannot attain 100% as there is no way to avoid cutting across flows. At the end of the evaluation process, the total residual imbalance is around 0.45% and the relative flow cutting rate reaches almost 0.13%. These tests were carried out over several runs and they produced results of the same quality.

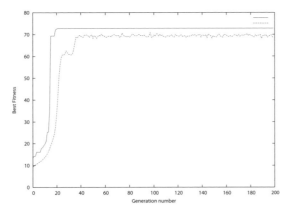

Figure 5.38. *Evolution of fitness in the case of the symmetric problem. The full line represents the fitness of the best individual and the dotted line represents the average fitness of the population*

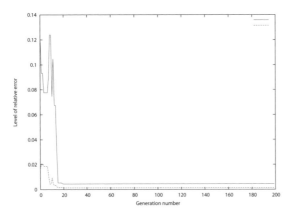

Figure 5.39. *Evolution of criteria in the case of the asymmetric problem. The full line corresponds to the balancing criterion (y_1) and the dotted line corresponds to the criterion associated with divided flows (y_2)*

5.5.5. *Conclusion*

This new approach allows us to synthesize sectors which respect all of our operational constraints without including constraint relaxation principles in the criterion. The tests proposed correspond to realistic instances on the scale of a country such as France.

5.6. Accounting for the dynamic aspect

Over the course of a day of normal traffic, the control workload fluctuates based on traffic demands between various origin-destination pairings. As the traffic across the network is dynamic, we might consider producing a new sectorization every hour with a number of sectors suited to the network load. In practice, this approach is not possible as controllers need a minimum training period to acquire the control reflexes needed for their specific sector (several months). However, in spite of this limitation, it is possible to adapt capacity to demand using a dynamic grouping principle. In the current operational system, the number of controllers varies in line with traffic fluctuations. Thus, during the night, the number of control teams is reduced as there is much less traffic. Sectors are then grouped into threes or fours at night, with each group assigned to a team of controllers. This grouping is carried out empirically by each regional control center, where experts group and ungroup sectors in anticipation of traffic flows. Every morning, for example, sectors are degrouped just before the rush linked to the opening of airports. The work presented in the rest of this chapter concerns the optimization of this grouping principle.

We will begin by presenting the mathematical modeling of this problem in terms of an objective function, state space and constraints. Two resolution methods (continuous and discrete) will then be presented with examples of results.

5.6.1. *Formalization of objectives and associated mathematical model*

As our problem concerns an optimal grouping of sectors, we require an initial description of these sectors. We consider that each sector is summarized by its barycenter, to which we associate a control workload. The properties of a good grouping are the same as those required in sectorization. We therefore wish to synthesize groups of sectors with balanced control workloads and which minimize the remaining coordination workload (inter-group coordination). One example of sector grouping is shown in Figure 5.40.

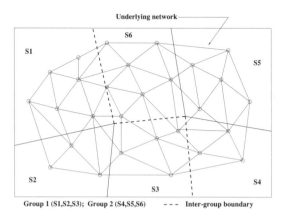

Group 1 (S1,S2,S3); Group 2 (S4,S5,S6)   - - - Inter-group boundary

Figure 5.40. *Example of grouping for $K = 6$ sectors and $N_g = 2$ groups*

As we see, the grouping $\{(S_1, S_2, S_3); (S_4, S_5, S_6)\}$ removes the coordination workload associated with the previous sector borders: $(S_1, S_2); (S_2, S_3); (S_4, S_5); (S_5, S_6)$. Thus, our problem may be formalized in the following manner:

Let us take a transportation network in a 2D space with traffic flows which generate a control workload distributed across the space which we will suppose to be divided into K sectors. We wish to find the optimal grouping of these sectors into N groups, balanced in terms of control workload and minimizing the required coordination effort.

REMARK 5.1.– For this type of problem, we have limited ourselves to networks in 2D, but the principle may be extended to a 3D framework. The proposed grouping must also respect the following connectivity constraint:

Sectors belonging to the same group must be connected.

This constraint avoids cases where a controller must, for example, manage a portion of traffic around Lille (northern France) and another in Marseille (on the south coast); this would be an aberration in terms of air traffic control, causing a loss of homogeneity of traffic in the sectors managed by the same control team, while also generating unnecessary coordination.

From a mathematical perspective, our problem consists of minimizing a criterion y, which is a combination of two subcriteria y_1 and y_2 corresponding, respectively, to the control workload and the coordination workload in each group. We obtain:

$$y = \alpha y_1 + (1 - \alpha)y_2$$

with

$$y_1 = \sum_{n=1}^{N} \frac{|w(g_n) - \frac{M}{N}|}{\frac{M}{N}}; \; y_2 = \sum_{n=1}^{N} w_{co}(g_n)$$

where α is a weighting parameter fixed by the user, $w(g_n)$ is the control workload in group g_n and $w_{co}(g_n)$ is the coordination workload associated with group g_n.

The mathematical description of our objective is very close to that used in the sectorization problem. The essential difference between the two problems resides in the description of the associated search space. In the sectorization problem, the space was continuous and the generated sector borders could be placed anywhere in the geographical space. The search space linked to the grouping problem, however, is a discrete space in which the borders of the new groups must follow the borders of the existing sectors (each group brings together a number of pre-existing sectors without creating any new sectors). Our grouping problem can thus be considered as a classification problem.

5.6.1.1. *Complexity of the grouping problem*

The combinatorics of our problem are presented in the following form:

Taking a set of K elements, how many different ways are there to create N_g ($N_g \leq K$) non-empty groups?

In our application, K is the total number of sectors and N_g is the number of groups created.

The number of possible cases is given by the second Stirling number $S_K^{N_g}$:

$$S_K^{N_g} = \frac{1}{N_g!} \sum_{i=1}^{N_g} C_{N_g}^i \cdot (-1)^{(N_g-i)} \cdot \left(i^K\right)$$

For N = 600 and K = 200 (average grouping of three sectors):

$$S_{600}^{200} \simeq 0.8 \ 10^{1001}$$

Our search space is therefore enormous.

If we now take into account the connectivity constraint, the search space is reduced. To study the induced complexity, we model the problem as follows: In a Euclidean space, we construct a graph in which each node represents the barycenter of each sector in the initial sectorization, and each link shows the *shared border* relationship (Figure 5.41).

Our problem thus requires us to find an optimal $N_g\_$partitioning of a graph of K nodes in connected components, which is NP-hard. As our problem is of large dimensions (K = 600, N_g = 200), we only envisage stochastic resolution techniques.

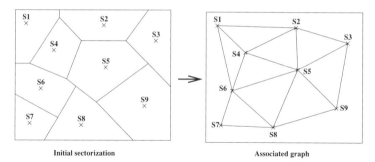

Initial sectorization   Associated graph

Figure 5.41. *Graph associated with a sectorization*

5.6.2. *Optimization using a genetic algorithm: continuous approach*

Coding the chromosome. To randomly generate N_g groups of sectors, we distribute N_g points (group centers) in the geographic space. The coordinates follow the law of uniform distribution. We then aggregate each sector barycenter to its closest group center (Figure 5.42 shows an example of a two-group grouping in a rectangle divided into five sectors).

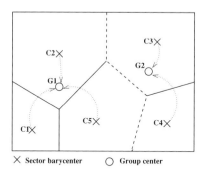

$\times$ Sector barycenter $\bigcirc$ Group center

Figure 5.42. *Example of a "2_grouping" of a "5_partition" of a rectangle*

In this way, we are able to synthesize groups which always respect the connectivity constraint: as the graph created using the barycenters of sectors contained in the group is connected, the associated sectors are guaranteed to be connected. We thus use a chromosome coding identical to that used for the continuous sectorization problem; in this case, we use the coordinates of the group centers. This allows us to use the same crossover and mutation operators.

5.6.2.1. *Results*

As with our sectorization problems, we validate the performances of the algorithm using an artificial network for which we have a clear solution. In this case, we have used an 81-sector sectorization of a regular grid (see Figure 5.43). In this figure, the nodes represent the barycenters of sectors. The flows between different sectors are shown as links in the network (when there is no flow between two sectors, there is no link). Using this sectorization, we wish to obtain nine balanced groups with minimal coordination. The evident solution to this problem is to generate nine subnetworks of nine sectors each.

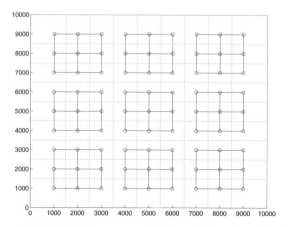

Figure 5.43. *Divided test network (dotted lines show the edges of the initial sectors)*

A genetic algorithm with simulated annealing crossover operator was used for these evaluations. The parameters used for this genetic algorithm are shown in Table 5.2.

Population dimension	: 200
Number of generations	: 100
Probability of crossover	: 0.6
Probability of mutation	: 0.06

Table 5.2. *Parameters of the genetic algorithm*

As we see from the statistics on the evolution of the normalized fitness (see Figure 5.44), an optimal solution is found at generation 50. A physical representation of this solution is shown in Figure 5.45.

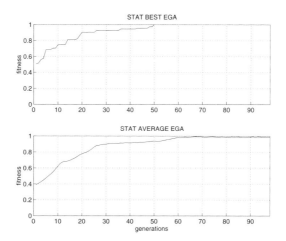

Figure 5.44. *Evolution of the normalized fitness. The evolution of the fitness of the best individual is shown at the top of the diagram with average fitness shown below*

The obtained results may seem surprising at first glance, but we should remember that the algorithm works with sector barycenters and not with the centers themselves. When a sector barycenter is assigned to a group, the whole sector is attached to this group. Returning to the initial definition of the sectors, we obtain the grouping shown in Figure 5.46 which corresponds to the expected result.

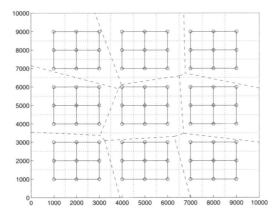

Figure 5.45. *Physical structure of the solution. Dotted lines show the boundries of the groups*

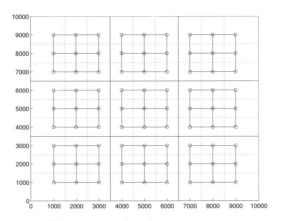

Figure 5.46. *Resulting grouping*

The drawback of the coding used in this case is that it generates groups with a quasi-convex form. Effectively, the principle of group construction by aggregating sector barycenters naturally leads to compact forms, thus reducing the possibilities of the state space.

Using the neighborhood graph of the control sectors, it is possible to use the synthesis of connected components to generate richer sector groups. This approach will be described in the following section.

5.6.3. *Optimization using a genetic algorithm: discrete approach*

5.6.3.1. *Introduction*

To overcome this limitation of the continuous model, the approach proposed here consists of working directly on the neighborhood graph of the control sectors. In this graph, the nodes represent sector barycenters and the links symbolize the relationship "is a neighbor of". An example of this type of graph is shown in Figure 5.47.

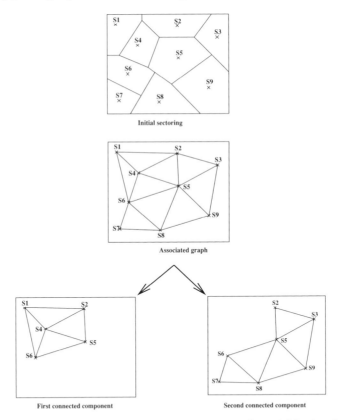

Figure 5.47. *Construction of groupings using the neighborhood graph associated with sectors*

As in the case of discrete sectorization, we wish to identify a set of connected components which will allow us to create sector groupings suited to a given traffic distribution. These components may take any form. This approach extends directly into 3D (see Figure 5.48).

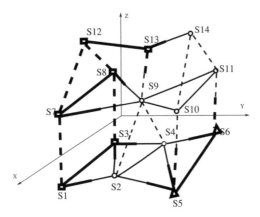

Figure 5.48. *In this illustration, 14 sectors $(S_1, ..., S_{14})$ are assigned to three groups, marked with circles, squares and triangles, respectively*

The model used for this problem is the same as that developed for discrete sectorization (see section 5.4). We can therefore use the same coding and mutation operators, with the exception of the weak mutation operator which is meaningless for this graph. This operator is used to modify the cutoff distance in relation to the nodes in cases where a link is shared by two components. Using a neighborhood graph, only the information concerning the dividing point is relevant.

5.6.3.2. *Results*

This algorithm has been tested on a network with 64 sectors, the structure of which is shown in Figure 5.49. This network presents symmetries which make it easy for us to identify optimal solutions in order to judge our algorithm.

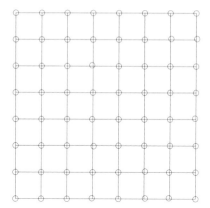

Figure 5.49. *64 node network*

Using this network, we developed six configurations corresponding to six time periods. These situations are shown in Figures 5.50 and 5.51. In these figures, all the nodes have the same weighting and all links have the same flow, with the exception of links which cut across borders, shown in dotted lines, for which the flow is fixed at zero. In these figures, it is easy to identify an optimal two-group solution in cases (a) and (b), four groups in case (c), eight groups in cases (d) and (e) and, finally, 16 groups in case (f).

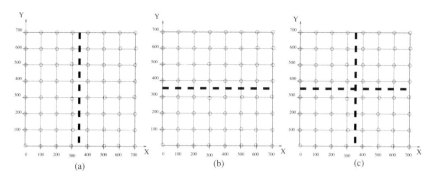

Figure 5.50. *Configurations with two groups (a,b)
and four groups (c)*

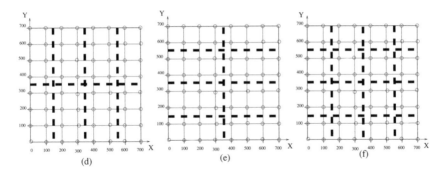

Figure 5.51. *Configurations with eight groups (d,e) and sixteen groups (f)*

As in the previous cases, an optimal solution (without coordination and completely balanced) has a fitness equal to 1.

At the beginning of each period, the desired number of groups is communicated to the algorithm. This situation corresponds to an operational case where we wish to distribute a group of sectors to a group of controllers.

The parameters used for these simulations are shown in Table 5.3.

Population dimension	: 100
Number of generations	: 100 (for each period)
Probability of mutation	: 0.7
Elitism	: yes

Table 5.3. *Parameters of the genetic algorithm*

Three situations were compared in order to verify the relevance of the mutation operators. In the first situation, only the strong mutation operator was used. Figure 5.52 shows the results of this simulation for the six periods. This operator only gives us an optimal solution for the first two periods, corresponding to the simplest configurations.

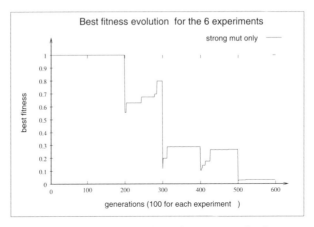

Figure 5.52. *Results of the algorithm using only the strong mutation. For the first 100 generations, the algorithm processes the first two-group problem but after it has not enough time to identify the exact solution*

For the second version of the algorithm, we add the medium mutation, which is only used once (when it is selected). The result of this experiment is shown in Figure 5.53, where we see that the algorithm produces an exact solution, except for the last period.

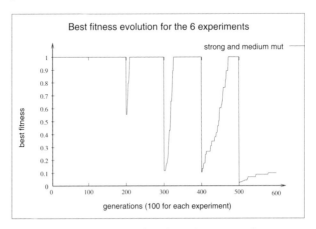

Figure 5.53. *Results of the algorithm using the strong and medium mutations*

Finally, in the third version of the algorithm, the medium mutation operator is used several times, and the process benefits from the group balancing heuristic. As we see from Figure 5.54, the algorithm is now capable of finding the exact solution rapidly for the six periods.

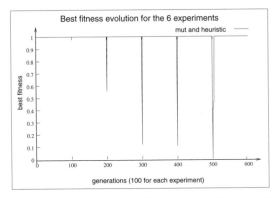

Figure 5.54. *Results of the algorithm with multiple applications of the medium mutation operator*

5.6.3.3. *Conclusion*

The results of these evaluations indicate that genetic algorithms are well suited to solving grouping problems. Despite the restriction of the state space associated with the chromosome coding in the continuous case, in the majority of cases, the solutions produced by the algorithm are of a very high quality.

The behavior of genetic algorithms in the context of realistic instances of sectorization problems has been shown to be highly effective. We have proposed both continuous and discrete modeling methods. Finally, a 3D extension taking into account the operational constraints of air traffic management allows us to produce sectors with a shape suitable for use in air traffic control.

Chapter 6

Contribution to Traffic Assignment

As we have already seen, airspace congestion is linked to the simultaneous presence of aircraft in the same zone of airspace. To reduce congestion, we must therefore separate these aircraft, in terms of time and/or space. To do this, we modify the departure time and/or the routes taken by aircraft in order to respect sector and airport capacities. Working with aircraft in flight, it is also possible to modify the speed of an airplane within certain limits. It is important to maintain equity between users of the transport system when carrying out these modifications.

The principles of traffic assignment consist of modifying airplane trajectories (in space and/or time) in order to reduce airspace congestion while best respecting airline aims. The first section of this chapter presents a summary of traffic assignment methods developed within the domain of transportation network theory. The second section considers other approaches proposed to deal with this problem.

The third section of this chapter covers two contributions in the areas of macroscopic (flow) assignment and microscopic (individual) assignment of air traffic. The fourth section considers the problem of assignment of a group of aircraft to a set of runways. A fifth and final section will present two trajectory planning approaches from a tactical perspective.

6.1. Summary of traffic assignment methods based on transportation network theory

This section presents a summary of traffic assignment methods. We will begin by considering approaches based on transportation network theory.

Any given transportation network will involve two opposing factors: demand and the ability of the network to respond to this demand (capacity). Traffic assignment problems consist of distributing flow across the network in order to optimize a certain number of predetermined criteria (journey time, distance, etc.). There are two broad classes of optimization problems, depending on whether the network is autonomous (users move across the network at will) or subject to the actions of an external flow direction agent (this involves the cooperation of users, who must obey orders from the manager, and constitutes a piloted network). Furthermore, depending on the nature of the demand, we can distinguish between two main categories of traffic assignment:

– static assignment ⇒ traffic demand is constant over time;

– dynamic assignment ⇒ traffic demand varies over time.

The rest of this section will introduce transportation networks, the assignment of static traffic and the assignment of dynamic traffic.

6.1.1. *Transportation networks*

A considerable number of human activities require the movement of people, goods, energy or information in order to maintain communication between different geographical sites. Examples include telephone networks, the distribution of energy from power stations, road networks, etc. In all of these cases, the transport generates a cost (transport cost), which we always wish to minimize. Even at individual level, holidaymakers minimize their transport cost by choosing the most suitable itineraries and times for their journeys. The notion of transport cost is subjective, and depends on the users of the network. Thus, certain entities will aim to minimize consumption; others will aim to minimize journey time, etc. A mathematical theory has been developed in order to optimize network transport costs, in the form of the transportation network theory. This branch of mathematics progressed rapidly in the latter half of the 20th Century; Euler's work in graphs was only published after WWI, and no significant results appeared before the 1950s. This activity continues to develop, as we identify more and more systems with characteristics identical to those which mathematicians associate with networks.

A transportation network can be modeled using a triplet $\{G, \vec{c}, \mathcal{D}\}$ where:

– G: oriented graph associated with the network, made up of two groups: $G = \{\mathcal{N}, \mathcal{A}\}$:

- $\mathcal{N}$: the nodes (with their geographical position, if the network is located in a space including distance). In a transportation network, nodes fall into two categories:

- centroid nodes: nodes that absorb or generate traffic,

- transit nodes: nodes for which the Kirchoff laws are respected:

$$\sum \text{input flow} = \sum \text{output flow}$$

- $\mathcal{A}$: the links. Each link describes an oriented link between two nodes (a link is thus a node pairing).

– $\vec{c}$: vector of the transport costs associated with each of the network links: $\vec{c} = (c_1, c_2, ..., c_{|\mathcal{A}|})$. (Another notation exists, using a matrix of link costs: $C = [c_{ij}] =$ [cost associated with the link connecting nodes (i, j)]). Transport costs are expressed per unit of flow.

– $\mathcal{D}$: all of the traffic demand, noted d_{pq}, between origin-destination node pairs (noted OD from now on); $\mathcal{D} = \{..., d_{pq}, ...\}$ where d_{pq} represents the traffic demand between the centroid nodes p and q (from p toward q). These traffic demands are routed through the network using assignment algorithms. Demand is generally expressed as the number of mobile units wishing to link an origin-destination pair in a given time period. We may distinguish two types of demand:

- static demand: d_{pq} fixed;

- elastic demand: d_{pq} is a function of the transport costs: $d_{pq} = g_{pq}(\vec{\pi})$ where $\vec{\pi}$ represents the cost vector of the shortest paths for all of the OD ($\vec{\pi} = (\pi_1, \pi_2, ..., \pi_{|\mathcal{D}|})^T$).

We say that a transportation network is congested if the cost function associated with a link is increasing in relation to the flow along the link.

Finally, depending on the nature of the interdependence of the link costs in the network, we can group networks into three categories. To do this, we define a Jacobian matrix of the costs:

$$\frac{\partial \vec{c}}{\partial \vec{f}} = [J_{ij}] = \mathbf{J} = \left[\frac{\partial c_i(\vec{f})}{\partial f_j} \right]_{i,j=1,...,|\mathcal{A}|}$$

where $\vec{f}$ is the vector of the flows through all of the links in the network.

1) Networks with separable link costs:

$$\Rightarrow \frac{\partial c_i(\vec{f})}{\partial f_j} = 0 \;\; \forall \;\; i \neq j \Rightarrow (\mathbf{J} \quad \text{diagonal})$$

2) Networks with non-separable symmetrical link costs:

$$\Rightarrow \frac{\partial c_i(\vec{f})}{\partial f_j} = \frac{\partial c_j(\vec{f})}{\partial f_i} \;\; \forall \;\; i, j \Rightarrow (\mathbf{J} \quad \text{symmetrical})$$

3) Networks with non-separable asymmetric link costs:

$$\Rightarrow \exists \;\; i, j \;\; | \;\; \frac{\partial c_i(\vec{f})}{\partial f_j} \neq \frac{\partial c_j(\vec{f})}{\partial f_i} \Rightarrow (\mathbf{J} \quad \text{asymmetric})$$

In the context of our application to air traffic, situations (2) and (3) are best suited to modeling the interaction of air traffic flows along airways.

6.1.2. *Static assignment*

We define a flow using paths $\vec{F}_{pq}$ (not to be confused with the flows across all the links of the network, $\vec{f}$, presented above) by the number of vehicles traveling from an origin centroid p toward a destination centroid q (these vehicles may follow different paths):

$$\vec{F}_{pq} = (F_{pq1}, F_{pq2}, ... F_{pqr}, ...)^T$$

where F_{pqr}: number of vehicles traveling from centroid p toward centroid q along route r. This flow must respect a conservation law in relation to the traffic demand d_{pq} between centroids p and q:

$$\sum_{k \in \mathcal{R}_{pq}} F_{pqk} = d_{pq},$$

where $\mathcal{R}_{pq}$ represents the set of possible routes leading from p to q. We define the transport cost along route k connecting nodes p and q:

$$C_{pqk} = \sum_{a \in \mathcal{A}} \delta_{pqak} c_a$$

where $\delta_{pqak} = 1$ if link a is part of the route k connecting the pair (p, q) (0 otherwise).

The flow along link a is the sum of the flow of routes containing this link:

$$f_a = \sum_{k \in \mathcal{R}_{pq}} \delta_{ak} F_k = \sum_{p,q \mid d_{pq} \in \mathcal{D}} \sum_{k \in \mathcal{R}_{pq}} \delta_{pqak} F_{pqk}$$

In the general case of an elastic demand, an interaction takes place between the flow and the demand through the intermediary of the cost function. We thus arrive at an equilibrium point where the flow present in the network fixes a global cost, which itself then fixes a new demand, etc. In the case of a demand that is independent of the associated transport cost, only the distribution of the flow across the network will be determined at this point.

In determining the obtained flow, we need to use two preliminary hypotheses:

1) each user has full knowledge of the network (links, routes, associated costs) with variable precision;

2) all users behave in the same way.

The precision with which a user knows the network determines whether we speak of deterministic or stochastic equilibrium.

a. Deterministic equilibrium

Using this model, we consider that each user has perfect knowledge of the network and is able to correctly estimate the costs associated with different routes.

Route selection principle: using the deterministic hypothesis, each user effectively chooses the route with the minimum cost. We reach a point of equilibrium when no user is able to reduce their transport cost by choosing a route different to that which they are already on. In these conditions, all routes of a pair OD, which are used, have the same cost, and those that are not in use have a higher cost. This type of equilibrium is summarized by Wardrop's first principle (1952) [LEB 84, WAR 52]:

The journey times in all routes actually used are less than those which would be experienced on unused routes.

Wardrop's equilibrium is, in fact, a Nash equilibrium (1951)[1] [NAS 51] between network users. When this user equilibrium is reached, the routes used are effectively the shortest in terms of transport cost.

Using the hypothesis that an agent outside the network can operate on the flows (users are not autonomous) to minimize the overall transport cost, we reach a point of system equilibrium as expressed in Wardrop's second principle:

The average journey time for all users is minimum.

Using this hypothesis, not all users take the shortest route. In the resulting flow, the marginal costs on the routes used

---

1 Nash's equilibrium describes the outcome of a non-cooperative game in which no player has anything to gain by changing their own strategy, taking account of the strategies of the other players.

to connect an OD pair are equal and lower than those of the unused routes between the same OD pair. The marginal cost $\bar{c}_a$ associated with a link a is given by:

$$\bar{c}_a(f_a) = \frac{d[c_a(\vec{f}).f_a]}{df_a} = c_a(\vec{f}) + \frac{d[c_a((\vec{f}))]}{df_a} \cdot f_a$$

In its general form, the search for user equilibrium is formalized using a variational inequality for which we seek a fixed point. The theory of variational inequality was introduced by Hartman and Stampacchia (1966) [HAR 66] as a tool for studying partially differential equations, applied mostly in the field of mechanics. The inequalities used in these cases were of infinite dimensions. Dafermos adapted the method to finite dimension spaces in 1980 [DAF 80]; Dafermos identified a structure for variational inequalities in the context of equilibrium problems for transportation networks. This marked the beginning of the use of variational inequalities in transportation network theory.

The variational inequality problem noted $VI(\vec{F}, \mathcal{K})$ consists of determining a vector $\vec{x}^* \in \mathcal{K} \subset \mathbb{R}^n$, verifying

$$\langle \vec{F}(\vec{x}^*)^T, (\vec{x} - \vec{x}^*) \rangle \geq 0, \quad \forall \vec{x} \in \mathcal{K} \qquad [6.1]$$

where $\vec{F}$ is a continuous function of $\mathcal{K}$ toward $\mathbb{R}^n$, $\mathcal{K}$ is a closed convex set and $\langle ., . \rangle$ represents the scalar product in $\mathbb{R}^n$.

In geometric terms, the equation [6.1] indicates that $\vec{F}(\vec{x}^*)^T$ is orthogonal to set $\mathcal{K}$ at point $\vec{x}^*$. Variational inequations allow us to model a variety of mathematical problems for which the solution can be expressed in the form of a search for a fixed point.

Effective solution principles have been proposed by D. Bernstein *et al.* [BER 93a, WIE 95, FRI 93b] for small-scale networks.

In the case of networks with separable link costs, Prager [PRA 54] demonstrated in 1954 that the problem of seeking user equilibrium is equivalent to a convex optimization problem. In 1956, Beckmann *et al.* [BEK 56] also identified an optimization problem for networks with elastic demands and separable link costs.

When we reach system equilibrium, the flow minimizes the total transport cost:

$$\min J_s(\vec{f}) = \sum_{a \in \mathcal{A}} c_a(f_a) \cdot f_a$$

In this case, the marginal costs are equal on the routes actually used; these costs are smaller than those calculated for unused routes. The equations linked to system equilibrium are thus the same as those for user equilibrium, but with marginal costs replacing real costs.

In addition, we can show that:

– user and system equilibria exist if and only if $d_{pq}(C_{pqk})$ is a positive or constant continuous function, and if $c_a(f_a)$ is a non-decreasing function;

– these equilibria are unique when $C_a(f_a)$ is a strictly increasing function;

– system equilibrium always gives a lower overall cost than that produced by user equilibrium;

– user equilibrium gives lower performances (in terms of overall cost) but ensures equity between users;

– system equilibrium is optimal, but not necessarily fair (certain users will be routed along non-optimal routes).

Resolution methods

The assignment of static and deterministic traffic was the first case to be dealt with in equilibrium studies for transportation networks. For this reason, the available bibliography on this subject is abundant, including high-performance algorithms, even for networks of large dimensions. The following works are devoted to deterministic assignment:

– Non-congested networks:

- non-congested networks with unlimited link capacity [DET 58];

- non-congested networks with limited link capacity: [MER 71].

– Congested networks:

- mono-class traffic:

i) J diagonal [ARE 90, BIE 80, DAF 72, DAG 80, FUK 84, GAL 86, HEA 86, LEB 85, LEB 75, LEV 73, MAR 65, NGU 76, TSI 86, VAN 87, ZEN 91];

ii) J symmetrical [DAF 80, MAR 83, NAG 84, NGU 76, POW 82, SMI 79, SMI 81];

iii) J asymmetric [AAS 79, DAF 71, DAF 80, DAF 92, DAF 69b, FIS 82, FLO 82, GAR 80, HEA 90, HEA 84, LAW 84, LAW 83, MAR 83, MAR 85, NAG 86, POW 82, SMI 83].

- multi-class traffic [NET 70];

- multi-class traffic and elastic demand [AAS 79, DAF 82a, DAF 82b, FIS 82, NAG 86, SHE 85].

The most widely used algorithms include: algorithm based on the Frank-Wolfe optimization method (1956 [DAF 69a, FRA 56]; descent algorithm), algorithm based on

Dijkstra's shortest path search principle (distribution of demand by flow increment across paths with minimum cost) and the Dafermos algorithm (1982 [FRA 82], consisting of iteratively moving flows between the currently used path with the highest maximum marginal cost to the path with the minimum marginal cost, so as to minimize the overall congestion of the network).

b. Stochastic equilibrium

We will now look at a more realistic situation, where the link costs are random variables and where users perceive cost with a degree of error, which varies between individuals [DAG 77]. We thus have two random variables linked to link costs:

1) an error from the network, symbolizing the flaws in the model;

2) an error due to the poor perception of cost values by users.

In addition, we consider that these perception errors are specific to classes of users. Figure 6.1 gives a summary of this principle.

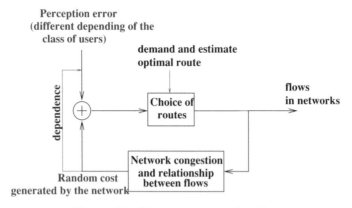

Figure 6.1. *Cost generation principle*

Problem: several user groups exist linking OD pairs (specific to their class) in a stochastic network. Each route connecting an OD pair is associated with a set of links of which the costs are random non-negative values. Each user perceives a transport cost on their route with their own level of error, which is a random value of which the characteristics are linked to the class of the user. The problem thus consists of determining the stochastic equilibrium of the resulting flow in the network (GTESP, Generalized Traffic Equilibrium problem on Stochastic Networks [MIR 87]).

In addition, we suppose that each user behaves in a different manner depending on the traffic they may encounter on their route. This behavior is modeled using a repugnance function.

Equilibrium study: using the stochastic framework presented in the previous text, it is possible to find a situation of equilibrium that takes the form of a generalization of Wardrop's first principle:

– at the point of equilibrium, for any OD pair, the flow in the stochastic network is such that the expected value of the repugnances perceived by users on current routes are equal and lower to those on unused routes.

Resolution algorithms: unlike the deterministic case, where practically all possible cases have been solved, the problem of equilibrium in stochastic networks remains unsolved in numerous situations. The main assignment algorithms for static stochastic traffic are described in references [DAG 83, FIS 80, MIR 87, SOR 90, SOR 85, VON 66].

c. Conclusion

The stochastic formulation is most realistic, but its resolution requires a far larger computation effort than in deterministic cases. However, it is possible to show that, for heavily congested networks, stochastic and deterministic equilibrium are practically equivalent. Nevertheless, in the context of air traffic, we cannot truly speak of heavily congested networks and the stochastic hypothesis is thus more suitable; unfortunately, as we have seen, very few resolution algorithms exist for these cases.

A static approach is suitable to describe macroscopic phenomena for which the notion of flow is meaningful. When we wish to obtain a more precise adjustment of demand to capacity, we need to account for the temporal evolution of traffic in the network, in order to represent microscopic relationships between demand and capacity. In these cases, we use the principle of dynamic assignment.

6.1.3. *Dynamic assignment*

Dynamic assignment consists of predicting the evolution of traffic in a congested network, for which traffic demand and link costs vary in space and time. We distinguish between two classes of assignment:

– optimal dynamic assignment from the user perspective, in which users attempt to minimize their own transport cost;

– optimal dynamic assignment from the system perspective, which allows overrall minimization of transport costs.

These forms of assignment can be used in both deterministic and stochastic cases.

a. Deterministic dynamic assignment

Resolution methods adapted to these models seek, for each network user, a departure time and a route producing user equilibrium. Unfortunately, the complexity inherent in these problems greatly reduces resolution algorithm possibilities, especially if we wish to optimize routes and departure times at the same time. This problem is NP-hard [BEN 91, DEP 90] and multimodal [GHA 95]. The proposed approaches only allow a partial solution to the problem:

– Ben Akiva [BEN 85]: one origin and one destination, optimization of departure time.

– Hendrickson *et al*. [HEN 81]: n origins and n destinations, system equilibrium in a network with simple link costs; departure time optimization (analytical approach).

– Mahmassani *et al*. [CHA 88a, JOU 93, MAH 84]: one origin and one destination; analytical approach using simple link costs; departure time optimization.

– Merchant *et al*. [MER 78a, MER 78b]: network with separable link costs; route optimization (heuristic approach).

– Alfa [ALF 89]: optimization heuristic for departure times and routes; convergence to a fixed point not guaranteed.

– Arnott *et al*. [ARN 90]: n parallel routes optimization of routes and departure times, separable link costs.

– Ho [HO 90]: optimization of routes, separable link costs, decomposition method.

– Bell [BEL 95]: optimization of routes, links with capacity, separable link costs.

– Carey [CAR 87]: optimization of routes, separable link costs, determination of system equilibrium by convex programming.

Further dynamic assignment methods are given in [FRI 93a, LAF 93, SMI 93a].

b. Stochastic dynamic assignment

In the case of static assignment, the user was simply required to choose a route. In the case of dynamic assignment, users also need a departure time. The user decision variable is thus made up of a pair (k, h), that is the chosen route and the departure time [ALF 86, CAS 89a, SHE 82, SMA 82]. The user associates utility value with each pair (k, h), which is, in fact, a random variable:

$$\tilde{U}_{kh} = \overline{V}_{kh} + \tilde{\varepsilon}_{kh};$$

with $\overline{V}_{kh}$: expectation of utility.

At this level, two different approaches may be used to optimize user decisions [BEN 86a].

– *Equilibrium-based model*: using this model, we seek an optimum flow on different routes in order to attain equilibrium. This equilibrium constitutes a generalization of Wardrop's first principle [WAR 52]:

In an equilibrium configuration, no user can increase their perceived utility value by leaving earlier or later or by selecting a different route.

At the time of writing, a mathematical demonstration of the existence and uniqueness of a state of equilibrium has yet to be established, but we know that this state of equilibrium does occur from observations of simulation [BEN 86a].

– *Model based on stochastic processes*: this model is an extension of the model described previously with a demand that varies from day to day. In this case, we consider that the cost and journey time on route k at instant h on day n is a function of the costs and journey times observed over the m previous days. The complexity created by a bi-allocation problem in large-scale networks with non-separable asymmetric link costs has led researchers to prefer simulation-based approaches, with the aim of producing solutions close to user or system equilibrium. The main advantage of these methods is their ability to account for real characteristics of a problem and the fact they are suitable for use with large-scale networks. Cascetta *et al.* [CAS 87, CAS 89a, CAS 91, CAS 93], Cantarella *et al.* [CAN 95] and Vythoulkas [VYT 90a] use a simulation in the following manner:

A set of departure times and a set of alternative routes are associated with each network user. Each user randomly selects a route and a departure time from these two sets, and traffic is simulated for the entire period under consideration (generally a day). Following this simulation, a utility function is computed for each network user. The following day, user choices are biased by the utility values from the previous day. The process of examining utility values from previous days is repeated, limiting the number of past days for examination (N days). We thus create a learning process with limited memory (for a day k, we observe the utility values of days $k - 1, ..., k - N$). This stochastic process may be shown to be a stationary Markov chain with a stable fixed point, but with a distance from user (or system) equilibrium, which is impossible to quantify, as this distance depends essentially on the initial conditions. Other simulation-based approaches are proposed in [BEN 86b], [BEN 94], [BIR 93], [CAS 89b], [CHA 88b], [MAH 92b], [MAH 86], [MAH 91b], [MAN 90], [VAN 79] and [VYT 90b].

c. Conclusion

As we have seen, transportation network theory proposes different modeling frameworks adapted to most of the situations encountered in reality. Unfortunately, some of these problems are so complex that no algorithms are available to solve them.

None of the assignment methods described above take account of the requirement for equity between airlines and therefore cannot be applied to our problem, as they are based on Wardrop's principles that, by definition, produce assignments with segmented flows[2].

Transportation network theory covers most traffic assignment methods, but our problem has also been approached in the context of other academic disciplines. The following section presents other methods that can be used when considering a traffic assignment problem.

6.2. Other approaches to traffic assignment

In this section, we will present other approaches to solving the traffic assignment problem, essentially based on the temporal extension of the network, optimal control and dynamic programming.

6.2.1. *Temporal extension of the network*

This technique consists of carrying out a temporal extension of each node and each link of a network in order to apply static assignment methods. If there are N time periods, the network is duplicated N times. The time increment is dimensioned based on the granularity of the desired equilibrium and the speed of vehicles in the network, in order to avoid missing critical network events. This approach is described in [DRI 92], [HEL 92], [JAY 95], [KAU 92], [ZAW 87] and [ZEN 91]. This approach, by its very nature, can only be applied to small-scale networks.

---

2 We see that in the context of congested networks (our case), a segmented flow assignment always produces better results, in terms of the overall network cost, than a non-segmented assignment. These techniques are essentially applied to road traffic, for which flows are naturally segmented by users; there is no prior justification for the development of assignment methods with non-segmented flow as these methods are known to reduce the capacity of transportation networks.

6.2.2. *Optimal control*

Approaches based on optimal control have been proposed in the context of small-scale networks. In general, the state variables are the flow along the links over a period δ_t and the associated control variables are the input flows along these links over the same period. The principle approaches carried out in this domain are as follows:

– Wie *et al.* [WIE 94]: n origins with one destination, route assignment, system equilibrium, network with separable link costs;

– Wie *et al.* [WIE 90]: n origins with m destinations, route assignment, user equilibrium, network with separable link costs;

– Papageorgiou [PAP 90]: route assignment, user and system equilibrium, network with separable link costs;

– Ran *et al.* [RAN 93]: n origins with m destinations, route assignment, user equilibrium, network with separable link costs;

– Friesz *et al.* [FRI 89]: n origins with one destination, route assignment, user and system equilibrium, network with separable link costs;

– Leblanc *et al.* [LEB 92]: description of a route and departure time assignment model aiming to obtain user equilibrium (no resolution algorithm);

– Janson *et al.* [JAN 93]: bi-allocation (route-time), network with separable link costs.

6.2.3. *Dynamic programming approaches (ground holding problem)*

The formulation of the slot allocation problem[3] by dynamic programming was initially proposed by Odoni [ODO 87].

The initial form consisted of optimizing the landing of N aircraft at the same airport within a given period, using the following model:

a. Hypotheses and data

– N airplanes (flights $F_1, ..., F_N$) are expected to land at airport Z from S departure airports.

– The destination airport is the only resource with limited capacity.

– The departure time and journey length of each aircraft are deterministic and known in advance.

– The considered time period $[0, T]$ is divided into P time slots $(T_1, T_2, ..., T_P)$.

– The capacity of airport Z is known for each of these time slots $(K_1, K_2, ..., K_P)$.

– For each flight F_i, we know the arrival time at airport Z and thus the associated time slot T_i. Furthermore, for each flight F_i, it is possible to calculate the cost associated with a delay of t slots $Cg_i(t)$ on the ground.

– C_{ij} represents the cost associated with flight i when it lands during period j.

– In addition, we suppose that flights that have been unable to land during one of the periods $T_1, T_2, ..., T_P$ will be able to land during the final period T_{P+1} ($K_{P+1} = \infty$).

– We wish to minimize the delay allocated to each flight which allows us to avoid exceeding the capacity of airport Z.

---

3 A slot is a departure time range.

b. Mathematical modeling

Let $d_1, d_2, ..., d_N$ be the set of delays associated with our N flights (variables to optimize). Introducing binary variables x_{ij}, with $x_{ij} = 1$ if aircraft i lands during period j (0 otherwise), the criterion to minimize is given by the following expression:

$$\min \sum_{i=1}^{N} \sum_{j=1}^{P+1} C_{ij}.x_{ij}$$

With the addition of our constraints, we obtain the following model:

$$\min \sum_{i=1}^{N} \sum_{j=1}^{P+1} C_{ij}.x_{ij}$$
$$SC$$
$$\forall (i,j) x_{ij} \in \{0,1\}$$
$$\forall i \in \{1, N\} \sum_{j=1}^{P+1} x_{ij} = 1$$
$$\forall j \in \{1, P\} \sum_{i=1}^{N} x_{ij} \leq K_j$$

Andreata and Romanin-Jacur [AND 87] began by developing a resolution principle associated with this basic model in the case of N flights arriving at the same airport during the same period, using a deterministic capacity. The stochastic case consists of envisaging several capacity scenarios, which mainly depend on weather conditions, and weighting them by level of probability. The different capacity scenarios for an airport (deterministic or stochastic) are described in [GIL 93].

Terrab and Odoni [TER 93] extended the previous model to cases with several time periods for the arrival airport and stochastic capacities. The algorithm they proposed did not allow treatment of large instances of the problem, and an improvement was later put forward by Richetta and Odoni [RIC 93, RIC 94].

Vranas et al. [AND 93, VRA 94a, VRA 94b] looked at the case of multiple airports in the deterministic case with connected flights (hub phenomenon[4]; note that, without this connection constraint, the problem becomes separable and may be treated independently for each individual airport).

Bertsimas and Stock [BER 94] proposed a binary programming approach, which extends the previous approach by adding en route-type constraints at sector level (limited sector capacity), but only consider the case of delay allocation. The same extension has also been proposed by Maugis [MAU 96], but using a more robust model of sector workload.

Finally, a first attempt of bi-assignment (routes and slots) has been developed by Tosic [TOS 97]; in this method, each airplane can choose a route from a set of options. The combinatorics involved mean that the results only deal with the case of two routes per airplane, working with small instances of the problem.

6.2.4. *Conclusion*

As we have already seen, two approaches may be used to reduce congestion in a transportation network:

1) Adaptation of capacity to demand (redimensioning the system);

2) Adaptation of demand to capacity (traffic assignment).

---

4 To increase the number of possible destinations at a reduced cost, an airline assigns the role of "hub" to an airport in its network, and organizes arrival and departure times so that stopovers will be as brief as possible for passengers. This reduces the number of segments involved, but requires precise management of synchronism and careful treatment of disturbances (particularly those caused by weather conditions). Certain American companies (Delta, American Airlines, etc.) use a "multi-hub" network, which requires elaborate supervision methods.

The traffic assignment problem is a key point in the reduction of congestion. A considerable number of research projects have been carried out on this problem, producing solution principles that are effective on simplified formulations. These methods distribute demand across several routes in order to minimize a criterion (user or system). In the case of system equilibrium, certain users are penalized in order to minimize an overall congestion criterion; this leads to a loss of equity. In the context of air transport, the notion of equity is important as there is fierce competition between airlines operating between the same origin-destination pairings. In the case of road traffic, this notion is not critical and assignment methods naturally distribute demand across several routes connecting the same OD pairs. This is known as segmented flow. For air traffic, and in the context of route assignment, two approaches may be used to recover equity:

1) All aircraft connecting the same OD pair are assigned to the same route. This is known as *all-or-nothing traffic assignment* and involves strong combinatorics (discrete variables). We have therefore developed an approach to this problem based on artificial evolution, which will be presented in the next section;

2) Implementation of a congestion pricing principle. This approach was studied in the thesis of Karine Deschinkel [DES 01].

In the case of bi-allocation (route and slots), the methods presented above can only be applied to small-scale networks. The problem remains difficult due to the combinatorics involved. An approach based on genetic algorithms, which has produced satisfactory results using realistic instances of the problem, will be presented later in this chapter.

6.3. Using artificial evolution in all-or-nothing traffic assignment

All-or-nothing traffic assignment (which involves non-segmented flows) aims to assign demands between each OD pair to a single route, minimizing overall congestion in the network. In practice, this approach ensures equity between users of a same OD pair; it is therefore appropriate for contexts where there is considerable competition, as in the case of airlines. However, the resulting assignment generally creates more congestion than in the case of segmented flows. The difference becomes more significant when more choices are available for each OD pair. All-or-nothing assignment involves a considerable combinatoric aspect, and we will consider a resolution method based on artificial evolution below.

6.3.1. *Mathematical formalization of objectives*

Our objective is to minimize a criterion C, which is the weighting of two criteria (C_1, C_2) linked, respectively, to the interests of network users (airlines) and the interests of the network manager (the Air Traffic Control (ATC) system), in the knowledge that C_1 and C_2 are not independent. We then construct a global objective function, which is the weighting of C_1 and C_2:

$$C = \alpha C_1 + (1 - \alpha)C_2; \ 0 \leq \alpha \leq 1;$$

where:

– C_1: average extension (in terms of cost) in relation to the shortest route in the sense of geographical distance covered:

$$C_1 = \frac{1}{|\mathcal{A}|} \left(\sum_{(i,j)\in\mathcal{A}} \left[\frac{a.d_{ij}.f_{ij} + b.f_{ij}^2}{\bar{f}} \right] - \sum_{\substack{(i,j)\,\in\,\mathcal{A} \\ \text{assignment to} \\ \text{to minimum} \\ \text{distance}}} \frac{a.d_{ij}.f_{ij}}{\bar{f}} \right);$$

In this expression:

– the second summation represents the transport cost linked to distances, i.e. when we assign all flows to the shortest routes.

– d_{ij} is the geographical distance separating nodes i and j.

– f_{ij} is the flow along the link connecting nodes i and j.

– $a.d_{ij}.f_{ij}$: cost linked to the distance traveled along a link (i,j).

– bf_{ij}^2 models the congestion along a link.

– Coefficients a and b are calculated so that the cost linked to the distance is dominant in relation to the congestion cost for average traffic flows (this choice is realistic as, unlike the road network, the air transportation network is not particularly congested).

However, for heavily loaded links ($f_{ij} = 10$ times the average fij), we need to increase the importance of the congestion term. For this reason, we have used the following values for coefficients a and b:

$$a = \frac{1}{\bar{d}}; \ b = \frac{1}{4\bar{f}};$$

where

$$\bar{d} = \frac{\sum_{(i,j)\in L} d_{ij}}{|\mathcal{A}|} \text{average link length}$$

$$\bar{f} = \frac{\sum_{(i,j)\in L} f_{ij}}{|\mathcal{A}|} \text{average flow along a link}$$

− C_2 is proportional to the overall congestion in the airspace:

$$C_2 = \sum_{k=1}^{k=K} \{a_1.f[C_{mo}(k)] + a_2.g[C_{co}(k)] + a_3.h[C_{cf}(k)]\}$$

where:

- K: number of sectors;

- $C_{mo}(k)$: monitoring workload in sector k;

- $C_{co}(k)$: coordination workload in sector k;

- $C_{cf}(k)$: conflict workload in sector k;

- f, g, h: quadratic functions;

- a_1, a_2, a_3 weighting coefficients pre-determined by the user.

This final point allows us to model congestion in the sectors used.

The criterion defined in this manner generates an underlying non-separability between links in the networks. Even in the absence of the canonical form of a network with non-separable link costs, we have:

$$C = \sum_{(i,j)\in L} C_{ij}(\vec{f});$$

where $\vec{f}$ is the vector containing all the flows of the links in the network. Criterion C_2 introduces dependency between links.

We will now present the way in which we used genetic algorithms to solve this problem.

6.3.2. *Coding and operators of the genetic algorithm*

a. Chromosome coding

The coding used for this algorithm consists of defining the list of nodes making up the path, which will carry the flow for each OD pair.

This coding means that the dimension of the chromosome varies as a function of the length of the paths included, as we can see from the example shown in Figure 6.2. In this example, airplanes connecting airport 1 to airport 16 are routed along the path $\{1, 4, 3, 7, 12, 16\}$. Aircraft traveling in the opposite direction are routed along the path $\{16, 11, 6, 3, 4, 1\}$, etc.

b. Initial population generation principle

To use a genetic algorithm correctly, we require an initial population of individuals containing a set of randomly initialized paths. For each individual, we consider the initial graph, for which link costs are determined using a geographical distance, subjected to noise using a Gaussian distribution (costs must remain positive). For each origin-destination pair contained in the chromosome, we look for the shortest path using a Dijkstra algorithm [DIJ 59] (complexity $O(N^2)$, where N is the number of nodes in the network). The deviation of the Gaussian distribution determines how different the generates paths will be from the shortest geographical path in the network before noise was applied [DEL 95a]. This initialization principle avoids purely random generation of paths in the network, which would create aberrations in navigational terms (such as a path linking Madrid and London via Moscow).

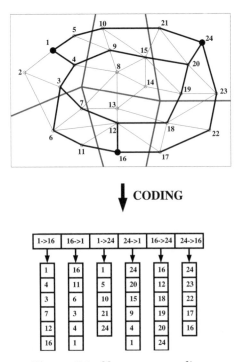

Figure 6.2. *Chromosome coding*

Once we have a non-homogeneous population, we need to define the associated crossover and mutation operators, which will be used to generate new elements within the population.

c. Crossover operator

For this application, we chose to use a slicing crossover. To carry out a crossover using this method, we randomly select a position in the chromosome, then exchange the two sets of terminal paths (see Figure 6.3).

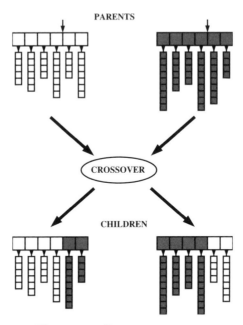

Figure 6.3. *Crossover operator*

d. Mutation operator

The mutation operator allows us to enrich the diversity of the population by creating new paths. To do this, the mutation operator randomly selects an origin-destination pair in the chromosome and applies the same random path generation process used in the creation of the initial population, but with a stronger standard deviation.

e. Calculation and normalization of fitness

First, we will consider the transportation network without traffic. For each origin-destination pair contained within the chromosome, we assign the corresponding demand to the path described by the associated list of nodes. We thus obtain the distribution of flows along each of the links of the network, which enables us to calculate the assignment sub-criterion C_1 and the overall control workload C_2 (and thus criterion C).

The number of operations needed to evaluate a fitness depends on the size of the network and varies in terms of $O(N_{od} + L + K(N + L))$ (N_{od}: number of origin-destination pairs, L: number of links in the network, K: number of sectors, N: number of nodes).

6.3.3. *Introduction of an inter-chromosome distance for sharing*

To carry out sharing (see section 2.2.2), we need an inter-chromosome distance in order to evaluate the level of aggregation of individuals in the state space. To determine this distance between paths, we directly consider the geographical space, using the coordinates of nodes rather than their indexes. We then define the distance between two paths by the closed surface they enclose (see Figure 6.4).

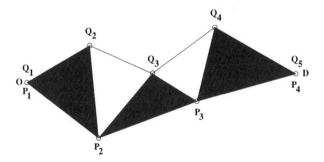

Figure 6.4. *Surface delimited by two paths*

This surface is calculated taking the sum of the surfaces of the triangles constructed using the nodes of each of the paths $\{P_1, P_2, ..., P_m\}$ and $\{Q_1, Q_2, ..., Q_n\}$ ($m \leq n$ and $n \geq 3$) as shown in Figure 6.4 (case where $m = 4$ and $n = 5$). The closed form expression of this surface is given by the following formula:

$$S \;=\; A(P_1, P_2, Q_2) + \sum_{i=2}^{m-1} \{A(P_i, Q_i, Q_{i+1}) +$$

$$A(P_i, P_{i+1}, Q_{i+1})\} + \sum_{i=m}^{n-2} \{A(P_m, Q_i, Q_{i+1})\}.$$

What happens when paths cross over?

In general, this pseudo-distance increases the area included between the two paths (see Figure 6.5); in the particular case of our planar transportation network, where routes cross at nodes, the pseudo-distance is always equal to the area enclosed by the two paths (see Figure 6.6).

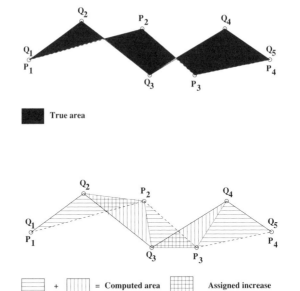

Figure 6.5. *Surface delimited by two paths with any intersection*

Using the distance between two paths, we calculate the distance between two chromosomes by taking the sum of the respective distances associated with each of the pairs of paths contained in the chromosome.

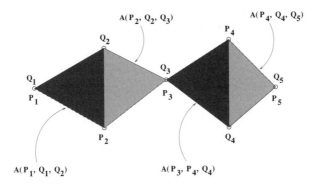

Figure 6.6. *Surface delimited by two paths intersecting at nodes*

a. Calculation of the barycenter between two chromosomes

To use clustered sharing (see section 2.3.1), we need to be able to calculate the barycenter of a set of chromosomes. As for the calculation of the distance between chromosomes, we need to work in the underlying geographical space of the network to calculate the barycenter between two paths.

Let us take two paths:

$$Ch_1 = \{P_1, P_2, ..., P_m\}; Ch_2 = \{Q_1, Q_2, ..., Q_n\}\, n \geq 3;\ m < n$$

with $P_1 = Q_1$ and $P_m = Q_n$. Let n_1 and n_2 be the barycentric coefficients associated with paths Ch_1 and Ch_2, respectively. The barycentric path is thus given by:

$$Ch_B = (\vec{P_1}, \frac{n_1\vec{P_2} + n_2\vec{Q_2}}{n_1 + n_2}, \frac{n_1\vec{P_3} + n_2\vec{Q_3}}{n_1 + n_2}, ...,$$

$$\frac{n_1\vec{P_{m-1}} + n_2\vec{Q_{m-1}}}{n_1 + n_2}, \frac{n_1\vec{P_{m-1}} + n_2\vec{Q_m}}{n_1 + n_2}, ..., \frac{n_1\vec{P_{m-1}} + n_2\vec{Q_{n-1}}}{n_1 + n_2}, \vec{Q_n})$$

In this expression, $\vec{P}$ represents the geographical position of node P.

An example of a barycentric path is shown in Figure 6.7 with $m = 5$, $n = 6$, $n_1 = 2$ and $n_2 = 1$.

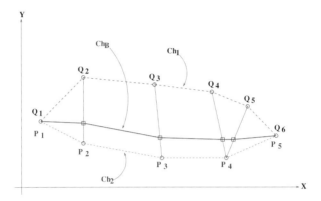

Figure 6.7. *Example of a barycentric path*

To determine the barycenter between two chromosomes, we must simply apply this process to each pair of paths representing the same OD in the two chromosomes.

6.3.4. *Example of results*

To evaluate our algorithm, we have used a test network for which we already have an optimal assignment solution (see Figure 6.8).

In this network, the nodes on the first diagonal represent airports, and those on the second diagonal are beacons. We wish to assign a constant, symmetrical traffic demand between each pair of airports (each airport generates a demand to be assigned to the symmetrical airport. Both generate and receive the same quantity of traffic).

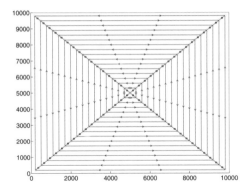

Figure 6.8. *Test network*

In this example, the congestion coefficient is chosen in such a way that no two traffic flows can take the same link; in the same way, no two flows will meet head-on along a link. The criterion is thus presented in the following manner:

$$C = \alpha \sum_{(i,j)\in\mathcal{A}} C_{ij}(f_{ij}) + (1 - \alpha) \sum_{(i,j)\in\mathcal{A}} \gamma f_{ij} f_{ji}$$

As we can see, there is no sectorization, but the form of the criterion is similar to that described earlier and has no effect on the generality of the algorithm.

The parameters used for our experiments are given in Table 6.1.

Population dimension	: 400
Number of generations	: 300
Probability of crossover	: 0.6
Probability of mutation	: 0.06

Table 6.1. *Parameters of the genetic algorithm*

For this test, we used a genetic algorithm with simulated annealing in the crossover operator in order to improve its convergence performance. The evolution of the fitness (normalized between 0 and 1) of the best individual and the average fitness of the whole population as a function of the generation are shown in Figure 6.9.

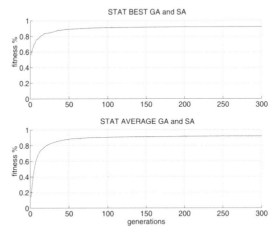

Figure 6.9. *Evolution of normalized fitness*

As we can see, an optimal solution is reached from generation 180, for which only the part of the criterion linked to the journey distance is used. The assignment corresponding to this solution is shown in Figure 6.10.

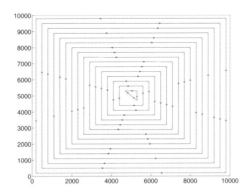

Figure 6.10. *Resulting assignment*

During this evaluation process, we noted that the performances of this algorithm are highly sensitive to the magnitude of the standard deviation of the distribution used to add noise to link costs in the process of generating random paths. For each problem, this parameter must be selected in order to obtain random paths which are different to the optimal path, in terms of distance, but which do not introduce excessive penalties in terms of the extra length involved. One solution would be to code this parameter into the chromosome and allow it to be adjusted adaptively by the genetic algorithm.

6.3.5. *Conclusion*

The equity constraint prevents us from using classic traffic assignment methods for networks with non-separable link costs and introduces a high level of complexity, pushing us to use stochastic optimization methods. Having developed suitable chromosome coding and appropriate operators, we see that genetic algorithms provide an effective means of treating these problems, on condition that the random path generator is suitable for the transportation network in question.

A major drawback of the equity constraint, which guarantees free competition between airlines, is that it reduces our search space and prevents us from accessing certain zones of the state space where the criterion would certainly be better. We see that, when the criterion to optimize is quadratic, rather than linear, in relation to the flow along paths, it would be better to segment flows in order to increase the capacity of the system.

This approach remains macroscopic and produces a crude assignment suitable for use with flows. To obtain a finer assignment, we need to look at a microscopic level, taking account of the dynamic aspects of demand. However, as we have seen, the problem of bi-allocation remains open in the context of large-scale networks. In the following section, we will present a realistic bi-allocation approach, based on artificial evolution, which presents considerable reductions in airspace congestion.

6.4. Allocation of routes and slots using artificial evolution

The work presented in this section was carried out in the context of a thesis by Sofiane Oussedik [OUS 00a]. The aim of this research was to reduce airspace congestion by modifying take-off slots and routes for a set of flights on a country-wide scale. We thus considered a sectorized airspace and a set of flight plans for a given day. For each flight, we defined a set of alternative routes and a set of possible take-off slots. Our goal was to produce an optimal assignment to minimize airspace congestion. Using realistic subsets of routes and slots allowed us to reduce the domain of instances of our problem, including only possibilities that would be realistic at operational level (negotiated with airlines). This reduction is justified by the choice of airlines concerning routes and slots (choices which are, in reality, limited), allowing us to develop an optimization satisfactory to both ATC and the airlines operating center (AOC).

Our problem can be presented as follows:

– We consider all of the flight plans associated with the airspace of a country.

– For each airplane k, we suppose that the following elements are known:

    - a set of possible routes (+ associated costs);

    - a set of possible takeoff times (+ associated costs);

- the set of flights connected with flight k at departure and arrival points (hub phenomenon).

We wish to obtain the configuration that allows us to reduce airspace congestion, minimize cost and respect connection plans.

We will begin our study by presenting the simulation principles used in generating the set of aircraft trajectories which constitute the basis of our system. We will then describe the way in which the objective function was calculated, along with two implementations of genetic algorithms. Finally, we will consider a "dynamic" version of the algorithm using sliding time windows and a multi-objective extension to the method.

6.4.1. *System architecture*

The architecture of the chosen approach (see Figure 6.11) is made up of a traffic simulator and a genetic algorithm (GA).

The simulator is used in pre-treatment to obtain the data needed for optimization. It receives flight plans (airplane identification, airplane type, origin-destination, departure time, flight profile, route as a set of beacons) and constructs airplane trajectories, while saving the necessary data (sector input and output, flight position and direction every minute, etc.).

The genetic algorithm then manipulates a population of possible plannings, represented by disturbances, in terms of routes and slots, to the initial flight plans.

The GA generates plannings which are increasingly efficient in terms of minimizing congestion. The best planning is then put forward as the result of the optimization process.

Below, we will consider the various components of the system, beginning with the principle used to generate alternative routes.

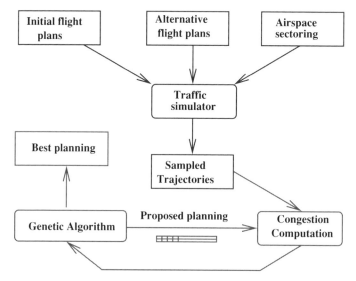

Figure 6.11. *Evolutionary algorithm using a simulated adaptation function*

a. Generation principle for alternative routes

The generation of alternative routes (between each origin O and destination D) to spread traffic across the network is a very important aspect of the optimization process.

Several approaches have been proposed to obtain these alternative routes:

– filtering real flight plans;

– use of a shortest path search algorithm;

– use of a GA.

These methods are presented below:

Filtering existing flight plans: this method is very simple and involves filtering existing flight plans to obtain the different possible routes used between a same origin-destination pairing. The main advantage of the method is that the routes obtained in this way are known to be valid (accepted by airlines) and respect constraints linked to the type of aircraft used on the route. However, route possibilities are limited to current existing routes and to the information contained in the chosen flight plan data, which reduces the number of proposed alternatives.

Use of a shortest path search algorithm: we begin by generating a subnetwork of beacons for a given origin-destination (OD) pairing. We then use a shortest path search algorithm ($A^\star$ [NIL 80], Dijkstra [DIJ 59], Bellman-Ford [BEL 58], etc.) to find the shortest path. For each iteration, we exclude certain portions of the airspace (sectors) by eliminating all of the links that cut across them (see Figure 6.12). We also remove at least one link belonging to the previous route, generated by the previous iteration. This requires pre-processing of all of the links and involves crossed sectors. Thus, in [DEL 94a] and to obtain different routes, a Gaussian noise is used to modify link costs after every use of the Dijkstra algorithm.

The main limitation of these methods is that it is difficult to integrate real constraints, such as limited changes in direction by airplanes; it is sometimes necessary to attempt to use the algorithm several times before obtaining a useable route.

Alternative route searches using genetic algorithms: in this case, routes are obtained using a minimum distance between routes in terms of crossed sectors and of surface. Using this method, route generation takes account of navigational constraints, such as the maximum angle for a change in direction between two consecutive segments and the longest possible route length. Only part of the beacon set is concerned by the alternative route generation process. We can eliminate all beacons which would introduce unacceptable lengthening, retaining only those belonging to the domain of an ellipse (see Figure 6.13) centered in the middle of segment OD (with a given eccentricity chosen by the user).

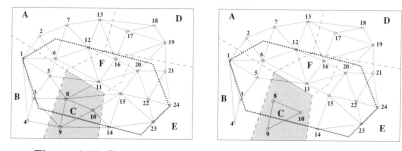

Figure 6.12. *Domain of generation of alternative routes. In this example, one search for alternative routes between nodes 1 and 24*

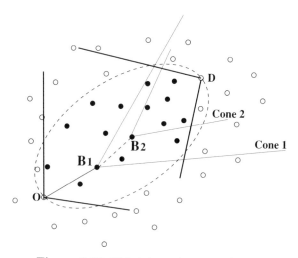

Figure 6.13. *Obtaining a beacon sub-set*

A greedy construction process is then used to generate alternative routes.

From the origin O, a beacon (belonging to the ellipse) is chosen at random (beacon B_1 in Figure 6.13). A cone (cone 1) is then opened (its axis is co-linear to vector $\vec{OB_1}$), allowing construction of a new subset of beacons (elements of the cone and of the ellipse). Another beacon (B_2) is then drawn from this subset, and the process is repeated until the destination is reached. The introduction of the cone ensures that the variation in direction between successive segments will be acceptable.

The distance between B_2 and D is smaller than the distance $B_1 D$. If the subset of attainable beacons is empty, the route is completed using a direct segment toward the destination D.

This process generates routes which respect the direction constraint. Note that other constraints (additional distance, zone avoidance, etc.) are relaxed and taken into account in the objective function:

$$f(R) = \text{length}(R) + \alpha.(\delta_R^S)$$

where:

– R is the route (list of beacons);

– δ_R^S is the Kronecker symbol, which is equal to one if part of route R is in a forbidden zone S (zero otherwise);

– α is a penalty parameter chosen by the user.

Due to the combinatorics involved, we then use a genetic algorithm to automatically generate a set of alternative routes of good quality. The key operator in this algorithm is the sharing, as it guides the emergence of distinct alternative routes in terms of geometric aspects and of sector differentiation. This approach, which permits automatic generation of alternative results, is described in detail in reference [OUS 00b].

6.4.2. *The fitness function*

The fitness function is based on the relationship between the congestion associated with an individual and the congestion in the reference planning. When computing congestion, we must take account of uncertainties concerning flights. In reality, flights are subject to disturbances (forecasting errors), which modify their take-off times or the moment at which they enter a sector.

These variations can be due to weather conditions, speed limitations or problems specific to the airline. Solutions obtained by any system ignoring these incertitudes will be fragile and often impossible to implement in practice.

We thus need to use a method to account for these incertitudes, known as *temporal smoothing*.

Smoothing allows discrete events to be averaged out over time, thus allowing us to account for forecasting errors in terms of flight positions. Solutions obtained using this method are more robust.

The mathematical form of the smoothed workload of sector s for period t, $\widetilde{W_{st}}$ is given by the following formula:

$$\widetilde{W_{st}} = \frac{1}{2.D+1} \sum_{x=t-D}^{t+D} W_{sx}$$

where W_{sx} is the instantaneous workload and D is the size (in slots) of the smoothing window.

To calculate the fitness function, we calculate the congestion rate for the day obtained using the initial planning (required by airlines):

$$W(\text{ref}) = \sum_{s \in P} \left\{ \left[\sum_{t=0}^{T} \widetilde{W}_{st,\text{ref}} \right]^{\phi} \times \left[\max_{t \in [0,T]} \widetilde{W}_{st,\text{ref}} \right]^{\varphi} \right\}$$

where $\widetilde{W}_{st,\text{ref}}$ is the smoothed reference workload (departure plan required by airlines) of sector s during period t, T represents the set of time periods for consideration, P the set of airspace sectors and ϕ, φ coefficients fixed by the user.

The first term represents the average congestion and the second term corresponds to the maximum congestion. This last term allows us to remove congestion peaks occurring over a short period, which cannot be taken into account for the first term. We then calculate the congestion associated with the planning contained in an individual:

$$W(\text{ind}) = \sum_{s \in P} \left\{ \left[\sum_{t=0}^{T} \widetilde{W}_{st,\text{ind}} \right]^{\phi} \times \left[\max_{t \in [0,T]} \widetilde{W}_{st,\text{ind}} \right]^{\varphi} \right\}$$

The fitness function is defined by the relationship between the two previous functions,

$$fitness = \frac{W(\text{ref})}{W(\text{ind})}$$

This fitness function needs to be maximized. If $fitness > 1$, then the congestion associated with the individual is lower than the congestion in the initial planning.

a. Taking account of the cost of alternative routes and delays

The cost of delays and alternative routes is unknown, as these costs depend on a number of parameters which are inherent to airlines. From an economic perspective, the information needed to account for these costs is incomplete. Costs are therefore dependent on fluctuations, meaning that they are random variables.

For our application, we have used an average cost unit.

The cost of a 1 min delay in flight is considered to be 3.5 times higher [FRO 98] than that of a 1 min delay on the ground. Route lengthening is also considered as a form of delay.

Thus, to minimize delay and route lengthening costs, we need to minimize $\sum_i C_{d_i}^2$ where $C_{d_i} = C.(d_i + (3.5.d_{r_i}))$ and d_{r_i} is the delay (if one exists) linked to the lengthening caused by the use of route r_i in relation to the route length requested by the airline. The cost function is therefore quadratic $(C_{d_i}^2)$ in order to promote equity between flights. If the route is shorter, no cost is paid by the airline.

6.4.3. *Simple genetic algorithm*

a. Coding and generation of an initial population

The *coding* of a solution is represented by a full planning of flights for a day of traffic. Each flight i is subject to a shift δ_i in relation to the planned takeoff time (see Figure 6.14) which is chosen from a set of possible (past or future) shifts (Δ_i) and a route r_i is chosen from a set of possible alternatives (R_i).

The *initial population* is generated by random assignment of past or future shifts and alternative routes for each flights, with a probability of p_δ and p_r, respectively.

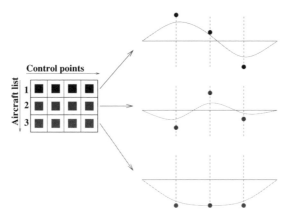

Figure 6.14. *Structure of an individual*

b. Flight connections

Flights are often connected to other subsequent flights. The phenomenon of hubs, which has emerged in recent years, creates waves of arrivals followed by waves of departures for certain airports.

Figure 6.15 shows a situation where four flights (A, B, C, D) are connected to a fifth flight E. The centers of the intervals represent the initial arrival times (flights A, B, C, D) or the initial departure time (flight E). The intervals are ranges within which times may be adjusted. τ_E is the minimum time required between the arrival of the last connected flight and the departure of the following flight (turnaround constraint). The arrows on the intervals represent the effective arrival times. Finally, through the minimum turnaround time constraint, these effective times modify the interval of possibilities associated with flight E.

To guarantee the possibility of allocating a departure time to flight E, the sets of time shifts used must satisfy the following constraint:

$$\delta_p^E > \max_{k \in \{A,B,C,D\}} \left(\delta_p^k + \tau_E \right)$$

where δ_P^k is the flight arrival time, determined using the delay and the initial forecasted arrival time, and δ_p^E is the departure time of flight E. τ_E is the turnaround time necessary between two flights.

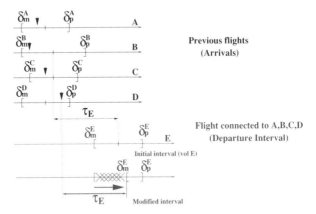

Figure 6.15. *Example of connection between flights*

Before assigning a delay to a connected flight, we must first verify that previous flights have assigned delays. This ensures coherency in the assignment of a delay to flight E.

c. Recombination operators

The following mutation and crossover operators are used:

Mutation: mutation occurs with a probability p_m of mutating a flight in a planning. It is carried out by assigning a new route and/or take-off slot to each flight with probability p_m.

Crossover: in this case, we use uniform crossover (see Figure 6.16); a planning is selected for crossover with probability p_c.

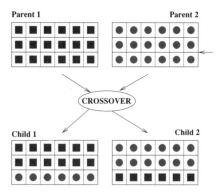

Figure 6.16. *Uniform crossover. The genes of the children are a copy of the genes of one of the two parents. A parent is chosen at random for gene copying*

d. First results

Tests were carried out using real traffic data corresponding to 6381 flights using French airspace on 21 June 1996.

89 elementary sectors were used.

The results use the principle of elitism (transfer the best individual from any population to the following population). These are preliminary results using time shifts (solution to the problem using slot assignment alone).

Parameters

– size of the smoothing window: $D = 5$ min;

– size of population $pop_{taille} = 50$;

– discretization $dt = 1$ min;

– number of generations: 300;

– maximum past or future slot shift: 45 min;

– the initial population was created by giving random shifts to different flights with a probability of 0.5;

– probability of chromosome crossover $P_c = 0.3$;

– probability of gene mutation $P_m = 0.02$ (for each flight).

The first results obtained were not satisfactory, demonstrating the ineffectiveness of a "naive" modeling of genetic algorithms. Nevertheless, the behavior of the algorithm modeled in this way did reduce congestion by a factor of 1.7. The curves in Figures 6.5 and 6.6 show the evolution of average fitness and best fitness using this model (SGA).

Given the complexity of the problem, we now need to introduce problem-specific knowledge in the chromosome.

6.5. Modification of the algorithm – adaptive modifications

These modifications were made with the aim of designing suitable operators to take account of congestion encountered by flights and of trends to advance or delay flights in order to reduce congestion (user optimization). We will begin by presenting the two concepts involved: the level of observed congestion and the stochastic trends.

6.5.1. *Establishing congestion levels in the chromosome*

In the previous algorithm, we mutated flights encountering heavy congestion and flights encountering no congestion (night flights, for example) in the same way. To take account of these differing congestion levels, we have developed a function to calculate the level of congestion encountered by each flight. This function is an *a posteriori* indicator (to minimize) indicating the quality of the past choice concerning each flight (in the planning to which it belongs). However, it must be used in a stochastic manner in order to avoid local optima. To estimate the level of congestion encountered, we take each flight plan (after simulation) and save the congestion encountered using this planning, considering only the congestion taking place between the input time t_{in} and the output time t_{out} of the sectors traversed by the flight. We obtain an *encountered congestion function*, which depends on the maximum encountered congestion and the average accumulated congestion for the flight.

$$NC_i = \sum_{s \in P_i} \left\{ \left[\sum_{x=t_{in,s}}^{t_{out,s}} \widetilde{W}_{sx,ind} \right]^{\phi} \times \left[\max_{\substack{x \in I \\ s \in P_i}} \widetilde{W}_{sx,ind} \right]^{\varphi} \right\}$$ [6.2]

where:

– P_i: set of sectors traversed by flight i;

– $I = [(t_{in,s}), (t_{out,s})]$;

– $t_{in,s}$: time of entry into sector s;

– $t_{out,s}$: time of exit from sector s.

For each flight, we then determine a level of encountered congestion which will direct (statistically) the next reproduction (mutation or crossover). The probability of mutation of a flight i is then given by the following expression:

$$C_{ri} = \frac{NC_i}{\max_{j \in V} NC_j}$$

where NC_i is the congestion encountered by flight i, $\max_{j \in V} NC_j$ is the maximum congestion encountered by a flight in the planning (V set of flights). We thus obtain $C_{ri} \in [0,1]$. The real mutation of flight i will, however, be limited to $\alpha \times C_{ri}$ in order to avoid premature convergence to local minima; we selected $\alpha \in [0.5, 1]$.

6.5.2. *Establishment of trends*

The effect on congestion of delaying or advancing a departure time is not symmetrical, and it is sometimes more advantageous to advance a flight than to delay it (see Figure 6.17).

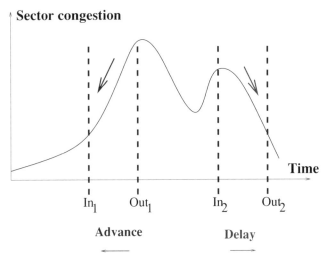

Figure 6.17. *Trends. If an airplane enters into a sector where congestion is increasing, it is better to advance its departure time, and if congestion is decreasing in the sector, it is preferable to delay the flight*

In the example shown in Figure 6.18, it is more advantageous to advance the flight by one time step (flight shown in gray) than to delay it, as the delay required in this case (supposing that all other flights are fixed) would be 7 time steps.

Based on this observation, we have been able to develop a concept of stochastic trends. Before any mutation, we apply a probabilistic bias to the direction of the assignment of the delay (advancement or delay). A case study has enabled us to identify three trends (see Figure 6.17):

– If the entry or exit of a flight from a sector coincides with an increase in congestion, that is if $f' = \frac{\widetilde{W_s}(t) - \widetilde{W_s}(t+\delta)}{\delta} > 0$, it is preferable to advance the flight.

– If the entry or exit of a flight from a sector coincides with a reduction in congestion, ($f' < 0$), it is preferable to delay the flight.

– In all other cases, the sense of assignment of a delay is chosen at random.

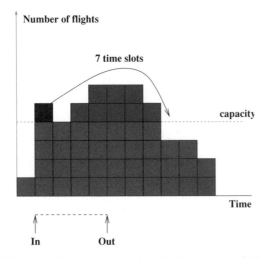

Figure 6.18. *Asymmetry in relation to time shifts*

In the considerations set out above, δ is chosen to be equal to the smoothing window.

These trends are summarized in the following table:

	$f' > 0$	$f' < 0$
Entry	Advance	Delay
Exit	Advance	Delay

To generalize this concept for all sectors traversed by the flight, we have developed functions that depend on the congestion encountered in the sector and the direction of increase or reduction in congestion. We thus generate general trends (noted Te_{flight}) for the delay or advance of each flight.

$$f_{flight_s}{'} = \frac{f'_{flight_{t_{in},s}} + f'_{flight_{t_{out},s}}}{2}$$

with $f'_{flight_{t_{in},s}}$ derived from the congestion of sector s; the flight ($flight$) enters the sector at instant t_{in}, $f'_{flight_{t_{out},s}}$, ditto for the instant the flight exits the sector s, and $f_{flight_s}{'}$ is the associated average value.

$$Te_{flight} = \frac{\sum_{s \in P} (f'_{flight_s} \times \widetilde{W}_{s,flight})}{|\sum_{s \in P} (f_{flight_s} \times \widetilde{W}_{s,vol})|}$$

where:

$$\widetilde{W}_{s,flight} = (\sum_{x=t_{in,flight}}^{t_{out,flight}} \widetilde{W}_{sx})^\phi \times (\max_{x \in [(t_{in},s),(t_{out},s)]}$$

$\widetilde{W}_{sx,flight})^\varphi$ is the congestion encountered by the flight in sector s.

$Te_{flight} \in [-1, 1]$ is such that:

– if Te_{flight} is close to 1, it is "advisable" to bring forward the flight;

– if Te_{flight} is close to -1, it is "advisable" to delay the flight.

This leads to the following mutation choices:

$$\text{Stochastic choice} = \begin{cases} Te_{flight} > \text{Rand}[0,1] & \text{(randomly advance flight)} \\ Te_{flight} < -\text{Rand}[0,1] & \text{(randomly delay flight)} \\ \text{otherwise} & \text{no preference} \end{cases}$$

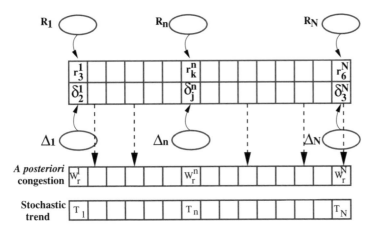

Figure 6.19. *New coding*

6.5.3. *New coding and biased initial population*

In the new coding (Figure 6.19), the two new indicators – encountered congestion and the stochastic trend – are added to the chromosome and calculated after each evaluation of fitness. Thus, the initial population is generated by disturbance of the take-off slots and flight routes of those flights which contribute most to congestion; this disturbance is carried out in a stochastic manner (the departure time and/or the flight route will be modified based on a probability, which increases in line with encountered congestion).

6.5.4. *New crossover operator*

This new operator involves the following steps:

– Two parents are selected based on their fitness function.

– We calculate the congestion C_{ri} encountered by each flight.

– The different flights are then arranged in the following manner:

- flight plan n in parent 1 is considered to be "better" than flight plan n in parent 2 if $C_{rn}^1 < \eta \times C_{rn}^2$ where $\eta \in [0.8, 0.95]$;

- flight plan n in parent 2 is considered to be "better" than flight plan n in parent 1 if $C_{rn}^2 > \eta \times C_{rn}^1$, where we recommend the value of the parameter $\eta \in [0.8, 0.95]$;

- the two flight plans are said to be equivalent if neither of the above relationships is verified.

– If a flight plan is "better" in parent 1, it is copied into both children.

– If a flight plan is "better" in parent 2, it is copied into both children.

– If the two flight plans are "equivalent", they are exchanged in the children with a probability of 0.5.

6.5.5. *New mutation operator*

This operator most often mutates flights using congested sectors. It works on the following principle:

– Calculate the congestion C_{ri} encountered by each flight i.

– Calculate the stochastic trends T_i of each flight i.

– If the individual is selected for mutation, we go through all flights (i) belonging to this planning. For each flight, we randomly apply (probability $1/2$):

- if $\frac{C_{ri}}{max_i C_{ri}} > \text{Rand}[0, 1]$ and $\text{Rand}[0, 1] < \omega$ (parameter fixed beforehand), where $\text{Rand}[0, 1]$ represents the random selection of a real number between 0 and 1 inclusive, we apply the following procedure:

1) if $T_i > \text{Rand}[0, 1]$, assign a future take-off slot d_i (stochastic trend);

2) if $T_i < \text{Rand}[0, 1]$, assign a past take-off slot d_i;

3) Otherwise, assign a past or future take-off slot with the same probability 0.5.

- Assign a new route with probability p_r (determined beforehand by the user).

The parameter ω is used to control the number of mutated genes for an individual.

6.5.6. *New results*

The new crossover and mutation operators permit significant improvements in the quality of our results. Thus, a comparison between the simple genetic algorithm (SGA) and the genetic algorithm with modified operators (OGA) shows (see Figure 6.5) that the congestion indicator was divided by 1.74 using the SGA and by 2.40 using the OGA. These results are also promising in light of the small size of the populations used (200 individuals in Figure 6.5) and the size of individuals (6,381 flights).

From Figure 6.21, we note that the maximum workload of the most congested sector is divided by 3.07 using the OGA and by 1.78 using the SGA. Figure 6.22 shows a zoomed-in view of the largest congestion peak in Figure 6.21. As predicted, the load is smoothed around the peak.

The SGA was executed more than 1,000 generations to allow more precise comparison with the OGA.

– The best fitness function reached 2.02, remaining inferior to that produced by the OGA.

– The number of flights moved for the SGA was 4,120, compared with 3,510 using the OGA.

– The total of all flight shifts, in minutes, was 126,508 for the SGA compared with 107,782 for the OGA.

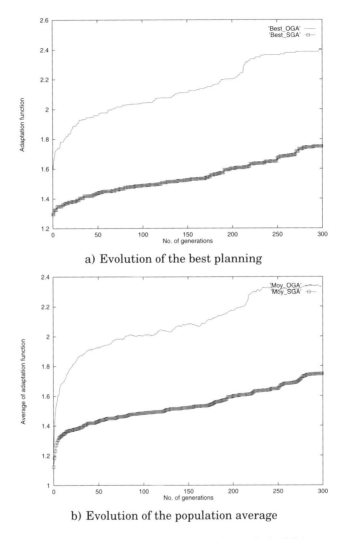

a) Evolution of the best planning

b) Evolution of the population average

Figure 6.20. *Comparison of the OGA and the SGA*

The lower quality of the SGA results presented is due to the fact that the mutation and crossover operators used in this method are either unsuitable or random. When these operators are applied, they can affect flights which are not concerned by congestion.

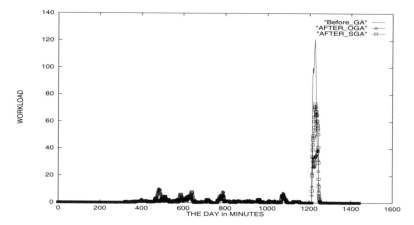

Figure 6.21. *Sector congestion*

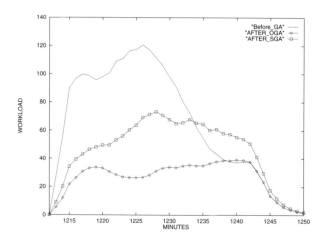

Figure 6.22. *Zoomed-in view of sector congestion*

6.5.7. *Dynamic bi-allocation*

The evolutionary algorithm model presented in the previous section can be used from several days to a few months before the traffic day in question, with the objective of spreading the congestion forecast. It is important to note that the forecast in this case is a key element in the future application of the results of the optimization. A poor forecast can lead to results that are impossible to apply in practice. We need to predict capacities and take-off times in the most effective manner possible, referring, for example, to days of similar traffic. On the given day, as time passes, the error in the traffic demand reduces; we are then able to correctly apply the previous algorithm to a shorter time range for which the demand predictions are reliable. In order to benefit from high quality forecasting, and consequently accelerate the execution of the algorithm, we have used the principle of dividing the day into partially overlapping time periods. As the day and the flight take-off times approach, the quality of forecasts improves, increasing the quality of our solutions. A GA is used to treat each time period $[T_0, T_1]$ of the day in order to reduce congestion and obtain a planning which takes account of flights registered by airlines only a few hours before take off.

The main steps of the model are as follows:

– Choose a size for the time window (3 h seems reasonable).

– Each time period $[T_0, T_1]$ is partially covered by the next time window (see Figure 6.23).

– The overlap period is larger than the maximum period of delay and advance.

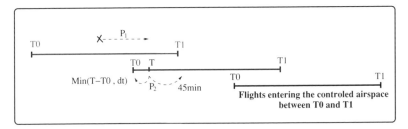

Figure 6.23. *Overlapping time windows*

This time division principle corresponds to a breakdown of the problem into several subproblems. When we execute a GA for a time window, certain flights may be delayed into an extended window $[T_0, T_1 + dt]$, where dt is the maximum admissible delay for a flight.

However, some flights, having had their take off delayed during the previous time window, may be delayed or advanced once again (in the new window), within a limit of $t \in min(T - T_0, dt)$, where T is the flight take-off time.

The choice of a suitable breakdown method is a guarantee of success in relation to the operational use of the method. We have chosen to break down the problem using time windows, with:

– 3 h for each time window and an overlap of 1 h between successive windows;

– the maximum delay and advance are fixed at 45 min, guaranteeing that a flight delayed after limit T_1, or during the overlap window, can be advanced or delayed a second time during the next treatment (i.e. during treatment of the following time window) within a limited domain $[-\min(T - T_0, dt), dt]$ where T is the time the flight enters into the control airspace.

To test the performance of dynamic planning, several tests were carried out using 1,066 flights. The first test used the static method and the second used a dynamic approach with sliding time windows. These tests showed that the dynamic approach using the parameters described above is able to provide almost the same levels of congestion reduction. The details of this approach are given in reference [OUS 99].

6.5.8. *Multi-objective approach*

The simultaneous minimization of congestion, delays and route lengthening presents contradictory objectives, which we have optimized using an MOGA-type multi-objective genetic algorithm [FON 93]. Delays and route lengthening were fused to form a single objective, using the following weighting rule: 1 min of in-flight delay has approximately the same cost as a delay of 3 min on the ground. We thus obtain an optimization problem with two objectives (minimization of delay and minimization of congestion).

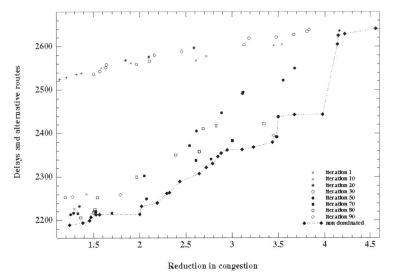

Figure 6.24. *Evolution of non-dominated solutions – September 1st, 1996. The ordinate axis represents the square root of the total number of minutes of delay (on the ground and in flight)*

The Pareto front regrouping the non-dominated solutions corresponding to September 1st, 1996 is shown in Figure 6.24. We thus have a panel of solutions allowing us to identify any compromise between congestion and delays. For example, we can reduce congestion by 4.58, but with a quadratic sum of delays (including time delays and route lengthening) of $(2,640)^2$, or reduce congestion by 2.87 with a quadratic sum of delays of $(2,358)^2$. In Figure 6.24, we note the evolution of non-dominated solutions over the course of the iterations of the GA, beginning with solutions of very low quality at iteration 1. Solutions then begin to appear which present a clear reduction in congestion with decreasing delay and route lengthening. The solutions on the Pareto front are updated for each iteration of the algorithm. Working from this figure, several choices are possible, of which one seems acceptable (congestion: 3.96, delays: $(2,442)^2$); for this choice, solutions which provide less reduction in congestion (given the slope of the curve) are practically identical in terms of delays, and the following solutions are much too costly in terms of delays without giving a noticeable reduction in congestion. This approach is described in detail in reference [DEL 05].

6.5.9. *Conclusion*

Artificial evolution is well suited to solving our traffic assignment problem. We have seen that this method is capable of managing real instances of the problem within a timeframe which is compatible with strategic planning. Moreover, the multi-objective approach to evolution allows us to identify several potential solutions, which can then be assessed by an expert.

6.6. Sequencing flights for landing

Artificial evolution has been used successfully for other assignment problems, particularly the problem of sequencing flights for landing. The efficient and effective use of airport capacity is a determining factor in reducing congestion in the air traffic system. The various models proposed are often based on simulations where models of deterministic queues use various priority rules (particularly first come, first served). Our approach, based on artificial evolution, provides an alternative to these rules.

6.6.1. *Introduction*

On entry into the terminal area of an airport, each aircraft is assigned a landing slot and a runway. Landing must occur in a pre-determined time window, bounded by an earliest landing time and a latest landing time. The earliest landing time represents a situation where the airplane flies at its maximum speed. The latest time corresponds to the opposite situation (the aircraft travels at minimum speed). We therefore wish to modify the landing sequence by modifying aircraft speeds in the terminal area in order to maximize the number of landings for a given period (this is the area where we have most room to maneuver in terms of varying aircraft speeds).

When a controller asks a flight to slow down or speed up in a terminal area, this action induces a cost (for the company) which increases as a function of the shift in relation to the planned landing time. We say that a runway is well supplied (in a congested situation) when the time during which the runway is unoccupied is very small. When dealing with a set of airplanes, this equates to minimizing the landing slot of the last aircraft. This minimization creates more or less significant modifications for preceding flights, thus increasing the cost values. We therefore have two conflicting objectives, corresponding to the interests of airlines and of the ATC.

In the context of a series of landings, a minimum separation time is necessary in order for wake turbulence to disperse. This time is a function of the type of aircraft. A Boeing 747, for example, creates significant turbulence, which can destabilize an aircraft coming too close behind, particularly if the airplane in question is small. A small aircraft, on the other hand, creates little disturbance, and another aircraft may land after a shorter period of time.

From now on, we will limit ourselves to optimizing the runway feed (the ATC objective).

6.6.2. *Single runway formulation*

For this single runway formulation, we will use the following notation for the problem data:

– P: number of aircraft;

– E_i: earliest landing time (dependent on the maximum speed of aircraft i);

– L_i: latest landing time (dependent on the minimum speed of flight i);

– t_{ij}: required separation time between the landing time of airplane i and that of airplane j.

Our optimization variables are t_i: landing time of aircraft i ($i = 1, ..., n$). Their domain of definition, $t_i \in [E_i, L_i]$ induces $t_1 < t_2 < t_3 < ... < t_n$.

Our objective is to minimize the time when the runway is unoccupied, i.e. to minimize the landing time of the last airplane. The objective function is therefore expressed by:

$$F_{\text{obj}} = (t_n - t_1) + \sum_{i=1}^{n-1} t_{i,i+1}$$

where t_n is the landing time of the last airplane in the queue and t_1 is that of the first aircraft. The first term represents the overall performance of the sequence. The second allows us to structure the sequence in order to minimize separation time.

The extension of this method to cases with multiple runways is described in detail in reference [GUI 99].

The airplane landing sequence problem is NP-hard (it can be reduced to the traveling salesman problem [GUI 99]), and we will use GAs to treat it.

6.6.3. *Modeling using GA*

The GA used is modeled in the following manner:

Each individual represents a sequence of flights coming in to land. The aim of the genetic algorithm is to determine the "best" sequence (permutation) of aircraft. The landing time of an airplane is then determined by a greedy deterministic procedure.

The specific operators of the GA are described below.

a. Coding and initial population

As the aim of the flight landing sequence problem is to find a real possible permutation (traveling salesman problem), the natural coding of the solution is as a permutation of flights. For certain pairs of aircraft (i, j), we can immediately decide whether flight i should land before or after flight j by referring to the time windows of the two flights. In this case, an individual is a permutation of flights, and each flight has a fixed maximum position, deduced by reference to other flights. The initial population is a set of possible permutations.

b. Operators

– Crossover

The crossover method used here is one often encountered in solving the travelling salesman problem [LAR 99].

Taking two individual candidates: P_1 = (1,2,3,4,5,6,7) and P_2 = (2,3,7,5,4,6,1), a crossover point is selected at random; the two children C_1 and C_2 are then filled in using the second sections of parents P_1 and P_2, respectively.

Thus, in the case above, if the third position is selected at random (C_1 = (.......,4,5,6,7) and C_2 = (.......,5,4,6,1)), the children are completed by reference to the parents (the same order of the associated parent is retained).

We obtain:

C_1 = (**2,3,1**,4,5,6,7) and C_2 = (**2,3,7**,5,4,6,1).

This crossover guarantees that each airplane will be in a valid position in relation to its maximum position in the sequence.

– Mutation

This operator randomly switches two airplanes in a sequence, while keeping each in a feasible position (with regards to its maximum place in the queue). Thus, not all permutations will necessarily be authorized. The mutation principle is set out below:

- An airplane p is selected along with another airplane p_v in the vicinity ($p_v \in [1, \max(p)]$ where $\max(p)$ represents the maximal position of airplane p).

- The initial position of p must be a possible position for p_v ($p \in [1, \max(p_v)]$).

- The positions of the two airplanes are switched.

We can differentiate between two types of mutations:

- Local mutations, where an airplane is switched with another aircraft in its immediate vicinity (the next or previous airplane in the sequence, if this position is possible).

- Global mutations, where two airplanes from any position in the sequence are switched (while still respecting the maximum position possible for each aircraft).

– Construction of a solution (decoding)

After crossover and/or mutation, we obtain a new population of individuals. Each individual is then used to construct a solution using the following greedy heuristic:

- Assign the first airplane to its earliest possible landing time t_1.

- The landing time $t_2 \in [E_2, L_2]$ of the second airplane is calculated in a way which respects the minimum separation time with airplane 1. If the separation time cannot be respected in relation to the domain of performance of airplane 2 ($[E_2, L_2]$), the associated aircraft pairing is penalized.

- Step 2 is repeated for the pairing 2 and 3 and so on until the whole sequence has been processed.

– Fitness

In the case of an feasible solution, the objective for minimization is defined (as described above) by:

$$F_{obj} = (t_n - t_1) + \sum_{i=1}^{n-1} t_{i,i+1}$$

In the opposite case, constraints are taken into account by relaxation (the penalization method uses the size of the largest feasible sequence to differentiate between different non-feasible solutions):

$$F = \begin{cases} F_{obj} \text{ if the sequence is feasible} \\ F_{obj} + \alpha \times (n_s + (n_s - l) \times log(2 + n)) \text{ otherwise} \end{cases}$$

where:

– n is the number of iterations of the GA: in the course of the iterations of the GA, non-feasible solutions are more and more heavily penalized.

– n_s is the size of the airplane sequence (size of an individual).

– l is the length of the largest feasible sequence.

– α is used to adjust the penalty. This depends on user choices and acts on the selection process.

As the chosen GA works by maximizing the objective function, we need to invert our criterion in order to define fitness.

$$\text{Fitness} = \frac{1}{F}$$

The curves presented below are associated with criterion F and not with fitness.

6.6.4. Results

Our tests were based on a data set concerning 43 airplanes. All airplanes were of the same type and had the same possibility of being moved into the past or the future. The aircraft had spatial positions within the interval [40 NM, 140 NM] representing the distance from the runway.

This data set was chosen to provide us with a problem for which, once again, an optimal solution is already known in order to successfully evaluate our methodology. The solution (given the equivalent characteristics of the aircraft) depends solely on the distance of the aircraft from the runway; thus, the closest airplane should land first, etc.

The temporal separation criterion between each pair of aircraft was fixed at 30 s ($t_{i,i+1} = 30$).

The parameters of the GA for the test are shown in Table 6.2.

Probability of mutation	$P_m = 0.45$
Probability of crossover	$P_c = 0.13$
Number of individuals	1,000
Number of iterations	500
Penalization factor	$\alpha = 1,000$
Elitism	yes

Table 6.2. *Parameters of the genetic algorithm*

For this test, we obtained solutions located at a distance of two permutations from the optimal solution. These permutations concerned two pairs of airplanes located at a quasi-equivalent distance from the runway.

Figure 6.25 shows the evolution of the best individual and of the average value of F. The rapid decrease represents the emergence of feasible solutions (which respect contraints). After 250 iterations, the population became homogeneous and the evolutionary process ceased to improve the fitness.

We then compared the effect of mutations (local and global) and of crossover on the behavior of the algorithm:

– crossover and mutation (local + global);

– global mutation alone;

– combination of mutations (global and local).

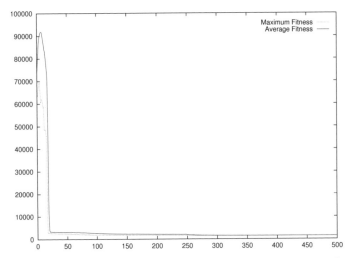

Figure 6.25. *Criterion of the best individual and average criterion of the population as a function of the generation number*

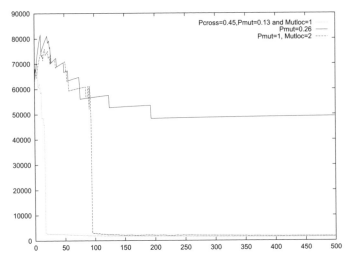

Figure 6.26. *Most rapid convergence using crossover and a combination of global and local mutations as a function of the generation number (dotted curve ....). No crossover (dashed curve - - - - -). Global mutation alone (solid curve)*

It is clear from Figure 6.26 that global mutation alone does not lead to the production of good solutions.

The combination of the two mutations gives very good results, but only after a relatively large number of iterations (100 iterations). The use of mutation with a well-defined crossover operator produces good solutions more rapidly (20 iterations). For this problem, the combined effect of mutations and crossover thus appears to be the most effective strategy. Other comparisons are given in reference [GUI 99].

In this section, we have presented a formulation of the flight landing sequence problem using a GA. Tests were carried out for a problem using a single runway, and airplanes were ordered to speed up or slow down in order to optimize the objective.

This method produces visibly better results than the current approach (first come, first served). However, the condition of equity between different airlines is not respected.

6.7. Trajectory planning

The latest work in the field of traffic assignment concerns the planning of trajectories in tactical and pre-tactical contexts. The objective of this type of planning is to determine an optimal trajectory shape (3D), departure time and speed profile in order to optimize a given criterion. Two similar approaches have been developed. The first uses an analogy with light propagation to generate optimal trajectories in terms of time (geodesic trajectories); the second generates trajectories with B-splines for which the control points are piloted using artificial evolution.

6.7.1. *Introduction*

Analysts working on the growth of air traffic have predicted that the number of flights will double in the next 20 years. The air traffic management (ATM) system therefore needs to increase airspace capacity, while maintaining security levels at least equivalent to those which currently exist. The European SESAR project was launched in order to propose solutions to this problem. This project is based on a new concept of traffic control, known as 4D trajectories, which consists of guaranteeing the position of aircraft at a given time. For each flight, a reference trajectory, known as the RBT[5], is required by the operating company. In the course of the flight, conflict situations may emerge for which it will be necessary to modify one or more trajectories in order to ensure respect of minimum separation distances between aircraft (currently 5 NM in the horizontal plane and 1,000 ft in the vertical plane). It is preferable for the new trajectories to remain as close as possible to the RBTs. Finally, the trajectories modified in this way must respect speed constraints linked to aerodynamics ($V \in [V_{min}; V_{max}]$).

The methods currently used to treat this problem can be grouped into two broad categories: genetic algorithms [DUR 04] and navigation functions [ROU 08]. The first approach considers a set of possible maneuvers for each airplane (offset or turning point) and solves the combinatorics by artificial evolution in order to produce a conflict-free solution respecting operational constraints. As artificial evolution is a stochastic method, there is no guarantee of optimality for a given run. The second approach, based on navigation functions, uses an electrostatic analogy in which an airplane is modeled as an electron moving in an electric field, synthesized by the other airplanes possessing a negative charge. The destination is represented as a positive attracting charge. Using this initial distribution of charges, the system is allowed to evolve in order to synthesize the trajectory of the airplane linking the origin to the destination while avoiding obstacles (other aircraft). Considering those

---

5 Reference Business Trajectory.

airplanes involved in conflicts sequentially (the first airplane is not modified, the second calculates its trajectory considering the first airplane as a constraint, etc.), the navigation functions generate a conflict-free set of trajectories with proof of convergence [ROU 08]. Unfortunately, the trajectories produced in this way present the following two drawbacks:

1) Non-bounded speeds: navigation functions do not ensure respect of aircraft speed limitations, so to resolve a conflict, an airplane may be required to slow down excessively.

2) Irregular trajectories: during resolution, certain trajectories take irregular forms (involving excessively sharp turns).

Each of these methods only provides a partial response to the problem. Genetic algorithms allow us to obtain an optimal solution in an asymptotic manner, but do not guarantee that we will obtain an admissible solution in limited time; navigation functions, on the other hand, guarantee the absence of conflict but generate trajectories, which are not necessarily flyable by an aircraft.

6.7.2. *The light propagation algorithm*

The objective of our proposed method, based on an analogy with optics, is to find an optimal 4D trajectory for each aircraft, which avoids conflicts and minimizes a criterion based on a local metric.

In the framework of geometrical optics, light propagates through space respecting Descartes' Law:

Let n_1 be the index of refraction of medium 1 in which the incident ray propagates and n_2 that of the medium in which the refracted ray propagates (medium 2). We obtain:

$$\begin{cases} n_1.\sin(\theta_1) = n_2.\sin(\theta_2) \\ v_1 = \frac{c}{n_1}, v_2 = \frac{c}{n_2} \end{cases} \qquad [6.3]$$

where v_1, v_2 are the speed values in media 1 and 2, θ_1 the angle of incidence, θ_2 the angle of the refracted ray and c the speed of light in a vacuum (see Figure 6.27).

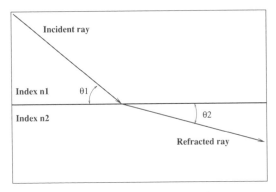

Figure 6.27. *Deviation of a light ray traversing two zones with different indices* (n_1, n_2)

For a given mobile, we wish to find the shortest path between two points of $\mathbb{R}^n$, taking account of a given metric (time, distance, etc.) while avoiding obstacles and respecting speed constraints. The trajectories produced must also respect a regularity criterion characterized by a maximum curvature value.

Two categories of obstacles are taken into account. The first category corresponds to obstacles that are static within the tactical timescale (10–20 min) representing, for example zones of congestion, storms or active military zones. Some of these obstacles may be traversed with the addition of a penalty (e.g. congestion zones) and are known as flexible obstacles. The penalty used in these cases is represented by a local increase in the metric for optimization. The second category covers dynamic obstacles, corresponding to the presence of other aircraft, which must, imperatively, be avoided (barrier obstacles).

For a given region, these obstacles are represented by a relief, $c(\mathbb{R}^n)$ the altitude of which is inversely proportional to the metric for optimization. This relief is synthesized in a 4D space (3D + time). Barrier obstacles are modeled as sudden peaks, while flexible obstacles take the form of hills.

Let $\vec{\gamma}(\vec{s}, \vec{d}, t)$ be the trajectory of a mobile object leaving from point $\vec{s}$ and arriving at point $\vec{d}$. We thus obtain $\vec{\gamma}(\vec{s}, \vec{d}, t_s) = \vec{s}$ and $\vec{\gamma}(\vec{s}, \vec{d}, t_d) = \vec{d}$.

The associated speed constraints are modeled by the following equation:

$$\left\| \frac{\partial \vec{\gamma}(\vec{s}, \vec{d}, t)}{\partial t} \right\| \in]V_{\min}, V_{\max}[\qquad [6.4]$$

For our problem, $\vec{V}_{\min}$ is the stalling point, and $V_{\max}$ corresponds to Mach 1 (speed for which the aircraft can be disintegrated).

The curvature of a trajectory is given by:

$$K(\vec{\gamma}, t) = \frac{\| \vec{\gamma}'(t) \wedge \vec{\gamma}''(t) \|}{\| \vec{\gamma}'(t) \|^3} \qquad [6.5]$$

To obtain regular trajectories, this curvature must be bounded from above:

$$|K(\vec{\gamma}, t)| \leq K_{\max} \ \forall t \in [t_s, t_d] \qquad [6.6]$$

Finally, the objective function that we wish to minimize is:

$$f = \min_{\vec{\gamma}} \int_{t=t_s}^{t=t_d} c(\vec{\gamma}(\vec{s}, \vec{d}, t)) dt \qquad [6.7]$$

The light propagation phenomenon thus appears suitable for use in modeling the search for a solution to the above problem. In practice, we simply need to model obstacles by a relief in the index, which the light will naturally avoid in an optimal manner. By controlling the maximum value of this index relief, we ensure, moreover, that the speed of mobile objects traveling along the produced trajectories remain above $V_{\min}$. In the same way, regions containing no obstacles will have an index fixed at 1, guaranteeing that airplanes will remain at the maximum speed determined by the flight profile.

We begin by positioning a light source at the departure point $(\bar{s})$, which emits rays in a hemisphere oriented toward the destination point (this restriction prevents the generation of unrealistic trajectories that begin by turning $180°$ before turning back toward the destination). The path followed by the first beam to reach the arrival point corresponds to the geodesic trajectory we wish to obtain. The light seeks to avoid zones with high index values, that is flexible obstacles, and is stopped by barrier obstacles (with very high index values). Thus, an airplane may traverse a congested zone, accepting the associated penalty, but will never be able to traverse zones with barrier indices, thus guaranteeing that conflicts will be resolved.

We suppose that the value of the criterion for optimization is an application that associates a C^1 class curve of $\mathbb{R}^3$ with a real positive value obtained by integrating a local metric along this curve. By carefully choosing the local metric, it is possible to optimize the length, journey time or an airline cost associated with a trajectory. The determination of an optimal trajectory thus comes down to seeking a geodesic.

To generate a trajectory, we use a wavefront propagation algorithm in 2D + time (in order to conform to operational practice, we carry out resolution in terms of heading, but with a detection method, which takes account of altitude) with temporal sampling (the wave is propagated with a time step dt). To avoid a combinatory explosion, propagation is coupled with a branch and bound (B&B) algorithm to avoid launching rays uselessly. The initial B&B tree is constituted by a single node representing the departure point. The branching rule consists of launching light rays from the current node, within the opening cone directed toward the destination (see Figure 6.28).

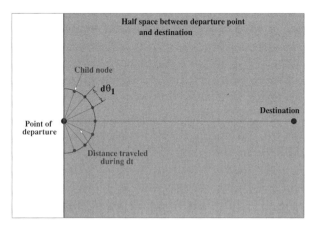

Figure 6.28. *Launching rays from the departure point. The points reached in this way constitute the initial wavefront*

For each of the child nodes, the algorithm then calculates an approximate lower bound, which is used to select the most promising candidate. This bound is calculated using the sum of two terms (see Figure 6.29):

$$lowerBound := TimeToNode + TimeToDest.$$

The first term, *TimeToNode*, represents the time taken to reach the current node from the origin. The second, *TimeToDest*, represents the time taken to reach the destination from the current node, taking account of the index along the direct route:

$$TimeToDest := \alpha * integTime + (1 - \alpha) * maxSpeedTime \quad [6.8]$$

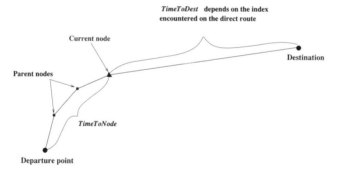

Figure 6.29. *Calculation of the lower bound. For a given node, the bound is calculated by adding the time to reach the node and the time to reach the destination along a direct route*

TimeToDest is a weighting of two terms: the first, *integTime*, is the time needed to reach the destination along a direct route while subjected to the effects of the encountered index, and the second, *maxSpeedTime*, is the time needed to reach the destination along a direct route without taking account of this index (the index is thus considered to be equal to one). Finally, α is a coefficient fixed by the user. Strictly speaking, this does not correspond to an exact bound, but this pseudo-bound produces very good results in the problems we have treated. More precisely, the term *TimeToDest* is developed as follows:

$$TimeToDest = \alpha * \int_{t_s}^{t_d} c(\vec{\gamma}_{direct}(t)) dt$$

$$+ (1 - \alpha) \frac{\|\vec{\gamma}_{direct}(t_d) - \vec{\gamma}_{direct}(\textbf{\textit{TimeToNode}})\|}{MaxSpeed}$$

where $\vec{\gamma}_{direct}$ represents the direct route to the destination and $MaxSpeed$ is the maximum speed in a vacuum.

The following node is then selected, and a new ray launch takes place from this node (see Figure 6.30).

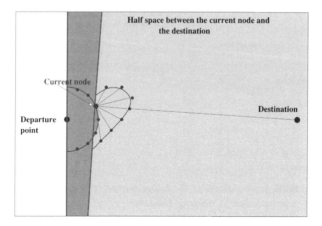

Figure 6.30. *Branching at the node with the best bound*

The tree is first explored in depth, beginning with the node with the lowest bound for nodes at the same level. The solution obtained in this way will be an approximate geodesic, guaranteeing a minimum speed, something that is critical for an airplane trajectory (see Figure 6.31).

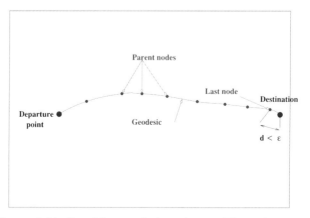

Figure 6.31. *Resulting geodesic trajectory. The trajectory is constructed when we arrive at a distance d lower than ϵ (fixed by the user) from the destination point*

To solve conflict situations involving several aircraft, we apply the algorithm sequentially for each airplane in a 4D space (3D + T, see Figure 6.32) in order to take account of the dynamic aspect of obstacles.

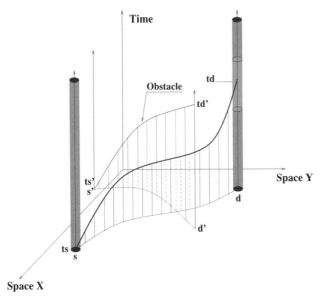

Figure 6.32. *Spatiotemporal extension. The full line represents the current trajectory, and the dotted line corresponds to a constraint. In the temporal domain, the destination takes the form of a segment centered on td*

In this case, we seek a geodesic linking a 4D point with a 4D segment (destination). If we simply extended the algorithm into 4D by connecting two 4D points, we would risk frequent violation of airplane speed constraints in order to guarantee that the craft would arrive at the destination point at a given moment. This problem is avoided by using a target segment for the destination in the temporal dimension (see Figure 6.32). Finally, the propagation of rays in this dimension is only permitted to evolve in a single direction (toward the future).

a. Examples of results

This algorithm was initially tested in the pre-tactical phase, where high-index zones were static (congestion and/or poor weather conditions). During the second stage of testing, the algorithm was applied to a problem of tactical conflict resolution. The parameters used in the algorithm were $d\theta_i = \frac{\Pi}{10}$ and $\alpha = 0.9$.

In the pre-tactical context, we synthesized refraction index maps using the following formula:

$$c(x, y) = \sum_{i=0}^{4} e^{-((x-a_i)^2 + (y-b_i)^2)/k}$$

with various values of a_i, b_i and k (see [DOU 11] for more details). The associated results are shown in Figure 6.33.

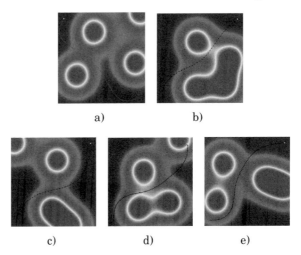

a)   b)

c)   d)   e)

Figure 6.33. *Approximate geodesics calculated by the algorithm. High values (flexible constraints) are shown in dark areas surrounded by white strips*

The computation time was around 5 s per trajectory using a Pentium 3.2 Ghz processor (Java coding). As we can see, the trajectories generated by our light propagation algorithm are geodesic approximations, which avoid zones with high indices, traveling, as predicted, through the "valleys".

We then tested the algorithm on conflict situations, beginning with artificial cases. We first considered a set of aircraft in conflict, for which we wished to find a solution respecting separation constraints, while introducing as small a route lengthening as possible and without changing the speeds of the aircraft. To solve this problem, the aircraft were treated sequentially. In this way, the first airplane was assigned a trajectory without modification. The trajectory of the second aircraft was then calculated, considering the first airplane as a constraint. The same process was repeated for the following aircraft up to the nth airplane, which took account of the $(n - 1)$ previous trajectories in the form of constraints. In cases of failure, the procedure was repeated again, changing the order of the aircraft.

An example of a solution is shown in Figure 6.34, where seven airplanes are positioned on a circle of radius 100 NM and converge on the center at the same speed (450 kts). The algorithm is applied sequentially to each of the aircraft (in a random order).

The chosen refraction index must guarantee avoidance of other aircraft, represented here as 4D tubes. The index inside these tubes is very high (outside, the index has a constant value equal to one).

As we see from Figure 6.34, the first aircraft to be treated are subject to fewer deviations than the last aircraft. This phenomenon is reproduced at operational level, when a controller solves a two-airplane conflict by modifying the trajectory of a single craft, allowing the other aircraft to continue along its trajectory. The time needed to obtain the solution involving seven airplanes was approximately 30 s, a time that is perfectly acceptable in relation to operational constraints.

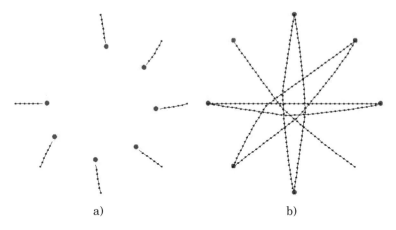

a)   b)

Figure 6.34. *(a) Conflict involving seven airplanes converging on the same point; (b) the solution*

This algorithm was then tested for a day of real traffic in French airspace. Using the flight plans for a day, we generated airplane trajectories (see Figure 6.35) using an arithmetic simulator (CATS: Complete Air Traffic Simulator [ALL 97]) developed by the former *Centre d'Etudes de la Navigation Aérienne* [Center for Air Navigation Studies] (CENA).

Using a sliding time window (21 min), we extracted a set of trajectory segments for which we then carried out conflict detection (see Figure 6.35) using inclusion boxes. Each segment was included in a box, for which we looked for intersections with other boxes. At points where boxes crossed, the trajectories were brought into the same cluster (see Figure 6.36) to which we applied the solution algorithm (see Figure 6.36).

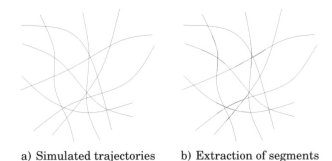

a) Simulated trajectories   b) Extraction of segments

Figure 6.35. *Simulated trajectories and segment extraction by temporal filtering*

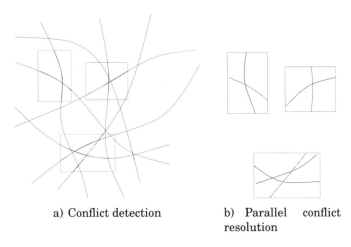

a) Conflict detection   b) Parallel   conflict
                                 resolution

Figure 6.36. *Detection of conflicts by box intersection and resolution of each conflict*

The trajectories where then updated using the solutions produced by the solver (Figure 6.37).

We then authorize the aircraft to fly for a fraction of the time window, 1/3 in our simulations, see Figure 6.37. The process is reiterated in the next window.

a) Updating trajectories   b) Following iteration

Figure 6.37. *Trajectory updates and shifting the time window*

All of the conflicts for the day of August 13, 2008 (around 4,000 conflicts) were solved, with 2,600 modified trajectories of 8,000.

On average, the length of the calculated trajectories was reduced by 3.46 NM, with a minimum length of 43 NM. Certain trajectories, however, were lengthened, with a maximum of 9.89 NM. The associated quantiles are shown below:

Quantile	Distance in NM
$\frac{1}{4}$ quantile	-4.55
$\frac{1}{2}$ quantile	-1.49
$\frac{3}{4}$ quantile	-0.1

The overall calculation time required for the day was around 12 h, using a Pentium 3.2 Ghz processor.

6.7.3. *Approach using genetic algorithms on B-splines*

The second approach we have developed to this problem of automatic conflict resolution is based on a summary of trajectories using B-splines of which the control points are piloted by a genetic algorithm [DEL 10].

The principle objective of B-splines is to produce a curve interpolating a set of points of $\mathbb{R}^2$ known as *control points*. This objective was then extended to approximation, allowing us to avoid undesirable oscillations inherent in interpolation. In our study, we will concentrate on this use of splines to approximate a set of control points. The *control polygon* is the piecewise linear curve linking control points, and entirely defines the obtained curve. The B-spline has the property of remaining in the convex envelope of its control points.

Figure 6.38. *Control points, control polygon and resulting B-spline*

B-splines are parametric curves, which generalize the concept Bzier curves. This mathematical tool produces an approximation constructed using polynomials, linked at certain parameter values known as *nodes*, which are stored in a *node vector*. To simplify, if we consider the set of control points $(X_i, Y_i) = P_i \in \mathbb{R}^2 (i = 0 : n)$ and the parameter u, we can define the B-spline as:

$$C(u) = (\sigma_x(u), \sigma_y(u)), u \in [a, b]$$

where $\sigma_x(u)$ and $\sigma_y(u)$ are B-spline approximations of pairs $(i, X_i)_{i=0:n}$ and $(i, Y_i)_{i=0:n}$ for $u \in [a, b]$.

We have chosen to use B-splines to build trajectories as they constitute an effective tool for the approximation of curves, in terms of both the quality of the approximation and the computation time. Moreover, B-splines present several interesting properties, such as C^2-continuity (essential in obtaining flyable trajectories), robustness and flexibility of use (if a control point is moved, only a small part of the curve will be affected).

In this case, the positions of the control points constitute our optimization variables. To determine the position of the control points, we use a classic genetic algorithm in which a chromosome represents the trajectory of N airplanes using a matrix of size $N \times N_c$ where N is the number of aircraft involved in the conflict and N_c the number of control points for each airplane. In a case where $N = 3$ and $N_c = 3$, for example, we code the chromosome in the following manner (see Figure 6.39):

$Airplane1$	P_{11}	P_{12}	P_{13}
$Airplane2$	P_{21}	P_{22}	P_{23}
$Airplane3$	P_{31}	P_{32}	P_{33}

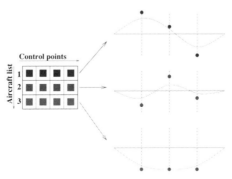

Figure 6.39. *Chromosome coding and corresponding B-splines. Trajectories are then adjusted as a function of the origin and destination points (dilation, rotation, translation)*

Clearly, the departure and arrival points of each airplane will not be coded in the chromosome as they do not move, and therefore do not constitute optimization variables.

Let us now define the way in which the control points P_{ij} will be specified. We wish to find a compromise between allowing the trajectory to deviate freely from the direct route to solve conflicts and retaining as much as possible of the direct route to minimize lengthening. With this in mind, we must define a maximal deviation band (D_{max}) around the direct route, within which control points are permitted to move.

Another issue associated with control points concerns their distribution along the trajectory in order to avoid large changes in direction. For this reason, control points are uniformly distributed along the direct route.

In summary, a control point is defined by a simple parameter, d, representing a percentage of the maximal authorized deviation band in the following manner: $\pm \dfrac{d}{D_{max}}\%$ (see Figure 6.40).

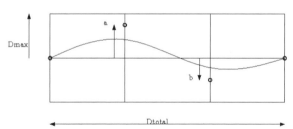

Figure 6.40. *Distribution of control points*

The associated crossover operator mixes the trajectories produced in this way using a classic chromosome slicing principle (see Figure 6.41).

The mutation operator randomly selects a control point and modifies its position using a uniform distribution (see Figures 6.42 and 6.43).

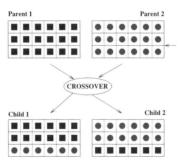

Figure 6.41. *Crossover operator. In this example, the third trajectory is exchanged between the two parents*

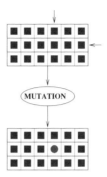

Figure 6.42. *Mutation operator. In this example, the fourth control point of the second trajectory is modified by the mutation operator*

The chromosome is then decoded into N trajectories in the aim of evaluating each individual. We calculate the number of conflicts between these N trajectories and the increase in distance in comparison with the direct routes. The number of conflicts is calculated using a division of the space into discrete square cells, the sides of which are half the length of the standard separation distance. Conflict detection takes place over two steps:

– For each cell through which an airplane passes, we memorize the entry and exit times and the aircraft ID.

– Once all of the airplanes have been covered in this manner, we look for squares that are traversed by one or more flights. We also check neighboring squares. In cases where several flights traverse neighboring squares, we check their traversal times and their altitudes in order to detect conflicts.

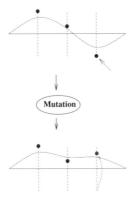

Figure 6.43. *Influence of the mutation operator on a trajectory*

The fitness used by the genetic algorithm is given by:

$$f(X) = -\left(CN + (\frac{NR}{DR} - N) \right) \qquad [6.9]$$

where CN is the number of conflicts, NR the sum of the distances of the new routes calculated by the algorithm, DR the sum of the distances of the direct routes and N the number of airplanes. The lower the number of conflicts and the increase in length, the better the chromosome is considered to be.

We will now look at the results obtained using the roundabout test problem. This academic problem consists of $N = 16$ airplanes, distributed uniformly across a circle of radius 100 NM (= 185,200 m), which must fly to the point diametrically opposite on the circle. Thus, each of the 16 points on the circle has an incoming and an outgoing trajectory. For this configuration, our method produces a conflict-free situation. The evolution of fitness as a function of time is shown in Figure 6.44. When the fitness belongs to $[-1, 0]$, the situation is conflict-free.

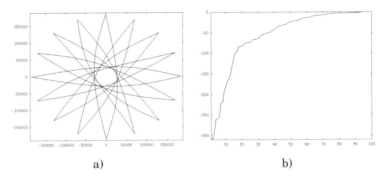

a)   b)

Figure 6.44. *a) Resolution of the roundabout problem and b) evolution of fitness as a function of the number of generations*

Although the solution to this problem can be found intuitively by human users due to its symmetry, computer processors are unable to use this symmetry. This result, obtained automatically, shows that our methodology is promising as the obtained solution is coherent with the expected result and corresponds to the practical approach of air traffic controllers. As in the case of the previous algorithm, this approach based on genetic algorithms will be tested using a day's worth of real traffic data. Moreover, the algorithm will be extended to take account of incertitudes linked to trajectory prediction.

These first approaches to trajectory planning currently produce very good results and allow us to treat realistic instances of problems, taking account of operational constraints. Only incertitudes linked to trajectory prediction are not taken into account, and the remainder of this work will be devoted to this aspect.

6.8. Conclusion

This research demonstrates that artificial evolution is extremely well suited to use with assignment problems in the context of air traffic. This approach allows us to take account of operational constraints in an effective manner without over simplifying the model. It produces highly satisfactory results, which are easy to reintegrate into their real-world context.

In both sectorization and assignment problems, the airspace congestion metrics used in optimization represent a key element in creating solutions. In our experiments, we have used operational metrics (number of aircraft in a given volume per unit of time), which are not ideal, due to the excessive levels of simplification involved; these metrics do not reflect the control workload that constitutes the limiting factor for sectors. This modeling fault has a clear impact on the optimization process, which consequently produces suboptimal solutions. We have therefore developed a set of more precise metrics, which give a more faithful representation of airspace congestion. These metrics will be presented in the next chapter.

Chapter 7

Airspace Congestion Metrics

In this chapter, we will present the congestion metrics that we have developed in order to improve the modeling of the objectives used in optimizing sectorization and traffic assignment.

We will begin by presenting a macroscopic metric based on traffic flows, and a microscopic geometric approach. We will then consider a trajectory-based metric using Lyapunov exponents.

7.1. Introduction

In a control sector, the higher the number of aircraft, the more the control workload increases (in a nonlinear manner). A limit exists after which the controllers in charge of a control sector are unable to accept additional aircraft, obliging these new aircraft to travel around the sector, moving through less-charged neighboring sectors. In this case, the sector is said to be saturated. This critical state should be avoided, as it provokes a cumulative overloading phenomenon in preceding sectors, which can backup as far as the departure airport. The saturation threshold is very difficult to estimate, as it depends on the geometry of routes traversing a sector, the geometry of the sector itself, the distribution of aircraft along routes, the performances of the control team, etc. One widely accepted threshold is fixed at 3 conflicts and 15 aircraft for a given sector. This maximum load should not last for more than 10 min as it places the controllers under considerable stress, with the risk that they will no longer be able to manage traffic in optimal safety conditions.

The control workload estimation is critical in many domains of Air Traffic Management (ATM) as it is central to the optimization processes. Examples include the following applications:

– Airspace comparison (US/Europe).

– Validation of future concepts (Single European Sky ATM Research (SESAR), Next Generation Air Transportation System (NextGen), etc.).

– Analysis of traffic control action modes (situation before and after control).

– Optimization of sectorization.

– Optimization of sector grouping and degrouping (pre-tactical alert: anticipation of an increase in congestion in a group of sectors in order to carry out ungrouping in an optimal manner).

– Optimization of traffic assignment.

– Determination of congestion pricing zones.

– Organic control assistance tools.

– Generation of four-dimensional (4D) trajectories.

– Prediction of congested zones, etc.

The operational capacity of a control sector is currently measured by the maximum number of aircraft able to traverse the sector in a given time period. This measurement does not take into account the orientation of traffic and considers geometrically structured and disordered traffic in the same manner. Thus, in certain situations, a controller may continue to accept traffic even if operational capacity has been exceeded (structured traffic); in other situations, the controllers may be bound to prohibit additional traffic even though operational capacity has not yet been reached (disordered traffic). Thus, a measurement in terms of the number of aircraft per unit of time constitutes an insufficient metric for the representation of the difficulty level associated with a particular traffic situation.

In the context of operational control, the ideal would be to find a metric that precisely measures the level of mental effort needed to manage a set of aircraft. Without going quite so far, it is possible to find complexity metrics that go beyond a simple measurement of the number of aircraft. We will begin by clarifying two essential notions for use in the remaining chapter:

– *Control workload*: measurement of the difficulty for the traffic control system treating a situation. This system may be a human operator or an automatic process. In the context of operational control, this workload is linked to the cognitive process of traffic situation management (conflict prediction and resolution, trajectory monitoring, etc.).

– *Traffic complexity*: intrinsic measurement of the complexity associated with a traffic situation. This measurement is independent of the system in charge of the traffic and is solely dependent on the geometry of trajectories. It is linked to sensitivity, to initial conditions and to the interdependency of conflicts. Incertitude with respect to positions and speeds increases the difficulty of predicting future trajectories. In certain situations, this incertitude regarding future positions can increase exponentially, making the system extremely complex in that it is virtually impossible to reliably extrapolate a future situation. When a future conflict is detected, a resolution process is launched, which, in certain situations, may generate new conflicts. This interdependency between conflicts is linked to the level of mixing between trajectories. As an example, Figure 7.1 shows three traffic situations classed according to increasing levels of difficulty as a function of the level of predictability and of interdependency between trajectories.

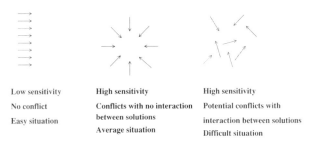

Low sensitivity   High sensitivity   High sensitivity

No conflict   Conflicts with no interaction   Potential conflicts with

Easy situation   between solutions   interaction between solutions

                         Average situation   Difficult situation

Figure 7.1. *Three traffic situations classed by increasing order of complexity*

One way of interpreting these notions is to imagine ourself being in charge of each situation in a context where the radar imaging equipment has ceased to work. Naturally, our attention is immediately focused on the situation on the right, as it is difficult to predict (in terms of the appearance of conflicts) and presents a high level of interdependency between trajectories. The middle solution, which presents a significant risk of conflict, is easy to manage as the same direction order must simply be given to all of the aircraft (+90° or −90°) in order to place them in safe roundabout trajectories. Finally, in the situation on the left, the trajectories do not present any difficulties and the relative distance between the aircraft will be maintained, at least for the immediate future.

Research into air traffic complexity metrics has attracted considerable attention in recent years, particularly in the United States and Europe. The first projects were launched in Germany in the 1970s, and since then the subject has continued to develop. Currently, National Aeronautics and Space Administration (NASA), Massachusetts Institute of Technology (MIT) and Georgia Tech are involved in work on the subject within the framework of the NextGen project. In Europe, the German Aerospace Center (DSNA), the Air Navigation Service Provider (DLR) and the Northern Aerospace Laboratory, Netherlands (NLR) are involved in similar activities linked to SESAR.

The objective of most of this work is to model the control workload associated with the given traffic situations. The main approaches are as follows:

– *Workload model based on the traffic level* [SCH 78]: this approach defines the workload as the proportion of control time over an hour, taking account of the average duration of routine control tasks for an aircraft, the average time taken to resolve conflicts per aircraft, the average rate of arrivals in a sector per hour and the average rate of conflicts in a sector per hour.

– *Queue-based model* [MAU 97]: in this case, a control sector is modeled as a system receiving an input (aircraft) and providing a service, allowing the aircraft to traverse the sector safely. The sector may then be modeled as a service center including one or more servers and an aircraft queue. By applying queueing theory, this approach allows us to determine a maximum acceptable arrival rate for a sector.

– *Model based on airspace structure* [JAN 91]: in this case, the capacity of a sector is based solely on its structure (flight levels, routes, route intersections, etc.).

– *Dynamic density* [LAU 98, SRI 01, CHA 01]: this model, developed by NASA, consists of measuring a set of traffic characteristics (number of changes in direction, changes in speed, changes in altitude, etc.) and the workload experienced by a controller, then carrying out linear regression in order to adjust the model to the experienced workload as precisely as possible.

This model of control workload presents the following two drawbacks:

1) incapacity for generalization to new sectors;

2) modeling is highly dependent on the controllers used to infer the model.

Other approaches [GRA 03, LEE 07] model the complexity of a traffic situation using automatic conflict resolution algorithms, for which we measure the number of trajectory modifications required in processing a given situation. In the same way as before, these methods are highly dependent on the type of algorithm used to resolve conflicts. These considerations have led us to develop intrinsic traffic complexity metrics that are only linked to trajectory structure, and not to the system used to process them. In the remaining chapter, we will propose the following three approaches:

– flow-based metrics;

– metrics based on the geometric distribution of speed vectors in the airspace;

– metrics using a dynamic system (linear or nonlinear) to model air traffic.

7.2. Flow-based approach

This control workload model is adapted for use with an air traffic model based on a transportation network, where nodes represent beacons or airports and the links represent airways. Flows of traffic circulate along these links and cross over at nodes. The model proposed is thus a macroscopic model that is suitable for quantifying the workload across large zones of airspace. Finally, this model is designed for use with en-route traffic.

Through questioning the controllers, we were able to see that the control workload is principally connected with the following quantitative criteria:

– conflict workload;

– coordination workload;

– monitoring workload.

Conflict workload: in a control sector, the conflict resolution workload is linked to the crossing of flows at nodes in the network. A simple geometric model allows us to quantify the average number of conflicts at the crossing point (j) of two airways for which the flows follow a Poisson process (means f_{ij}, f_{lj}) with a crossing angle of θ_{ijl} (see Figure 7.2):

$$N_c = \frac{2N_s \sqrt{V_{lj}^2 - 2.V_{lj}.V_{ij}.\cos\theta_{ijl} + V_{ij}^2}}{V_{lj}.V_{ij}.\sin\theta_{ijl}} \cdot f_{ij}.f_{lj}$$

where N_s is the standard separation norm, f_{ij}, f_{lj} are convergent flows associated with links (i,j) and (l,j), V_{ij}, V_{lj}, is the average speed of the aircraft along links (i,j) and (l,j) and θ_{ijl} represents the angle formed by links (i,j) and (l,j).

Supposing that the control workload for the crossing is proportional to the number of generated conflicts, we obtain $C_{cf} = \alpha(\theta_{ijl})f_{ij}f_{lj}$ in the case of a two-route crossing, where $\alpha(\theta_{ijl})$ is a weighting coefficient dependent on the angle of the crossing between the routes. When a crossing involves more than two incident routes, the conflict workload is the sum of the workloads induced by the links taken two by two. This gives us an expression for the conflict resolution workload for the node j:

$$C_{cf}(j) = \frac{1}{2} \sum_{\substack{i \in \mathcal{N} \\ i \neq j}} \sum_{\substack{l \in \mathcal{N} \\ l \neq i; l \neq j}} \alpha_{ijl} f_{ij} f_{lj}$$

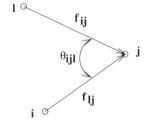

Figure 7.2. *Crossing of two routes*

If we only consider conflicts at the node j, we may take:

$$\alpha_{ijl} = \frac{2 N_s \sqrt{V_{lj}^2 - 2.V_{lj}.V_{ij}.\cos\theta_{ijl} + V_{ij}^2}}{V_{lj}.V_{ij}.\sin\theta_{ijl}} \Rightarrow N_C = \alpha_{ijl}.f_{ij}.f_{lj}$$

The conflict workload in a sector S_k is therefore the sum of the workloads for each node contained within the sector:

$$C_{cf}(S_k) = \frac{1}{2} \sum_{j \in \mathcal{N}_k} \sum_{\substack{i \in \mathcal{N} \\ i \neq j}} \sum_{\substack{l \in \mathcal{N} \\ l \neq i; l \neq j}} \alpha_{ijj}.f_{ij}.f_{lj}$$

where $\mathcal{N}_k$ represents the set of nodes located in the sector S_k.

Coordination workload: all the aircraft in the same sector use the same frequency to communicate with the controller in charge of a sector. When they change sector, they must change frequency, and a transfer of control takes place. This transfer is the subject of prior negotiations between the transferring and receiving controllers to ensure that the latter is able to accept the aircraft and to define the modes (flight level, etc.) of the transfer. A transfer requires a significant amount of work on the part of the two controllers; moreover, misunderstandings and errors can occur in the course of the process, causing accidental losses of separation. The workload induced by these transfers is known as coordination. In a sectorized transportation network, the coordination workload is proportional to the flows cut across sector boundaries. By studying the coordination workload generated by the link of a route (i, j), some or all of which belongs to a sector S_k, we can identify three possible cases:

1) The two extremities of the link belong to sector $S_k \Rightarrow i \in \mathcal{N}_k$ and $j \in \mathcal{N}_k$; the whole link is thus in sector S_k (as in the case of link (2,3) in the network shown in Figure 7.3).

$\Rightarrow C_{co} = 0$ (no intersection with the edge of the sector)

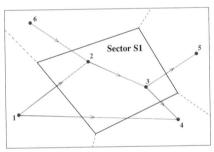

Figure 7.3. *Network showing three possible coordination situations*

2) Only one extremity of the link belongs to sector $S_k \Rightarrow i \in \mathcal{N}_k$ or (exclusive) $j \in \mathcal{N}_k$; there is therefore an intersection between link (i, j) and the edge of sector S_k, as in the case of link (3,4) in the network shown in Figure 7.3. We can represent the coordination workload of this link using the following expression:

$\Rightarrow C_{co} = \beta_{ij} f_{ij}$ (one intersection with the sector edge) where β_{ij} is a proportionality coefficient used to weight the influence of coordination in relation to the other aspects of the control workload.

3) The two extremities of the link are located outside the sector $S_k \Rightarrow i \notin \mathcal{N}_k$ and $j \notin \mathcal{N}_k$ but $(i,j) \in \mathcal{A}_k$ where $\mathcal{A}_k$ is the set of links with a segment in the sector S_k; in this case, the flow is cut twice, as shown in link $(1,4)$ in the network in Figure 7.3. We can model the coordination workload of this link using the following expression:

$$\Rightarrow C_{co} = 2\beta_{ij}f_{ij} \text{ (two intersections with the edge of the sector)}$$

Grouping these three cases together and considering all links intersecting with the sector S_k, we obtain the overall coordination workload associated with the sector S_k:

$$C_{co}(S_k) = \sum_{i \oplus j \in \mathcal{N}_k} \beta_{ij}f_{ij} + \sum_{\substack{i \notin \mathcal{N}_k \\ j \notin \mathcal{N}_k \\ (i,j) \in \mathcal{A}_k}} 2\beta_{ij}f_{ij}$$

where $\oplus$ represents the "exclusive" or logic function.

In the example shown in Figure 7.3 $C_{co}(S1) = \beta_{12}f_{12} + \beta_{62}f_{62} + \beta_{35}f_{35} + \beta_{34}f_{34} + 2\beta_{14}f_{14}$

Monitoring workload: in a control sector, aircraft that are not in conflict or involved in transfers require surveillance by the controller, who verifies the course of flight plans using a radar image and attempts to determine the risk of future conflicts involving these aircraft. Monitoring is the basic task carried out by the controllers and represents a significant source of stress. The monitoring workload is directly linked to the number of aircraft present in the control sector. For a sector S_k, this may be modeled by:

$$C_{mo}(S_k) = \eta \sum_{(i,j) \in \mathcal{L}_k} \frac{l_{ij}}{V_{ij}} f_{ij}$$

with:

– $\mathcal{L}_k$: set of network links with a non-empty intersection with sector S_k;

– l_{ij}: length of the link (i, j) contained within sector S_k (in Nautical Miles);

– V_{ij}: average flow speed along link (i, j) (in knots);

– η: proportionality coefficient.

7.2.1. *Mathematical modeling of the control workload*

The control workload in a sector is thus the sum of the conflict, coordination and monitoring workloads:

$$C(S_k) = C_{cf}(S_k) + C_{co}(S_k) + C_{mo}(S_k)$$

This control workload model is well suited to describing the air traffic system at a microscopic level, where the notion of flow has meaning (large time scale). This type of representation is therefore used in sectorization and assignment of traffic flows. For cases where the notion of flow is no longer appropriate, we have developed a set of geometric and trajectory-based metrics (based on dynamic systems), which allow us to take into account the microscopic events (at individual aircraft level).

7.3. Geometrical approaches

These metrics are calculated at a given instant using the positions and speed vectors of the aircraft present in the chosen geographical zone. Each of these geometrical metrics exhibits a particular characteristic associated with the complexity of the situation.

Before presenting these metrics, we should highlight a specific property of the separation distance between aircraft. Separation constraints are not the same in the horizontal and vertical planes, and consequently classical Euclidean notions of distances are not suitable for the measurement of relative distances between pairs of aircraft. In these cases, we use an "elliptical" or "reduced" distance of the type:

$$d_{ij}^{a,h} = \| \, \vec{p_i} - \vec{p_j} \, \|_{a,h} = \sqrt{\frac{(x_i - x_j)^2 + (y_i - y_j)^2}{a^2} + \frac{(z_i - z_j)^2}{h^2}}$$

[7.1]

where $\vec{p_i}$ and $\vec{p_j}$ are the positions of two aircraft i and j in a local earth referential, a is the horizontal separation distance and h is the vertical separation distance. Values generally admitted for en-route sectors are $a = 5$ NM and $h = 1{,}000$ ft. The use of this new distance allows us to give as much importance to a horizontal separation of 5 NM as to a vertical separation of 1,000 ft.

7.3.1. *Proximity metric*

a. Objective

Observation of the positions of aircraft in a volume of airspace allows us to determine a level of aggregation known as *proximity* that is used to characterize the geographical distribution of aircraft. Proximity allows us to identify spatial zones with high levels of aggregation in relation to their volume. Thus, for a constant number of aircraft in a sector, proximity is used to distinguish whether these aircraft are distributed homogeneously or in the form of clusters. We can then distinguish in a quantitative manner between the two situations shown in Figure 7.4.

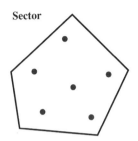 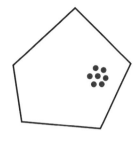

Sector

Figure 7.4. *On the left, we have five aircraft that are well distributed across the sector. In the situation represented on the right, the same five aircraft are aggregated in a reduced spatial zone*

b. Calculation method

For each aircraft under consideration, we open a spatial weighting window centered on that aircraft, making it the reference aircraft. We then calculate the relative distances of the other aircraft from the reference aircraft in order to calculate weighting coefficients using a spatial window:

$$f(d_{ij}) = e^{-\alpha d_{ij}^2}$$

where α is a parameter fixed by the user and d_{ij} is the normalized distance separating aircraft j from aircraft i. In this way, the distant aircraft are of less importance than the nearby aircraft. These factors are then added together in order to compute the proximity factor linked to the reference aircraft $P(i)$:

$$P(i) = \sum_{j=1}^{N} e^{-\alpha d_{ij}^2}$$

where N is the number of aircraft for consideration.

The proximity of a spatial zone is then calculated using the sum of the proximities of the aircraft present in that zone.

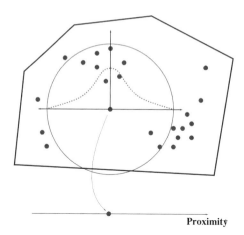

Figure 7.5. *Example of construction of a proximity scale*

Furthermore, each aircraft can be classified according to a proximity scale (see Figure 7.5). Depending on the distribution of aircraft in a sector, the value of this metric varies from N, when traffic is uniformly distributed, to N^2, when all of the aircraft are aggregated at the same point (where N represents the number of aircraft present in the sector at instant t)

$$N \leq P \leq N^2$$

For identical operational workloads, this indicator identifies sectors in which traffic distribution is not balanced across the space (sector with zones of dense traffic).

c. Examples and results

We calculated the evolution of this indicator for a day of traffic in France (see Figure 7.6). Using this curve, it is easy to identify moments of low traffic density (the night) and moments of clustering.

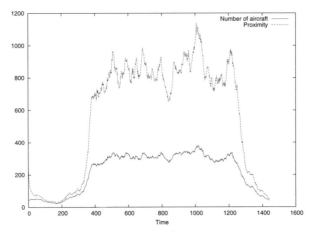

Figure 7.6. *Evolution of the number of aircraft and of proximity as a function of time*

The graph of the relationship between these two metrics (Proximity/Number of aircraft; see Figure 7.7) allows us to directly quantify the level of clustering as a function of time.

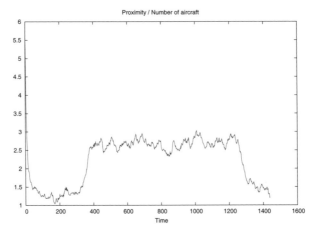

Figure 7.7. *Evolution of the (proximity) / (number of aircraft) relationship over time*

The results of this indicator clearly confirm its suitability to detect dense traffic structures. Finally, a cartographic version of proximity has been developed, an example of which is shown in Figure 7.8.

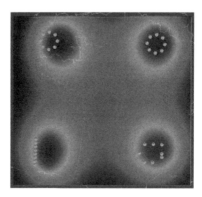

Figure 7.8. *This figure presents an artificial traffic situation with four groups of eight aircraft placed on a square. For each point in the space, we calculate the average level of proximity, considering the aircraft in the vicinity of the point*

As shown in Figure 7.8, the proximity indicator is able to identify areas where aircraft aggregate, but is unable to distinguish between situations using speed vectors. The two situations at the bottom of the figure are represented in the same manner, despite the fact that the situation on the right is much more difficult to manage. This consideration has led us to develop a convergence indicator, which takes account of the orientation of the speed vectors of the aircraft.

7.3.2. *Convergence*

a. Objective

The convergence indicator is used to quantify the geometric structure of the speed vectors of aircraft present in a sector. Thus, for identical proximity values, the convergence indicator allows us to distinguish between converging and diverging aircraft.

When a dense zone has been identified, it may be characterized using the rate of convergence of the aircraft present in this area. The higher the indicator, the closer the aircraft and the faster the convergence. Thus, in the example shown in Figure 7.9, the convergence indicator is used to provide an unambiguous classification of the eight situations. Each situation corresponds to two aircraft, for which the relative distance is constant (higher in the top four cases) and the relative speed varies from strong divergence to strong convergence. In the case of divergence, the indicator will be null, and for convergences, it will be increasingly high as the relative distance diminishes and the relative speed increases.

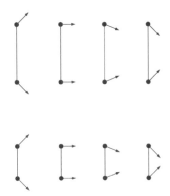

Figure 7.9. *The speed distributions are identical in the top four situations and the bottom four situations; however, the relative distance is smaller in the bottom four situations. The most critical situation is located at the bottom right (strong convergence and low relative distance)*

b. Calculation method

Let us take two moving points i and j (see Figure 7.10); the *level of variation of their relative distance* is:

$$r_{ij} = \frac{\partial}{\partial t}\left(d_{ij}\right) \tag{7.2}$$

where d_{ij} is their reduced relative distance. Thus, a pair of aircraft converges if, and only if, this level of variation is negative; convergence becomes increasingly rapid as the absolute value of this level increases.

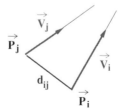

Figure 7.10. *The variation of the relative distance between two aircraft (d_{ij}) indicates whether or not they are converging, and at what speed*

Let $\vec{p_{ij}}$ be the reduced relative position vector and $\vec{v_{ij}}$ the reduced relative speed vector:

$$\vec{p_{ij}} = \begin{vmatrix} \frac{x_j - x_i}{a} \\ \frac{y_j - y_i}{a} \\ \frac{z_j - z_i}{h} \end{vmatrix} \qquad \vec{v_{ij}} = \begin{vmatrix} \frac{v_{xj} - v_{xi}}{a} \\ \frac{v_{yj} - v_{yi}}{a} \\ \frac{v_{zj} - v_{zi}}{h} \end{vmatrix}$$

r_{ij} is thus given by:

$$r_{ij} = \frac{\partial}{\partial t} \|\vec{p_{ij}}\|_2 = \frac{\partial}{\partial t} \sqrt{\vec{p_{ij}} \cdot \vec{p_{ij}}} = \frac{\vec{p_{ij}} \cdot \vec{v_{ij}}}{d_{ij}} \qquad [7.3]$$

In reality, the risk associated with the convergence of a pair of aircraft also depends on the relative distance between aircraft. We must therefore simultaneously account for the speeds and relative distances of each pair of aircraft. One possible form of a convergence indicator associated with an aircraft i is given by:

$$Cv(i) = \lambda_c \sum_{j/r_{ij} \leq 0} -r_{ij} \cdot e^{-\frac{1}{2}(\alpha_c \cdot d_{ij})^2} \qquad [7.4]$$

where λ_c and α_c are weighting coefficients.

Thus, for each aircraft i, it is possible to calculate a proximity value $P(i)$ and a local convergence level $Cv(i)$ in order to locate it in a referential whose axes are the proximity and the convergence level (see Figure 7.11).

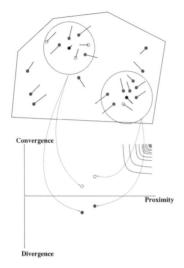

Figure 7.11. *In this figure, two aircraft are represented in a proximity / convergence referential. The aircraft located in the top right zone are the most critical (strong convergence with high proximity)*

c. Examples and results

We tested this indicator using the same simulation files as before. For all of the traffic in French airspace over the course of a day and for each time step, each aircraft present in the space is represented by a cross. The whole set of crosses is forming a cloud (see Figure 7.12) in which we are able to easily identify critical aircraft (top right).

As in the case of proximity, the convergence indicator can be mapped. The map associated with the artificial situation involving four groups of eight aircraft (as mentioned earlier) is shown in Figure 7.13.

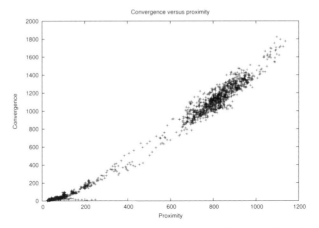

Figure 7.12. *Convergence and proximity calculated for a day of French air traffic*

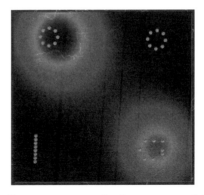

Figure 7.13. *Convergence map for four groups of eight aircraft*

From this figure, we show that only the two non-organized situations (pure conflict and random situation) are identified by the indicator.

The two indicators discussed above (proximity and convergence) are calculated by the aggregation of local influences between pairs of aircraft. This approach can prove limiting in certain situations, and as a result we have developed an extension of these principles to the level of aircraft clusters.

7.3.3. *Clusters*

a. Objective

This indicator allows us to directly account for multiple interactions between aircraft. Thus, if aircraft A is in interaction with aircraft B and aircraft B with aircraft C, we consider the cluster A, B, C using a pseudo-transitivity relation. It is possible to characterize a cluster using its construction in terms of relative distances and/or relative speeds.

b. Calculation methods

"Clusters" are small groups of neighboring aircraft, which appear when the airspace is heavily congested. In a cluster situation, the resolution of a conflict between two aircraft A_1 and A_2 must take into account the other individuals in the cluster:

– either because A_1 or A_2 is also involved in a conflict with other aircraft in the cluster;

– or because the possibilities for maneuver of A_1 or A_2 are limited by the presence of the other aircraft in the cluster.

To construct clusters, we calculate a clustering coefficient c_{ij} for each pair of aircraft present in the sector:

$$c_{ij} = a_{ij} \cdot b_{ij}$$

where a_{ij} is the spatial aggregation factor $a_{ij} = e^{-\frac{1}{2}(\alpha_p \cdot d_{ij})^2}$ and b_{ij}, is the associated convergence level:

$$b_{ij} = \begin{cases} r_{ij} = -\frac{d(d_{ij})}{dt} & \text{if} \quad \frac{d(d_{ij})}{dt} \leq 0 \text{ (convergence)} \\ 0 & \text{otherwise} \quad \text{(divergence)} \end{cases}$$

where r_{ij} is the level of variation of the reduced relative distance d_{ij}. Two aircraft i and j belong to the same cluster C if $c_{ij} \geq S$ (S clustering threshold).

Clusters are noted as CL_k^l ($l \in \{1, 2, ...N_k\}$) when N_k is the number of clusters at instant t_k. $\mathcal{C}_k^l$ is the intrinsic complexity value of the cluster CL_k^l, which is evaluated by the norm of the coefficient matrix c_{ij}:

$$\mathcal{C}_k^l = \alpha_c \|CL_k^l\|_T + \beta_c \|CL_k^l\|_1 \qquad [7.5]$$

with $\alpha_c > 0$, $\beta_c > 0$ and for a matrix C, the matrix norms $\|C\|_T$ and $\|C\|_1$ are defined in the following manner:

$$\|C\|_T = \sqrt{\sum_{i=1}^{i=n} \sum_{j=1}^{j=n} c_{ij}^2} = \sqrt{tr(C^T.C)}$$

$$\|C\|_1 = \max_j \left(\sum_{i=1}^{i=n} |c_{ij}| \right)$$

The section "norm-trace" indicates an average risk factor for all the aircraft in the cluster, whereas the section "norm l_1" indicates the risk of the most heavily penalized aircraft.

Another way to account for speed vectors is to calculate a pseudo-measurement of disorder by constructing the Grassmannian matrix[1] [SHA 94] associated with the relative speed vectors between pairs of aircraft.

---

1 The Grassmannian matrix associated with vector $\vec{V}$ is constructed in the following manner: $\vec{V}.\vec{V}^T$

7.3.4. *Grassmannian indicator*

a. Objective

When we observe a field of speed vectors, it is natural to imagine a measurement of the disorder of the speed vectors in order to differentiate between the two situations shown in Figure 7.14.

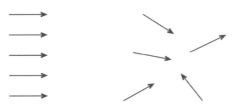

Figure 7.14. *This figure presents two extreme traffic situations. On the left, the aircraft are completely structured in terms of speed and the situation presents no difficulties. On the right, however, the situation is extremely disordered and will consequently be harder to manage*

We also need to take into account the relative distances between the aircraft in order to characterize only those situations that are disordered in a limited space. Thus, the larger the zone considered, the less the notion of complexity is relevant in relation to the associated complexity. The objective of this new metric is to provide a local measurement of disorder in the field of speed vectors, taking account of relative distances.

b. Calculation method

We begin by calculating all of the relative speeds associated with possible pairs of aircraft. These vector pairings are then weighted using a factor linked to the relative distance. We then construct the Grassmannian matrix of this new vector, for which we theoretically need to calculate the determinant representing the associated expansion rate. However, when aircraft are in cruise mode, the third dimension of the speed vectors cancels out, systematically canceling the determinant of the associated Grassmannian matrix. To avoid this problem, we begin by computing the singular values decomposition of the Grassmannian matrix, then we calculate the product of all singular values greater than 1. This allows us to avoid the problems associated with dimensions. The aggregated metric is then constructed by calculating the sum of the products of the singular values of the weighted Grassmannian matrices associated with each pair of aircraft.

We obtain the following mathematical formulation:

$$\vec{V}_{ij} = \vec{V}_j - \vec{V}_i = \begin{bmatrix} dv_x \\ dv_y \\ dv_z \end{bmatrix}$$

Let G_{ij} be the Grassmannian matrix associated with à $\vec{V}_{ij}$:

$$G_{ij} = \vec{V}_{ij}.\vec{V}_{ij}^T$$

The decomposition of the weighted Grassmannian matrix into singular values is thus written as:

$$\alpha_{ij}.G_{ij} = L_{ij}.S_{ij}.U_{ij}^T$$

where α_{ij} is the weighting coefficient associated with the relative distance of aircraft i and j ($\alpha_{ij} = \exp(-\alpha_p.\|\vec{d}_{ij}\|)$) and S_{ij} is a diagonal matrix containing the singular values.

The disparity factor of the relative speeds, c_{ij}, associated with the aircraft pair i, j is the product of the singular values greater than 1:

$$c_{ij} = \prod_{k,S_{kk}>1} S_{kk}$$

The overall factor is thus constructed by considering all pairs of aircraft:

$$C_{cov} = \sum_i \sum_{j,j\neq i} c_{ij}$$

c. Examples of results

A mapped version of this indicator was also developed, and an example is shown in Figure 7.15.

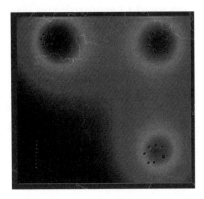

Figure 7.15. *Mapped Grassmannian indicator*

As is shown in the figure, this indicator clearly identifies zones where the speed vectors are not structured. For the situation in the top right, however, the indicator is unable to identify a rotation organization (situations that are rare in Air Traffic Control (ATC)). This consideration leads us to search for an indicator that would be able to show this type of organization while detecting the level of disorder of the speed vectors. More specifically, we have developed a metric based on Koenig's theorems of solid mechanics, which enables us to identify situations where traffic is organized in rotation. Other geometrical metrics are discussed in [DEL 04].

When a traffic situation is organized following any trajectory, these geometric metrics are unable to identify them. Moreover, they are only valid for a given instant, and are therefore unsuited to measuring the complexity of a set of trajectories over a given time period. These limitations naturally lead us to look at the theory of dynamic systems to infer a complexity metric suited to trajectories and not just to a set of speed vectors.

7.4. Approach based on dynamic systems

These metrics are used to quantify the level of disorder and interaction of a set of trajectories in a given zone of airspace.

7.4.1. *Linear dynamic systems*

This approach consists of modeling a set of trajectories using a linear dynamic system with the following equation:

$$\dot{\vec{X}} = \mathbf{A} \cdot \vec{X} + \vec{B} \tag{7.6}$$

where $\vec{X}$ represents the state vector of the system.

$$\vec{X} = \begin{bmatrix} x \\ y \\ z \end{bmatrix} \tag{7.7}$$

This equation associates a speed vector $\dot{\vec{X}}$ with each point in the state space $\vec{X}$.

The coefficients of matrix A determine the mode of evolution of the system in relation to its dynamics. More precisely, the eigenvalues of this matrix will determine the behavior of the system. Thus, the real part of the eigenvalues indicates whether the system is convergent or divergent in each of the eigenvectors. An eigenvalue with a positive real part produces a divergence, and an eigenvalue whose real part is negative produces convergence. The absolute value of these real parts is proportional to the level of contraction or expansion of the system. The imaginary part of the eigenvalues shows the tendency of the system to organize itself following a global rotation movement associated with each of the eigenaxes.

In the complex plane, it is then possible to identify the locus of the eigenvalues of matrix A associated with organized traffic situations (see Figure 7.16).

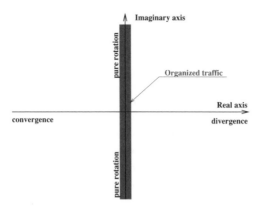

Figure 7.16. *Location of the eigenvalues of matrix A. The central rectangle corresponds to organized traffic situations (in pure rotation or in translation)*

Our problem therefore consists of determining the dynamic model that is closest to the observations that we have at a given instant. The least squares method is applied in order to adjust the model to the observations.

Let N be the number of observations at a given instant (number of aircrafts present in a sector at a given instant).

For each of these observations, we have a position measurement (see Figure 7.17):

$$X_i = \begin{bmatrix} x_i \\ y_i \\ z_i \end{bmatrix}$$

and a speed measurement:

$$V_i = \begin{bmatrix} vx_i \\ vy_i \\ vz_i \end{bmatrix}$$

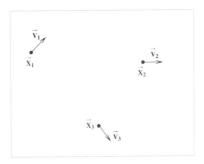

Figure 7.17. *Radar captures associated with three aircraft*

We thus wish to find the vector field described by a linear equation ($\dot{\vec{X}} = A.\vec{X} + \vec{B}$), which is best fitted to our observations. To illustrate this aspect, we construct a grid over the airspace (see Figure 7.18) on which we carry out regression of a vector field in such a way as to minimize the error between the model and the observation.

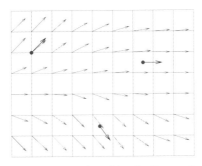

Figure 7.18. *Vector field produced by the linear dynamic system*

We then construct an error criterion E based on a norm (Euclidean, in our case), which should be minimized in relation to matrix A and vector $\vec{B}$, which represent the parameters of the model:

$$E = \sqrt{\sum_{i=1}^{i=N} \left\| \vec{V}_i - \left(A.\vec{X}_i + \vec{B} \right) \right\|^2}$$

We then insert the following matrices:

$$X = \begin{bmatrix} x_1 & x_2 & x_3 & \dots & x_N \\ y_1 & y_2 & y_3 & \dots & y_N \\ z_1 & z_2 & z_3 & \dots & z_N \\ 1 & 1 & 1 & \dots & 1 \end{bmatrix}$$

$$V = \begin{bmatrix} vx_1 & vx_2 & vx_3 & \dots & vx_N \\ vy_1 & vy_2 & vy_3 & \dots & vy_N \\ vz_1 & vz_2 & vz_3 & \dots & vz_N \end{bmatrix}$$

$$C = \begin{bmatrix} a_{11} & a_{12} & a_{13} & b_1 \\ a_{21} & a_{22} & a_{23} & b_2 \\ a_{31} & a_{32} & a_{33} & b_3 \end{bmatrix}$$

Criterion E may then be written in the following form:

$$E = \|V - C.X\|_F$$

where $\|\ \|_F$ represents the Frobenius norm[2].

Minimizing E is equivalent to minimizing $E^2 = \|V - C.X\|^2$. To do this, we calculate the gradient of E^2 in relation to matrix C:

$$\nabla_C E^2 = -2.(V - C.X).X^T$$

---

2 The Frobenius norm of a matrix A is equal to the sum of the squares of its elements: $\|A\|_F = \sum_i \sum_j A_{ij}^2$.

By canceling the above, we obtain:$\nabla_C E^2 = 0 \Leftrightarrow C.X.X^T = V X^T$, which then allows us to calculate C_{opt}:

$$C_{opt} = V.X^T.(X.X^T)^{-1}$$

The expression $X^T.(X.X^T)^{-1}$ is the pseudo-inverse of matrix X for which the singular values decomposition is given by:

$$X^T.(X.X^T)^{-1} = L^T.S^{-1}.R$$

where S is the diagonal matrix of the singular values. This decomposition allows us to control conditioning by only inversing singular values that are sufficiently distant from zero. Matrix C is thus given by:

$$C = V.L^T.S^{-1}.R$$

We then extract matrix A, for which we calculate the associated eigenvalues:

$$A = L.D.U^T$$

As an example (see Figure 7.19), the eigenvalues of matrix A have been calculated for a situation with three aircrafts located on a circle, for which only the orientation of the speed vectors is modified in order to create four traffic situations (organized traffic, convergence, divergence and rotation).

As shown in Figure 7.19, the two organized traffic situations have eigenvalues in the central band.

This approach, based on linear dynamic systems, thus produces a global measurement of the level of organization of a set of trajectories. As the number of the linear model's degrees of freedom is reduced, an error remains between the model and the observation when we increase the number of measurements. To increase the precision of this type of indicator, we have developed a spatial extension of the approach, which allows us to create complexity maps associated with a given airspace.

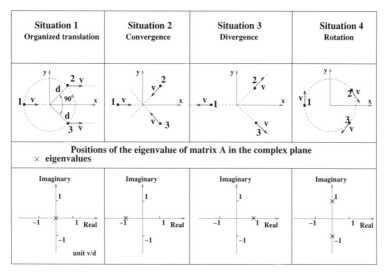

Positions of the eigenvalue of matrix A in the complex plane

Figure 7.19. *Representation of the eigenvalues of matrix A associated with four traffic situations*

7.4.2. *Spatial extension using nonlinear dynamic systems*

The previous metric can be improved by considering a nonlinear model of the associated dynamic system. The main difference between this and the previous approach is that a nonlinear system is located in a space. Thus, its value changes from one point to another in this space, whereas a linear system remains constant.

The nonlinear model takes the following form:

$$\dot{\vec{X}} = \vec{f}(\vec{X})$$

where f is a spatial evolution function of the dynamic model. We therefore wish to find a function $\vec{f}$ that minimizes the interpolation criterion E_1:

$$E_1 = \sum_{i=1}^{i=N} \| \vec{V_i} - \vec{f}(\vec{X_i}) \|^2$$

Note that it is always possible to determine a nonlinear dynamic system interpolating a set of data. In fact, an infinite number of functions $\vec{f}$ exist that allow us to minimize the criterion E_1 (with $min(E_1) = 0$).

To obtain a unique solution, we need to introduce an additional regularity criterion E_2:

$$E_2 = \int_{\mathbb{R}^3} \left\{ \alpha \, \|\nabla \text{div} \, \vec{f}(\vec{X})\|^2 + \beta \, \|\nabla \text{rot} \, \vec{f}(\vec{X})\|^2 \right\} . d\vec{X}$$

The joint minimization of E_1 and E_2 induces a unique function $\vec{f}$ [AMO 91]:

$$\vec{f}(\vec{X}) = \sum_{i=1}^{N} \Phi(\|\vec{X} - \vec{X}_i\|) . \vec{a}_i + \mathbf{A} . \vec{X} + \vec{B}$$

where $\vec{a}_i$ is the parameter vector. Matrix Φ (associated vector spline) is given by:

$$\Phi(\|\vec{X} - \vec{X}_i\|) = \mathbf{Q}(\|\vec{X} - \vec{X}_i\|^3)$$

where $\mathbf{Q}$ is the matrix operator:

$$\mathbf{Q} = \begin{pmatrix} \frac{1}{\alpha}\partial_{xx}^2 + \frac{1}{\beta}(\partial_{yy}^2 + \partial_{zz}^2) & (\frac{1}{\alpha} - \frac{1}{\beta})\partial_{xy}^2 & (\frac{1}{\alpha} - \frac{1}{\beta})\partial_{xz}^2 \\ (\frac{1}{\alpha} - \frac{1}{\beta})\partial_{xy}^2 & \frac{1}{\alpha}\partial_{yy}^2 + \frac{1}{\beta}(\partial_{xx}^2 + \partial_{zz}^2) & (\frac{1}{\alpha} - \frac{1}{\beta})\partial_{yz}^2 \\ (\frac{1}{\alpha} - \frac{1}{\beta})\partial_{xz}^2 & (\frac{1}{\alpha} - \frac{1}{\beta})\partial_{yz}^2 & \frac{1}{\alpha}\partial_{zz}^2 + \frac{1}{\beta}(\partial_{xx}^2 + \partial_{yy}^2) \end{pmatrix}$$

In the same way as in the linear context, regression of the nonlinear dynamic system is carried out using the least squares method, with the difference being that the number of parameters to be determined is much higher ($\Rightarrow$ $\mathbf{A}$, $\vec{B}$, $\vec{a}_i$ ($i \in \{1, .., N\}$), i.e. a total of $3N + 12$ parameters).

This model thus allows us to construct a regular field that is perfectly fitted to the observations ($\min(E_1) = 0$). Using this model, we can then apply the Lyapunov's exponent theory in order to quantify the local level of organization of the vector field. The principle of the Lyapunov exponents consists of measuring the sensitivity of the reconstituted vector field to initial conditions. To do this, we consider a point in the state space ($\vec{x_0}$) and we observe its trajectory (γ) when it is transported by the field (like a dust mote in a wind field). We thus obtain:

$$\gamma(t, \vec{x_0}) = \vec{x_0} + \int_0^t \vec{f}(u, \gamma(u, \vec{x_0}))du$$

We then consider a small disturbance ($\vec{\epsilon}$) of the initial position $\vec{x_0}$ for which we characterize the trajectory:

$$\gamma(t, \vec{x_0} + \vec{\epsilon}) = \gamma(t, \vec{x_0}) + \nabla_{\vec{x}}\vec{f}(\gamma(t, \vec{x})) \cdot \vec{\epsilon} + o(\|\vec{\epsilon}\|)$$

where $\nabla_{\vec{x}}\vec{f}(t, \gamma(t, \vec{x}))$ is the gradient of the field $\vec{f}$ at point $\vec{x}$. Next, we measure the distance between this new trajectory (taken from $\vec{x}$) and the reference trajectory in $\vec{x_0}$ (see Figure 7.20):

$$\|\gamma(t, \vec{x_0}) - \gamma(t, \vec{x})\| = D(t, \vec{x})$$

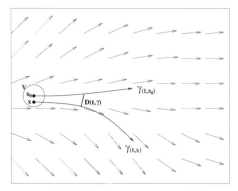

Figure 7.20. *Temporal evolution of the reference trajectory and a trajectory taken from the vicinity in $\vec{x_0}$.*

As $\gamma(t, \vec{x})$ is controlled by the vector field $\vec{f}$, we have:

$$\frac{\partial \gamma(t, \vec{x})}{\partial t} = \vec{f}(t, \gamma(t, \vec{x})) \quad \gamma(0, \vec{x}) = \vec{x}$$

It is thus possible to demonstrate that the distance $D(t)$ is also governed by a differential equation:

$$\frac{\partial D(t, \vec{x})}{\partial t} = \nabla_{\vec{x}}(t, \gamma(t, \vec{x})).D(t, \vec{x}) \quad D(0, \vec{x}) = \|\vec{x} - \vec{x}_0\|$$

As the previous equation is linear when considering the three dimensions of the space (x, y, z), it is possible to carry out a matrix extension (variational field equation):

$$\frac{dM(t)}{dt} = \nabla_{\vec{x}}(t, \gamma(t, \vec{x})) \cdot M(t) \quad M(0) = Id$$

This equation represents a linear dynamic system that forms a "tangent" to the initial system (at the point under consideration). We then calculate the decomposition of the matrix $M(t) = U^t(t)\Sigma(t)V(t)$ into singular values. The Lyapunov exponents are calculated by averaging the logarithms of these singular values over time (diagonal of matrix $\Sigma(t)$):

$$\kappa(\vec{x}) = -\frac{1}{T}\int_0^T \log(\Sigma_{ii}(t))dt \quad \forall \Sigma_{ii}(t) \leq 1$$

When an exponent has a high value, it shows a high sensitivity to initial conditions (deviation $\vec{\epsilon}$). In this case, the two trajectories $\gamma(t, \vec{x}_0)$ and $\gamma(t, \vec{x}_0 + \vec{\epsilon})$ taken by two particles in $\vec{x}_0$ and $\vec{x}_0 + \vec{\epsilon}$ are very different. The future situation is thus very difficult to predict in the zone of calculation of this exponent. On the other hand, a Lyapunov exponent with a low value shows a well-organized situation that is easy to predict. The map of the Lyapunov exponents allows us to identify zones of the airspace, where traffic is well organized (requires little monitoring), and zones of disordered traffic. In organized zones, the relative distances between aircraft remain stable over time, giving a stable situation with no modifications in the near future.

The following stages are involved in calculating a map of the Lyapunov exponents:

1) Regression of the nonlinear dynamic system using the N radar observations (position X_i and speed V_i). This allows us to fix the N coefficients $\vec{a}_i$, along with the matrix A and the vector $\vec{B}$.

2) Calculation of the gradient of the vector field for each point of a 3D grid: $\nabla_{\vec{x}}\vec{f}$.

3) Calculation of the Lyapunov exponents for each point of the grid using a Runge–Kutta integration:

$$\kappa(\vec{x}) = \frac{1}{L}\sum_{i=1}^{i=L}\|\nabla_{\vec{x}}(\gamma(t,\vec{x}))\|_2$$

$$\simeq \left(\frac{1}{L}\sum_{l=1}^{L}\log\left\{\max\left(\mathbf{Sing\ Value}\left(\nabla_{\vec{x}}(\gamma(t,\vec{x}))\right)\right)\right\}\right) \qquad [7.8]$$

where L represents the number of integration time steps.

The critical stage of this calculation is linked to the regression of the nonlinear dynamic system, of complexity $O[(3*(N+4))^3]$. Taking $\alpha = \beta$, we see that the differential matrix operator is considerably simplified:

$$\Phi(r) = Q(D)r^3 = \begin{bmatrix} \partial^2_{xx}+\partial^2_{yy}+\partial^2_{zz} & 0 & 0 \\ 0 & \partial^2_{xx}+\partial^2_{yy}+\partial^2_{zz} & 0 \\ 0 & 0 & \partial^2_{xx}+\partial^2_{yy}+\partial^2_{zz} \end{bmatrix}$$

The problem thus becomes:

$$\min E_1 = \sum_{i=1}^{i=N}\|\vec{V}_i - \vec{f}(\vec{X}_i)\|^2$$

and

$$\min E_2 \int_{\mathbb{R}^3} \|\Delta \vec{f}(\vec{x})\|^2 d\vec{x} \quad \text{with} \quad \Delta \vec{f} = \begin{bmatrix} \frac{\partial^2 f_x}{\partial x^2} + \frac{\partial^2 f_x}{\partial y^2} + \frac{\partial^2 f_x}{\partial z^2} \\ \frac{\partial^2 f_y}{\partial x^2} + \frac{\partial^2 f_y}{\partial y^2} + \frac{\partial^2 f_y}{\partial z^2} \\ \frac{\partial^2 f_z}{\partial x^2} + \frac{\partial^2 f_z}{\partial y^2} + \frac{\partial^2 f_z}{\partial z^2} \end{bmatrix}$$

where $\Delta \vec{f}$ represents the Laplacian of the vector field. From this, we deduce that

$$\Phi(r) = 12 \begin{bmatrix} r & 0 & 0 \\ 0 & r & 0 \\ 0 & 0 & r \end{bmatrix}$$

Under this form, the complexity is reduced to $O[3 * (N + 4)^3]$ and is thus divided by 9. Furthermore, it is possible to determine a closed form of the spatial gradient of the field:

$$\nabla_{\vec{X}} \vec{f}(\vec{X}) \begin{bmatrix} \frac{\partial f_x}{\partial x} & \frac{\partial f_x}{\partial y} & \frac{\partial f_x}{\partial z} \\ \frac{\partial f_y}{\partial x} & \frac{\partial \Phi_y}{\partial y} & \frac{\partial \Phi_y}{\partial z} \\ \frac{\partial f_z}{\partial x} & \frac{\partial f_z}{\partial y} & \frac{\partial f_z}{\partial z} \end{bmatrix} =$$

$$\mathbf{A} + \sum_{i=1}^{N} \begin{bmatrix} a_{ix} \\ a_{iy} \\ a_{iz} \end{bmatrix} \cdot \begin{bmatrix} \frac{\partial \Phi(r - r_i)}{\partial x} & \frac{\partial \Phi(r - r - i)}{\partial y} & \frac{\partial \Phi(r - r_i)}{\partial z} \end{bmatrix}$$

($\Phi(r)$ scalar function dependent on $r = \sqrt{x^2 + y^2 + z^2}$)

$$\frac{\partial \Phi(r - r_i)}{\partial x} = 12 . \frac{x - x_i}{\|\vec{X} - \vec{X}_i\|}$$

$$\frac{\partial \Phi(r - r_i)}{\partial y} = 12 . \frac{y - y_i}{\|\vec{X} - \vec{X}_i\|}$$

$$\frac{\partial \Phi(r - r_i)}{\partial z} = 12 . \frac{z - z_i}{\|\vec{X} - \vec{X}_i\|}.$$

The overall complexity of the algorithm is therefore:

– Regression: $3 * (N + 4)^3$ (most critical point).

– Reconstruction $N * M$ with M number of grid points.

– Estimation of the gradient M.

– Calculation of the Lyapunov exponents $M * L$ with L as the number of time steps used.

Note that the vector spline to solve this problem ($\Phi(r)$) is not located in space. Thus, the contribution of distant observations is more important than that of close observations. In the context of our application, and as an example, this means that to compute the vector field over New York, we need to take into account the distant traffic located over San Francisco, for example. The number of observations to take into consideration in the least squares regression cannot be reduced by considerations of spatial proximity.

a. Results using examples

The map (2D) of the Lyapunov exponents associated with our four different traffic situations is shown in Figure 7.21. In this figure, it is shown that the Lyapunov exponents are close for the pure conflict situation and the rotation situation. This phenomenon is entirely logical. When we do the summation of the Lyapunov exponents into a zone of the state space, the obtained value corresponds to the minimum quantity of information (in the Shannon sense) to provide to the system in order to configure it into a completely organized state (unidirectional field, null relative speeds). In the same way, the deviation of the sums of the Lyapunov exponents associated with two space state zones of the same volume corresponds to the minimum quantity of information to provide one situation in order to transform it into another. Thus, the pure conflict situation and the rotation situation are relatively close, in that we simply need to give the same direction change order to all aircraft to move from one situation to another (a heading change of $+90°$ or $-90°$); this constitutes a relatively small quantity of information.

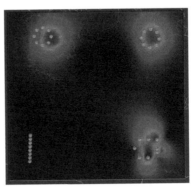

Figure 7.21. *Map of the Lyapunov exponents for four artificial traffic situations*

The Lyapunov exponents can be used to identify any organizational structure. Figure 7.22 shows a simulation of "Miles In Trail" traffic (aircrafts regularly spaced, flying at the same speed from the south-west to the north-east) traversing two zones of disordered traffic. As is shown the figure, a valley appears in the relief of the Lyapunov exponents where the organized traffic is located.

Generally, the Lyapunov exponents are able to identify all types of trajectory organization and not just structures following a straight line.

A simple spatial extension allows us to account for trajectories over a limited time period in a reasonable manner. If the temporal horizon is extended to the whole of the trajectory (several hours, in the case of air traffic), certain situations can generate results that have no real meaning in operational terms. Thus, if we consider an artificial situation where an aircraft travels in a loop in the horizontal plane (see

Figure 7.23), the spatial model may detect a conflict between the aircraft and itself due to the fact that observations are taken into account in the same manner with no consideration for time differences.

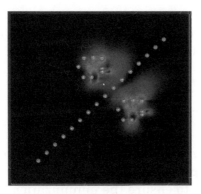

Figure 7.22. *The Lyapunov exponents have low values at the level of the "Miles In Trail" organized traffic, and high values in zones of disordered traffic*

Figure 7.23. *Looped trajectory in the horizontal plane*

To correct this limitation, we have developed a spatiotemporal extension to this approach.

7.4.3. *Spatiotemporal extension using nonlinear dynamic systems*

The purpose of this extension is to allow temporal localization of the regression carried out from our observations. A spatiotemporal dynamic system is governed by an equation with the form:

$$\dot{\vec{X}} = \vec{f}(\vec{X}, t)$$

We thus seek the vectorial function $\vec{f}(\vec{X}, t)$ that ensures the precise interpolation of our observations:

$$\min E_1 = \sum_{i=1}^{i=N} \sum_{k=1}^{k=K} \|\vec{V}_i(t_k) - \vec{f}(\vec{X}_i, t_k)\|^2$$

where $\vec{V}_i(t_k)$ represents the observation of aircraft i at instant t_k. As in the purely spatial case, an infinite number of functions $\vec{f}$ exist to ensure the minimization of E. To obtain a unique solution, we add a criterion of regularity in space and time:

$$\min E_2 \int_{\mathbb{R}^3} \int_t \|\Delta \vec{f}(\vec{x})\|^2 + \|\frac{\partial \vec{f}}{\partial t}\|^2 d\vec{x} dt$$

Using a spectral approach, we are able to identify a closed-form solution to the problem:

$$\vec{f}(\vec{X}, t) = \sum_{i=1}^{N} \sum_{k=1}^{K} \Phi(\|\vec{X}(t) - \vec{X}_i(t_k)\|, |t - t_k|).\vec{a}_{i,k} + \mathbf{A}.\vec{X} + \vec{B}$$

with

$$\Phi(r, t) = \mathbf{diag}\left(\frac{\sigma}{\sqrt{\pi}.r}.\mathbf{erf}\left[\frac{r}{\sigma.\sqrt{2 + \theta.|t|}}\right]\right)$$

and

$$\mathbf{erf}(x) = \frac{2}{\sqrt{\pi}} \int_0^x e^{-t^2} dt$$

When variable x is small in function "erf" is small, we use the following approximation:

$$\Phi(r,t) = \text{diag}\left(\frac{1}{\pi.\sqrt{2+\theta.|t|}}\right)$$

We are also able to identify a closed form of the spatial gradient of $\vec{f}$:

$$\nabla_{\vec{X}}\vec{f}(\vec{X}) = \mathbf{A} + \sum_{i=1}^{N}\sum_{k=1}^{K}\begin{bmatrix} a_{ikx} \\ a_{iky} \\ a_{ikz} \end{bmatrix}$$

$$.\left[\begin{array}{ccc} \frac{\partial\Phi((r-r_{ik}),(t-t_{ik}))}{\partial x} & \frac{\partial\Phi((r-r_{ik}),(t-t_{ik}))}{\partial y} & \frac{\partial\Phi((r-r_{ik}),(t-t_{ik}))}{\partial z} \end{array}\right]$$

$$\frac{\partial\Phi(\Delta_r,\Delta_t)}{\partial x} = \mu x - \eta x$$

$$\frac{\partial\Phi(\Delta_r,\Delta_t)}{\partial y} = \mu y - \eta y$$

$$\frac{\partial\Phi(\Delta_r,\Delta_t)}{\partial z} = \mu z - \eta z$$

with

$$\mu = \frac{\Phi(\Delta_r,\Delta_t)}{\Delta_r^2}$$

$$\eta = \frac{2\sigma}{\pi}.\frac{1}{\sqrt{2+\theta.|t|}}.e^{-\frac{\Delta_r^2}{\sigma^2.(2+\theta.|t|)}}$$

All of the approaches developed so far use noiseless observations, allowing us to generate instantaneous metrics. For certain applications, however, we need to take into account the stochastic aspect of observations in order to generate reliable metrics. As an example, we might consider the comparison of large-scale airspaces (US-Europe). For this type of application, we compute the map of the Lyapunov exponents for a given period (rush hour, for example) for each of the airspaces. To do this, we use a set of flight plans and an arithmetic trajectory simulator to produce observations. In the operational framework, however, we know that the position of an aircraft on its trajectory is affected by noise, particularly in the temporal dimension. Thus, the moment of passage of regular flights into a given control sector varies from day-to-day, based on weather conditions and operational criteria (regulations, passenger lateness, etc.). We will therefore concentrate on time shift phenomena, which represent the principal source of randomness in observations.

In the context of stochastic process theory, this phenomenon is known as clock shifting (the trajectory continues to conform to the flight plan in the spatial dimension, but the position of the aircraft on the trajectory may be subject to significant deviations in the temporal dimension). The distribution of these shifts is known (from laws, mathematical expectation, standard deviation, etc.) and can easily be introduced into an arithmetic simulator in order to produce realistic sets of observations. We may then construct an average mapping of the Lyapunov exponents using these trials in order to obtain robust comparisons between air-spaces.

A simplistic approach would consist of producing a set of trials, then calculating the map of the Lyapunov exponents associated with each of these selections before averaging out the maps. While this process produces precise results, it requires a level of CPU resources, which is too high for use with airspaces on a continental scale, where several tens of minutes are required to produce a single map.

Another approach consists of using a local linearization of the underlying dynamic system, which allows us to directly extract the mathematical expectation of the associated field gradient. This approach uses local linear models.

7.4.4. *Local linear models*

We have developed a local approximation method using only observations close to the evaluation point when calculating regression in order to accelerate the calculation of the field vector on the airspace grid. The calculation process consists initially of determining the average linear field ($\dot{\vec{X}} = A.\vec{X} + \vec{B}$) and subtracting it from each of the observations. For each measurement point, we obtain the deviation of the observation from the average field:

$$\vec{v}_i = \vec{V}_i - (A.\vec{X}_i + \vec{B})$$

The local approximation then consists of seeking a local linear model adjusted to each of the deviations $\vec{v}_i$.

The first-order approximation of the spatiotemporal field $\vec{f}$ is given by the following expression:

$$\vec{f}(t_0, \vec{X}_0) = \vec{f}(t, \vec{X}) + \frac{\partial \vec{f}(t,\vec{X})}{\partial t}(t_0 - t)+$$
$$+\frac{\partial \vec{f}(t,\vec{X})}{\partial \vec{X}}(\vec{X}_0 - \vec{X}) + O(|t_0 - t| + \|\vec{X}_0 - \vec{X}\|)$$

where $\frac{\partial \vec{f}(t,\vec{X})}{\partial t}$ is the temporal derivative of the field $\vec{f}$ and $\frac{\partial \vec{f}(t,\vec{X})}{\partial \vec{X}}$ is the associated spatial derivative.

This equation represents a local linear model of field $\vec{f}$ in the vicinity of point $(t, \vec{X})$.

We will now use this model to calculate an approximation of the field based on a set of local observations.

Let us consider a grid point $(t, \vec{X})$ in the state space and look for observations situated in the vicinity. The field is regressed in such a way as to minimize the error between the relative deviation $\vec{v}_i(t_i, \vec{X}_i)$ and the local linear model associated with field $\vec{f}$ at the grid point:

$$\vec{v}_i(t_i, \vec{X}_i) \simeq \vec{f}(t, \vec{X}) + \frac{\partial \vec{f}(t, \vec{X})}{\partial t}(t_i - t) + \frac{\partial \vec{f}(t, \vec{X})}{\partial \vec{X}}(\vec{X}_i - \vec{X})$$

$$= \vec{a} + \vec{b}.(t_i - t) + C.(\vec{X}_i - \vec{X})$$

with $\vec{a} = \vec{f}(t, \vec{X})$, $\vec{b} = \frac{\partial \vec{f}(t, \vec{X})}{\partial t}$ and $C = \frac{\partial \vec{f}(t, \vec{X})}{\partial \vec{X}}$

We now wish to find the vectors $\vec{a}$, $\vec{b}$ and the matrix C to minimize criterion J:

$$\min_{\vec{a}, \vec{b}, C} J = \sum_{i=1}^{N} \| \vec{v}_i(\vec{X}_i, t_i) - \left\{ \vec{a} + \vec{b}(t_i - t) + C.(\vec{X}_i - \vec{X}) \right\} \|^2 . \psi_i \quad [7.9]$$

where $\psi_i = \psi(t_i - t, \vec{X}_i - \vec{X})$ is a spatiotemporal weighting window used to select observations in the vicinity of the observed grid point.

Noting:

$$X = \begin{bmatrix} 1 & 1 & 1 & \cdots & 1 \\ (t_1 - t) & (t_2 - t) & (t_3 - t) & \cdots & (t_N - t) \\ (x_1 - x) & (x_2 - x) & (x_3 - x) & \cdots & (x_N - x) \\ (y_1 - y) & (y_2 - y) & (y_3 - y) & \cdots & (y_N - y) \\ (z_1 - z) & (z_2 - z) & (z_3 - z) & \cdots & (z_N - z) \end{bmatrix}$$

$$V = \begin{bmatrix} vx_1 & vx_2 & vx_3 & \cdots & vx_N \\ vy_1 & vy_2 & vy_3 & \cdots & vy_N \\ vz_1 & vz_2 & vz_3 & \cdots & vz_N \end{bmatrix}$$

$$M = \begin{bmatrix} a_x & b_x & C_{xx} & C_{xy} & C_{xz} \\ a_y & b_y & C_{yx} & C_{yy} & C_{yz} \\ a_z & b_z & C_{zx} & C_{zy} & C_{zz} \end{bmatrix}$$

and

$$\Psi = \begin{bmatrix} \sqrt{\psi_1} & 0 & 0 & \dots & 0 \\ 0 & \sqrt{\psi_2} & 0 & \dots & 0 \\ 0 & 0 & \sqrt{\psi_3} & \dots & 0 \\ 0 & 0 & 0 & \dots & 0 \\ 0 & 0 & 0 & \dots & \sqrt{\psi_N} \end{bmatrix}$$

criterion J takes the form:

$$J = \|\Psi(M) \cdot X - V\|_F^2 = (M \cdot X - V)^T \cdot \Psi \cdot (M \cdot X - V)$$

Deriving J in relation to matrix M, we obtain:

$$M_{opt} = V \cdot \Psi \cdot X^T (X \cdot \Psi X^T)^{-1}$$

As before, we use a singular values decomposition in order to avoid conditioning problems. The structure of the algorithm is therefore as follows:

---

1) Regression of the global linear dynamic system $(A \cdot \vec{X} + \vec{B})$.

2) Computation of relative observations $(\vec{v}_i - (A \cdot \vec{X} + \vec{B}))$.

3) For each grid point $\vec{X}(t)$, carry out:

i) Computation of the linear model $(\vec{a}, \vec{b}, C)$.

ii) Computation of the field $((A \cdot \vec{X} + \vec{B}) + \vec{b})$.

iii) Computation of the field gradient $A + C$.

4) Computation of the Lyapunov exponent map using Runge-Kutta integration.

Note that steps 3 and 4 may be executed in parallel.

7.4.5. *Stochastic extension*

When we wish to compare several airspaces, we need to consider several days of traffic for the same set of flight plans in order to smooth out the random effects linked to weather conditions. For all of these days, we compute the maps of the Lyapunov exponents, which we then average out. However, this precise approach requires considerable calculation time, particularly when dealing with large zones of airspace.

Another approach consists of calculating the average field, considering the position of the aircraft on their trajectories as random variables. To do this, we use a clock shift principle:

$$t_i \rightarrow t_i - \tilde{\tau}_i$$

where $\tilde{\tau}_i$ is a random variable (from now on, we will identify random variables using a tilde˜).

We thus obtain: $\tilde{\vec{X}}_i = \vec{\gamma}(\tilde{t}_i)$, $\tilde{\vec{v}}_i = \dot{\vec{\gamma}}(\tilde{t}_i) - A \cdot \tilde{\vec{X}}_i + \vec{B}$ et $\tilde{\psi}_i = \psi(\tilde{t}_i - t, \tilde{\vec{X}}_i - \vec{X})$, where $\vec{\gamma}(t)$ represents the trajectory of an aircraft.

As in the previous case, we wish to find the local linear model that minimizes the mathematical expectation of criterion $\tilde{J}$, which is now a random variable.

We thus seek $\vec{a}$, $\vec{b}$, C to minimize:

$$\min_{\vec{a},\vec{b},C} E[\tilde{J}] = \sum_{i=1}^{N} E\left[\| \tilde{\vec{v}}_i - \left[\vec{a} + \vec{b} \cdot (\tilde{t}_i - t) + C \cdot (\tilde{\vec{X}}_i - \vec{X}) \right] \|^2 . \tilde{\psi}_i \right]$$

$$[7.10]$$

Let $E[\tilde{V}], E[\tilde{X}]$ and $E[\tilde{\Psi}]$ be the mathematical expectations of the random matrices $\tilde{V}, \tilde{X}, \tilde{\Psi}$. Criterion $E[\tilde{J}]$ may then be written as:

$$E[\tilde{J}] = \| E[\tilde{\Psi}](M \cdot E[\tilde{X}] - E[\tilde{V}]) \|^2$$
$$= (M \cdot E[\tilde{X}] - E[\tilde{V}])^T \cdot E[\tilde{\Psi}] \cdot (M \cdot E[\tilde{X}] - E[\tilde{V}])$$

Deriving this expression in relation to M, we obtain:

$$M_{opt} = E[\tilde{V}] \cdot E[\tilde{\Psi}] \cdot E[\tilde{X}]^T (E[\tilde{X}] \cdot E[\tilde{\Psi}]E[\tilde{X}]^T)^{-1}$$

We then use the same algorithm as in the determinist case to extract the parameters of the model.

This approach is still in development at the time of writing, and should be tested on European and American airspaces in the near future.

Conclusion and Future Perspectives

The real-world optimization problems we have considered have shown the richness and complexity which make this research domain so appealing. When faced with a real problem, one of the most significant difficulties involved is linked to the development of a relevant mathematical model which best reflects the system in question. Using this model, we can identify properties in the state space, the objective space and constraints in order to develop an optimization algorithm which responds as effectively as possible to operational requirements. The complexity of these problems (non-convex, non-derivable, NP-hard, etc.) means that we often need to use stochastic methods to counteract this complexity while producing solutions of a very high quality. Our research activity has therefore focused on these methods, and in particular on artificial evolution. Alongside other researchers, we have proposed effective improvements to these algorithms in terms of crossover (using simulated annealing), clustered sharing (adaptive modification) and parallelism (using islets). We have also developed a new concept for genetic algorithms, working on domains evaluated using order statistics, which produces clear improvements in performance in the context of continuous spaces.

One of the great advantages of mathematical optimization is that it allows researchers in the domain to discover a wide range of application fields due to the quasi-universality of optimization requirements associated with human activities.

We thus began our research activity by looking at the problem of airspace sectorization. A first approach based on Voronoi diagrams with class centers driven by artificial evolution enabled us to treat the continuous two-dimensional (2D) form of this problem. A discrete development, working directly on the underlying network of air routes, allowed us to process larger networks with better results. These two modeling approaches were then extended to a three-dimensional (3D) context, ensuring that synthesized sectors conformed to operational constraints (cylindrical shaped sectors with an axis perpendicular to the ground). Finally, we proposed a dynamic adaptation of these algorithms, allowing us to account for traffic fluctuations in the context of sector grouping.

We then went on to consider traffic assignment as a means of reducing congestion in control sectors by modifying aircraft routes and departure times. Due to the combinatory nature of this problem, we proposed a number of different algorithms based on artificial evolution. Our first algorithm considered the macroscopic case, seeking a single path for all of the flows linking a same origin–destination pair. This approach ensures equailty between network users. A second approach looked at the microscopic context, optimizing routes and departure times for a set of flights at the level of a country or a continent. Once again, the combinatory nature of the problem meant that artificial evolution provides an effective means of addressing the issue. In order to regain equity between network users, we then added a congestion pricing principle. The extension to continuous cases, where we attempted to optimize the shape of airplane trajectories, gave promising results in tactical and pre-tactical contexts (algorithms based on a light propagation analogy and genetic algorithms using B-Splines) and is currently under development in a strategic context. Finally, we were able to show that the artificial evolution provides effective ways of treating traffic assignment in the terminal area, in the context of maximizing runway capacity by modifying airplane routes and speeds.

To improve the relevance of our optimization models, we then developed congestion metrics which are much more precise than those used in the field of operations. We first proposed metrics based on traffic geometry which show certain characteristics of the traffic (proximity, convergence etc.). Using dynamic systems theory, we then developed trajectory-based metrics, aggregating most of the characteristics of the previous geometric indicators. Using Lyapunov exponents, these indicators can be presented in the form of four-dimensional (4D) (3D+T) maps. We then proposed three variations: a spatial model, a temporal model and a stochastic extension using local linear models.

Optimization is a fascinating and rich research domain with applications in a wide variety of fields which make it a highly varied discipline.

Perspectives

Our short and mid-term research perspectives remain within the domain of application to air transport, but with increasing use of tools taken from the areas of approximation, statistics (such as order statistics), analysis of principal components, and analysis and support vector machines (SVMs).

We will look at these areas in greater detail in this final section.

To improve the results of sectorization and traffic assignment algorithms, we intend to use our airspace congestion model using nonlinear dynamic systems (Lyapunov exponents) in the objective function. In the context of sectorization, this modification should reduce the number of sectors and the disparities between associated control workloads. In terms of traffic assignment, the application of this new metric should allow us to generate better structured traffic which will be easier to control. We have recently begun a new study on strategic planning for European airspace with the aim of optimizing the routes and take-off times of a set of 3,000 airplanes per day in order to minimize the disorder in the associated trajectories.

Within the framework of mathematical optimization, we intend to continue working on the combination of order statistics with artificial evolution. When the objective function is costly to evaluate, it is possible to evaluate several subdomains using the same set of points in the state space. The extension of the algorithm thus consists of conserving a set of state space points, with which we evaluate multiple subdomains using order statistics (see Figure 8.1), renewing the set of points periodically, retaining good samples and enriching the set with new selections from the state space.

Later, it would be interesting to extend this approach to discrete spaces or even to multi-objective cases.

In the context of trajectory planning, we intend to continue our research on representation bases suited to air traffic; more specifically, we intend to develop a new approach based on the analysis of principal components. This decomposition would reduce the dimension of the state space in a quasi-optimal manner. It consists of transforming correlated variables into new, non-correlated variables. These new variables are known as "principal components". The planned approach would use a large set of radar data and begin by extracting trajectories for the same origin–destination pair for a given aircraft type. We would then carry out an analysis using principal components in order to determine the minimum number of coefficients required to explain 99% of the energy (we believe that around 20 coefficients will be enough). We then intend to determine the statistical distribution of these coefficients using estimation methods. These coefficients would be driven by a stochastic optimization process, producing realistic trajectories for the types of airplane considered. In parallel, we intend to look for other trajectory representation bases, some of which might be suitable for the flight phase in question. Airplanes flying in the terminal zone turn more often and thus require a richer representation to give an equivalent level of precision.

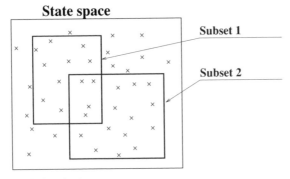

Figure C.1. *Use of a single set of state space points to evaluate multiple subdomains*

Staying within the domain of trajectory planning, we wish to improve the light propagation algorithm (LPA) presented in this book by linking it with a learning mechanism. The underlying idea is to record, after the event, the directions of ray launches which are most promising to ensure conflict resolution. Using a large number of situations resolved using the LPA, we would be able to use SVMs in order to identify the most favorable ray launch directions.

To take account of meteorological aspects, we have also started work on robust planning of trajectories in a wind field involving a deterministic and a stochastic component. Two different projects are currently under way in this context. The first project involves trajectory planning to reduce congestion while favoring geodesic trajectories between each origin–destination pair. The second project is devoted to optimizing airplane trajectories for oceanic transatlantic traffic. For this type of traffic, radar monitoring is not possible as the range of these instruments is limited to 300 nautical miles; a track system is used to structure the oceanic traffic (see Figure C.2). The position of these tracks is calculated and published on a daily basis and depends on the behavior of the jet stream altitude wind. The temporal separation between aircraft on the same track is currently fixed at 10 min, and when an airplane changes track, there must be no other aircraft within 15 min (see Figure C.3). These separation norms present considerable restrictions to track changing possibilities over the Atlantic. Let us consider the case of an airplane coming from Canada with a destination in Africa: the aircraft will enter the network on a northern track and will then attempt to move progressively south from track to track in order to approach its destination. Unfortunately, the density of traffic in the North Atlantic means it is rare for an airplane to be able to change tracks without violating separation constraints; so the length of the route taken by the aircraft will increase. Moreover, airplanes must wait to exit the network before continuing toward their destinations; this generates crossings between trajectories at the network exit point and increases airspace congestion. In the near future, all airplanes will be equipped with a new surveillance system known as the Automatic Dependent Surveillance-Broadcast (ADS-B). An airplane with ADS-B determines its position using a satellite positioning system (Global Navigation Satellite System (GNSS)), periodically transmitting this position and other information to ground control stations and to other aircraft with ADS-B traveling through the same zone. The introduction of this new system will allow the oceanic norms of 10 and 15 min described above to be reduced to 2 and 3 min, respectively. Aircraft will then be able to change tracks much more easily in order to reach the optimal exit track. This problem creates a considerable level of combinatorics, and we have begun work on optimizing this problem. The aim of this study is to find an oceanic trajectory plan which best satisfies the requirements of airlines, taking into account the oceanic winds and the new separation norms. We will then carry out a prospective study in order to quantify the gains associated with the removal of the oceanic tracks network.

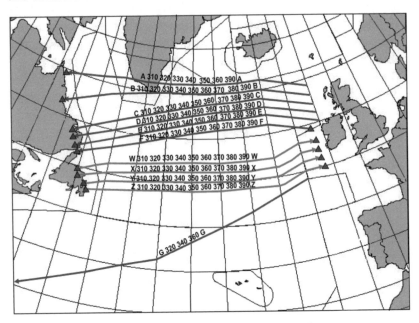

Figure C.2. *Structure of the transatlantic tracks system*

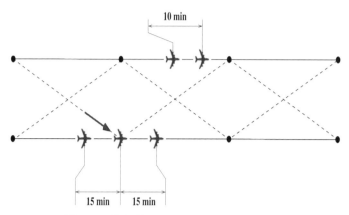

Figure C.3. *Time separation constraint*

Finally, in the longer term, we intend to start work on principles of self-organization for airplane trajectories. Using local knowledge of traffic and behavioral rules, we wish to infer an organized macroscopic structure for all trajectories. This adaptive structuring approach will increase the robustness of plans in the case of unexpected occurrences.

Bibliography

[AAR 89] AARTS E., KORST J., *Simulated Annealing and Boltzmann Machine*, John Wiley and Sons, 1989.

[AAS 79] AASHTIANI H.Z., The multimodal traffic assignment model with application to two ways traffic, PhD Thesis, Sloan School MIT, 1979.

[ADL 93] ADLER D., "Genetic algorithms and simulated annealing: a marriage proposal", *Proceedings of the 1993 IEEE International Conference on Neural Network*, ICNN, San Francisco, CA, 1993.

[ALF 85] ALFUFFI-PENTINI F., PARISI V., ZIRILLI F., "Global optimization and stochastic differential equations", *Journal of Optimization Theory and Applications*, vol. 47, pp. 1–15, 1985.

[ALF 86] ALFA A.S., "A review of models for the temporal distribution of peak traffic demand", *Transportation Research B*, vol. 20, pp. 477–479, 1986.

[ALF 89] ALFA A.S., "Departure rate and route assignment of commuter traffic during peak period", *Transportation Research*, vol. 23B, no. 5, pp. 337–344, 1989.

[ALL 93] ALLIOT J.M., GRUBER H., "Using genetic algorithms for solving ATC conflicts", *Proceedings of the 9th IEEE Conference on Artificial Intelligence for Application*, IEEE, Newport Beach, CA, USA, 1993.

[ALL 97] ALLIOT J.M., BOSC J.F., DURAND N., *et al.*, "CATS: a complete air traffic simulator", *Proceedings of the 16th DASC*, Irvine, CA, USA, 1997.

[AMO 91] AMODEI L., BENBOURHIM M.N., "A vector spline approximation", *Journal of Approximation Theory*, vol. 67, pp. 51–79, 1991.

[AND 87] ANDREATTA G., ROMANIN-JACUR G., "Aircraft flow management under congestion", *Transportation Science*, vol. 21, no. 4, pp. 249–253, 1987.

[AND 93] ANDREATTA G., ODONI A.R., RICHETTA O., "Models for the ground holding problem", in BIANCO L., ODONI A.R. (eds), *Large Scale Computation and Information Processing in Air Traffic Control*, Transportation Analysis, Springer-Verlag, pp. 125–168, 1993.

[ARE 90] AREZKI Y., VAN VLIET D., "A full analytical implementation of the PARTAN/Frank-Wolfe algorithm for equilibrium assignement", *Transportation Science*, vol. 24, no. 1, pp. 58–62, 1990.

[ARN 90] ARNOTT R., DE PALMA A., LINDSEY R., "Departure time and route choice for the morning commute", *Transportation Research*, vol. 24B, no. 3, pp. 209–228, 1990.

[BAC 91a] BACK T., HOFFMEISTER F., "Extended selection mechanisms in genetic algorithms", *Proceedings of the 4th International Conference on Genetic Algorithms*, ICGA, San Diego, CA, USA, 1991.

[BAC 91b] BACK T., HOFFMEISTER F., SCHWEFEL H.P., "A survey of evolution strategy", *Proceedings of the 4th International Conference on Genetic Algorithm*, ICGA, San Diego, CA, USA, 1991.

[BAC 92a] BACK T., *The Interaction of Mutation Rate, Selection and Self Adaptation within a Genetic Algorithm (in Parallel Problem Solving from Nature 2)*, Elsevier, 1992.

[BAC 92b] BACK T., "Self-adaptation in genetic algorithms", *Proceedings of the 1st European Conference on Artificial Life*, MIT Press/Bradford Books edition Paris, France, 1992.

[BAC 93] BACK T., "Optimal mutation rates in genetic search", *Proceedings of the 5th International Conference on Genetic Algorithm*, ICGA, Urbana-Champaign, IL, USA, 1993.

[BAK 85] BAKER J.E., "Adaptative selection methods for genetic algorithms", *Proceedings of an International Conference on Genetic Algorithms*, ICGA, Pittsburgh, PA, USA, 1985.

[BAL 93] BALA J.W., WECHSLER H., "Learning to detect targets using scale-space and genetic search", *Proceedings of the 5th International Conference on Genetic Algorithm*, ICGA, Urbana-Champaign, IL, USA, 1993.

[BEK 56] BEKMANN M.J., McCUIRE C.B., WINSTON C.B., *Studies in the Economics of Transportation*, Yale University Press, 1956.

[BEL 58] BELLMAN R.E., "On a routing problem", *Quarterly of Applied Mathematics*, vol. 16, pp. 87–90, 1958.

[BEL 95] BELL M.G.H., "Stochastic user equilibrium assignment in networks with queues", *Transportation Research*, vol. 29B, no. 2, pp. 125–137, 1995.

[BEN 85] BEN-AKIVA M., "Dynamic network equilibrium research", *Transportation Research A*, vol. 19A, no. 5, pp. 429–431, 1985.

[BEN 86a] BEN-AKIVA M., DE PALMA A., KANAROGLOU P., "Dynamic model of peak period traffic congestion with elastic arrival rates", *Transportation Science*, vol. 20, pp. 164–181, 1986.

[BEN 91] BEN-AKIVA M., DE PALMA A., KAYSI I., "Dynamic network models and driver information systems", *Transportation Research*, vol. 25A, no. 5, pp. 251–266, 1991.

[BEN 94] BEN-AKIVA M., KOUTSOPOULOS H.N., MUKUNDAN A., "A dynamic traffic model system for ATMS/ATIS operation", *IVHS Journal*, vol. 2, no. 1, pp. 1–9, 1994.

[BER 93a] BERNSTEIN D., FRIESZ T.L., TOBIN R.L., *et al.*, "A variational control formulation of the simultaneous route and departure-time choice equilibrium problem", *Transportation and Traffic Theory*, Elsevier, NY, 1993.

[BER 93b] BERTONI A., DORIGO M., "Implicit parallelism in genetic algorithms", *Artificial Intelligence*, vol. 61, no. 2, pp. 307–314, 1993.

[BER 94] BERTSIMAS D.J., STOCK S., The air traffic flow management problem with en-route capacities, Technical report, A.P Sloan School of Management. M.I.T, 1994.

[BER 99] BERTSEKAS D.P., *Nonlinear Programming*, Athena Scientific, 1999.

[BIE 80] BIELLI M., CALICCHIO G., NICOLETTI B., *et al.*, "Flow control of large scale air traffic systems", *Proceedings of the IFAC Symposium*, IFAC, Budapest, Hungary, 1980.

[BIR 93] BIRGE J.R., "Optimal flows in stochastic dynamic networks", *Operations Research*, vol. 41, no. 1, pp. 203–216, 1993.

[BOU 68] BOUDAREL R., DELMAS J., GUICHET P., *Commande optimale des processus Tome II. Programmation non linéaire et ses applications*, Dunod, 1968.

[BRI 91] BRIDGES C.L., GOLDBERG D.E., "An analysis of multipoint crossover", *Proceedings of the Foundation of Genetic Algorithms*, FOGA, Vail, Colorado, USA, 1991.

[BRO 70] BROYDEN C.G., "The convergence of a class of double-rank minimization algorithms", *Journal of the Institute of Mathematics and Its Applications*, vol. 6, pp. 76–90, 1970.

[CAN 95] CANTARELLA G.E., CASCETTA E., "Dynamic processes and equilibrium in transportation networks: toward a unifying theory", *Transportation Science*, vol. 29, no. 4, pp. 305–328, 1995.

[CAR 87] CAREY M., "Optimal time-varying flows on congested networks", *Operations Research*, vol. 35, no. 1, pp. 58–69, 1987.

[CAS 87] CASCETTA E., "Static and dynamic models of stochastic assignment to transportation networks", *Flow Control of Congested Networks*, vol. 38, pp. 91–111, 1987.

[CAS 89a] CASCETTA E., "A stochastic process approach to the analysis of temporal dynamics in transportation networks", *Transportation Research*, vol. 23B, no. 1, pp. 1–17, 1989.

[CAS 89b] CASCETTA E., CANTARELLA G.E., A doubly dynamic assignment model, Technical report, ACTS of PTRC Summer Annual Meeting, Brighton, UK, 1989.

[CAS 91] CASCETTA E., CANTARELLA G.E., "A day-to-day and within-day dynamic stochastic assignment model", *Transportation Research*, vol. 25A, no. 5, pp. 277–291, 1991.

[CAS 93] CASCETTA E., CANTARELLA G.E., "Modeling dynamics in transportation networks: state of the art and future developments", *Simulation Practice and Theory*, vol. 1, pp. 65–91, 1993.

[CER 85] CERNY V., "A Themodynamical approach to the travelling salesman problem", *Journal of Operations Research*, vol. 32, pp. 44–51, 1985.

[CER 94] CERF R., Une théorie asymptotique des algorithmes génétiques, PhD Thesis, University of Montpellier II (France), 1994.

[CET 93] CETIN B., BARHEN J., BURDICK J., "Terminal repeller unconstrained subenergy tunneling for fast global optimization", *Journal of Optimization Theory and Applications*, vol. 77, no. 1, pp. 97–126, 1993.

[CHA 88a] CHANG G.L., MAHMASSANI H.S., "Travel time prediction and departure time adjustment behavior dynamics in a congested traffic system", *Transportation Research*, vol. 22B, no. 3, pp. 217–232, 1988.

[CHA 96] CHARON I., GERMA A., HUDRY O., *Méthodes d'Optimisation Combinatoire*, Educational Telecommunication Series, Masson, 1996.

[CHA 01] CHATTERJI G.B., SRIDHAR B., "Measure for air traffic controller workload prediction", *Proceedings of the 1st AIAA Aircraft Technology, Integration, and Operation Forum*, AIAA, Los Angeles, CA, USA, 2001.

[CHE 92] CHENG C.K., "The optimal partitioning of networks", *Networks*, vol. 22, pp. 297–315, 1992.

[CHI 95] CHINRUNGRUENG C., SEQUIN C.H., "Optimal adaptive k-means algorithm with dynamic adjustment of learning rate", *IEEE Transaction on Neural Networks*, vol. 6, no. 1, pp. 157–169, 1995.

[COL 91] COLLINS R.J., JEFFERSON D.R., "Selection in massively parallel genetic algorithms", *Proceedings of the 4th International Conference on Genetic Algorithms*, ICGA, 1991.

[COL 92] COLIN DE VERDIÈRE D., Le systéme français de contrôle du trafic aérien: Le CAUTRA, Technical report, Air Navigation Research Center, Toulouse, France, August 1992.

[CON 09] CONN A.R., SCHEINBERG K., VICENTE L.N., *Introduction to Derivative-free Optimization*, MPSSIAM, Cambridge, 2009.

[DAF 69a] DAFERMOS S., SPARROW F., "The traffic assignment problem for a general network", *Journal of Research of the National Bureau of Standards*, vol. 73B, pp. 91–118, 1969.

[DAF 69b] DAFERMOS S.C., SPARROW F.T., "The traffic assignment for a general network", *Journal of Research of the National Bureau of Standards-B Mathematical Sciences*, vol. 73B, no. 2, pp. 91–112, 1969.

[DAF 71] DAFERMOS S.C., "An extended traffic assignment model with applications to two-ways traffic", *Transportation Science*, vol. 5, pp. 366–389, 1971.

[DAF 72] DAFERMOS S.C., "The traffic assignment problem for multiclass-user transportation networks", *Transportation Science*, vol. 6, pp. 73–87, 1972.

[DAF 80] DAFERMOS S.C., "Traffic equilibrium and variational inequalities", *Transportation Science*, vol. 14, no. 1, pp. 42–54, 1980.

[DAF 82a] DAFERMOS S.C., "The general multimodal network equilibrium problem with elastic demand", *Networks*, vol. 12, pp. 57–72, 1982.

[DAF 82b] DAFERMOS S.C., "Relaxation algorithms for the general asymmetric problem", *Transportation Science*, vol. 16, pp. 231–240, 1982.

[DAF 92] DAFERMOS S.C., MCKELVEY S.C., "Partitionable variational inequalities with application to network and equilibria", *Journal of Optimization Theory and Application*, vol. 73, no. 2, pp. 243–268, 1992.

[DAG 77] DAGANZO C.F., SHEFFI Y., "On stochastic models of traffic assignment", *Transportation Science*, vol. 11, pp. 253–274, 1977.

[DAG 80] DAGANZO C.F., "An equilibrium algorithm for the spatial aggregation problem of traffic assignment", *Transportation Research*, vol. 14B, pp. 221–228, 1980.

[DAG 83] DAGANZO C.F., "Stochastic network equilibrium with multiple vehicle types and asymmetric indefinite link cost Jacobians", *Transportation Science*, vol. 17, pp. 282–300, 1983.

[DAR 90] DARKEN C., MOODY J., "Fast adaptive k-means clustering: some empirical results", *Proceedings of the International Joint Conference on Neural Networks*, IJCNN, Washington, D.C, USA, 1990.

[DAV 91] DAVIS L., *Handbook of Genetic Algorithms*, Van Nostrand Reinhold, New York, NY, 1991.

[DEB 89a] DEB K., Genetic algorithms in multimodal function optimization, TCGA report no. 89002, TCGA, University of Alabama, 1989.

[DEB 89b] DEB K., GOLDBERG D.E., "An investigation of niches and species formation in genetic function optimization", *Proceedings of the 3rd International Conference on Genetic Algorithm*, ICGA, Fairfax, Virginia, USA, 1989.

[DEJ 75] DE JONG K.A., An analysis of the behavior of a class of genetic adaptative systems, PhD Thesis, University of Michigan, 1975.

[DEL 94a] DELAHAYE D., ALLIOT J.M., SCHOENAUER M., et al., "Genetic algorithms for air traffic assignment", *Proceedings of the European Conference on Artificial Intelligence*, ECAI, 1994.

[DEL 94c] DELAHAYE D., ALLIOT J.M., SCHOENAUER M., et al., "Genetic algorithms for partitioning airspace", *Proceedings of the 10th IEEE Conference on Artificial Intelligence for Application*, CAIA, San Antonio, TX, USA, 1994.

[DEL 95a] DELAHAYE D., Optimisation de la sectorisation de l'espace aérien par algorithmes génétiques, PhD Thesis, Automatic ENSAE, 1995.

[DEL 95b] DELAHAYE D., ALLIOT J.M., SCHOENAUER M., et al., "Genetic algorithms automatic regrouping of air traffic sectors", *Proceedings of the 4th International Conference on Evolutionary Programming*, Natural Selection Inc., San Diago, CA, USA, 1995.

[DEL 00] DELAHAYE D., PUECHMOREL S., "A new genetic algorithm working on state domain order statistic", *Proceedings of the 6th International Conference on Parallel Problem Solving from Nature*, 2000.

[DEL 04] DELAHAYE D., Métriques de complexité du trafic, Technical report CENA/NR04-806, Air Navigation Research Center, Toulouse, France, 2004.

[DEL 05] DELAHAYE D., OUSSEDIK S., PUECHMOREL S., "Airspace congestion smoothing by multi-objective genetic algorithm", *Proceeding of the 20th Annual ACM Symposium on Applied Computing*, Santa Fe, New Mexico, USA, 2005.

[DEL 10] DELAHAYE D., PEYRONNE C., MONGEAU M., et al., "Aircraft conflict resolution by genetic algorithm and b-spline approximation", *Proceedings of the 2010 International Conference on Evolutionary Computation*, ICEC, Valencia, Spain, 2010.

[DEN 90] DE NEUFVILLE R., *Applied Systems Analysis: Engineering Planning and Technology Management*, McGraw-Hill Company, 1990.

[DEP 90] DEPALMA A., HANSEN P., LABBÉ M., "Commuters' paths with penalties for early or late arrival time", *Transportation Science*, vol. 24, no. 4, pp. 276–286, 1990.

[DES 01] DESCHINKEL K., Régulation du trafic aérien par optimisation dynamique des prix d'utilisation du réseau, PhD Thesis, Ecole nationale supérieure de l'aéronautique et de l'espace, 2001.

[DET 58] Detroit area transportation study, vol. 2, pp. 79–107, 1958.

[DIJ 59] DIJKSTRA E.W., "A note on two problems in connexion with graphs", *Numerishe Mathematics*, vol. 1, pp. 269–271, 1959.

[DOU 11] DOUGUI N., DELAHAYE D., PUECHMOREL S., *et al.*, "A light-propagation model for aircraft trajectory planning", *Journal of Global Optimization*, vol. 2012, pp. 1–23, 2011.

[DRI 92] DRISSI-KAITOUNI O., HAMEDA-BENCHEKROUN A., "A dynamic traffic assignment model and a solution algorithm", *Transportation Science*, vol. 26, no. 2, pp. 119–128, 1992.

[DUN 05] DUNLAVY D., LEARY D., Homotopy optimization methods for global optimization, Technical report, SANDIA, Albuquerque, NM, 2005.

[DUR 94a] DURAND N., ALECH N., ALLIOT J.M., *et al.*, "Genetic algorithms for optimal air traffic resolution", *Proceedings of the 2nd Singapore Conference on Intelligence Systems*, SPICIS, 1994.

[DUR 94b] DURAND N., ALLIOT J.M., NOAILLES J., "Algorithmes génétiques: un croisement pour les problèmes partiellement séparables", *Journées évolution artificielle*, Ecole nationale de l'aviation civile, Toulouse, France, 1994.

[DUR 04] DURAND N., Algorithmes génétiques et autres méthodes d'optimisation appliqués à la gestion de trafic aérien, PhD Thesis, INPT, 2004.

[ESH 89] ESHELMAN L.J., CARUANA R.A., SHAFFER J.D., "Biases in the crossover landscape", *Proceedings of the 3rd International Conference on Genetic Algorithms*, ICGA, Fairfax, Virginia, USA, 1989.

[ESH 93] ESHELMAN L.J., SHAFFER J.D., "Crossover's niche", *Proceedings of the 5th International Conference on Genetic Algorithms*, ICGA, Urbana-Champaign, IL, USA, 1993.

[FIS 80] FISK C., "Some developments in equilibrium traffic assignment methodology", *Transportation Research B*, vol. 14B, pp. 243–255, 1980.

[FIS 82] FISK C., NGUYEN S., "Solution algorithms for network equilibrium models with asymmetric user costs", *Transportation Science*, vol. 16, no. 3, pp. 361–381, 1982.

[FLE 70] FLETCHER R., "A new approach to variable metric algorithms", *Computer Journal*, vol. 13, pp. 317–322, 1970.

[FLO 82] FLORIAN M., SPIESS H., "The convergence of diagonalization algorithms for asymmetric network equilibrium problem", *Transportation Research B*, vol. 16B, pp. 477–483, 1982.

[FLO 93] FLOCKTON S.J., WHITE M.S., "Pole-zero system identification using genetic algorithms", *Proceedings of the 5th International Conference on Genetic Algorithm*, ICGA, 1993.

[FOG 89] FOGARTY T.C., "Varying the probability of mutation in genetic algorithms", *Proceedings of the 3rd Conference on Genetic Algorithms*, ICGA, 1989.

[FOG 66] FOGEL L.J., OWENS A.J., WALSH M.J., *Artificial Intelligence Through Simulated Evolution*, John Wiley and Sons, NY, 1966.

[FOG 94] FOGEL D.B., *Evolutionary Computation. Toward a New Philosophy of Machine Intelligence*, IEEE press, 1994.

[FON 93] FONSECA C.M., FLEMING P.J., "Genetic algorithms for multiobjective optimization, formulation, discussion and generalization", *Proceedings of the 5th International Conference on Genetic Algorithm*, ICGA, Urbana-Champaign, IL, USA, 1993.

[FOR 93] FORREST S., SMITH R.E., JAKORNIK B., *et al.*, "Using genetic algorithms to explore pattern recognition in the immune system", *Evolutionary Computation*, vol. 1, no. 3, pp. 191–211, 1993.

[FRA 56] FRANK F., WOLFE P., "An algorithm for quadratic programming", *Naval Research Logistics Quarterly*, vol. 2, pp. 95–110, 1956.

[FRA 82] FRANK F., WOLFE P., "Relaxation algorithms for the general asymmetric traffic equilibrium problem", *Transportation Science*, vol. 16, pp. 231–240, 1982.

[FRE 83] FREIDLIN M.I., WENTZELL A.D., *Random Perturbations of Dynamical Systems*, Springer-Verlag, New York, NY, 1983.

[FRI 89] FRIESZ T.L., LUQUE J., TOBIN R.L., *et al.*, "Dynamic network traffic assignment considered as a continuous time optimal control problem", *Operations Research*, vol. 37, no. 6, pp. 893–901, 1989.

[FRI 93a] FRIESZ T.L., BERNSTEIN D., SMITH T.E., *et al.*, "A variational inequality formulation of the dynamic network user equilibrium problem", *Operations Research*, vol. 41, pp. 179–191, 1993.

[FRO 98] FRON X., "ATM performance review in Europe", *Air Traffic Management R and D Seminar*, Orlando, FL, USA, 1998.

[FUK 84] FUKUSHIMA M., "A modified Frank-Wolfe algorithm for solving the traffic assignment problem", *Transportation Research*, vol. 2, pp. 169–177, 1984.

[GAL 86] GALLO G., PALLATINO S., "Shortest path methods: a unifying approach", *Mathematical Programming Studies*, vol. 26, pp. 38–64, 1986.

[GAR 79] GAREY M.R., JOHNSON D.S., *Computers and Intractability. A Guide to the Theory of NP-Completeness*, W.H. Freeman and Company, 1979.

[GAR 80] GARTNER N.H., GERSHWIN S.B., LITTLE J.D.C., *et al.*, "Pilot study of computer based urban traffic management", *Transportation Research B*, vol. 14B, no. 1, pp. 203–217, 1980.

[GEN 94] GENDREAU M., HERTZ A., LAPORTE G., "A tabu search algorithm for the vehicle routing problem", *Management Science*, vol. 40, pp. 1276–1290, 1994.

[GHA 95] GHALI M.O., SMITH M.J., "A model for the dynamic system optimum traffic assignment", *Transportation Research*, vol. 29B, no. 3, pp. 155–170, 1995.

[GIL 93] GILBO E.P., "Airport Capacity: representation, estimation, optimization", *IEEE Transaction on Control Systems Technology*, vol. 1, no. 3, pp. 144–154, 1993.

[GLO 86] GLOVER F., "Future paths for integer programming and link to artificial intelligence", *Computers and Operations Research*, vol. 13, no. 5, pp. 533–549, 1986.

[GLO 88] GLOVER F., Tabu search, Technical report, CAAI Center for Applied Artificial Intelligence, Graduate School of Business, University of Colorado, Boulder, CO, 1988.

[GLO 91] GLOVER F., TAILLARD E., DE WERRA D., A user's guide to tabu search, Technical report, University of Colorado, Boulder, CO, and EPFL Lausanne, 1991.

[GLO 92] GLOVER F., LAGUNA M., Tabu search, modern heuristic techniques for combinatorial problems, Technical report, University of Colorado, Boulder, CO, 1992.

[GOE 94] GOEMANS M.X., WILLIAMSON D.P., "Improved approximation algorithms for maximum cut and satisfiability problems using semidefinite programming", *Proceedings of the 26th Symposium on the Theory of Computing*, Canada, 1994.

[GOL 87] GOLDBERG D.E., RICHARDSON J.J., "Genetic algorithms with sharing for multimodal function optimization", *Proceedings of the 2nd International Conference on Genetic Algorithm*, ICGA, MIT, Cambridge, MA, USA, 1987.

[GOL 89] GOLDBERG D.E., *Genetic Algorithms in Search, Optimization and Machine Learning*, Addison Wesley, Reading MA, 1989.

[GOL 91a] GOLDBERG D.E., "Real-coded genetic algorithms, virtual alphabets and blocking", *Complex Systems*, vol. 5, pp. 139–167, 1991.

[GOL 91b] GOLDBERG D.E., DEB K., "Adaptative selection methods for genetic algorithms", *Proceedings of the Foundation of Genetic Algorithms*, FOGA, 1991.

[GOL 91c] GOLDBERG D.E., DEB K., CLARK J.H., Genetic algorithms, noise and the sizing of population, Report 91010, University of Illinois, Bloomington, Indiana, USA, 1991.

[GOL 92] GOLDBERG D.E., RICHARDSON J.J., *Massive Multimodality, Deception and Genetic Algorithms (in Parallel Problem Solving from Nature 2)*, Elsevier, Brussels, Belgium, 1992.

[GOL 70] GOLDFARB D., "A family of variable metric updates derived by variational means", *Mathematics of Computation*, vol. 24, pp. 23–26, 1970.

[GRA 03] GRANGER G., DURAND N., "A traffic complexity approach through cluster analysis", *Proceedings of the US Europe ATM Seminar*, Eurocontrol-FAA, Budapest, Hungary, 2003.

[GRE 86] GREFENSTETTE J.J., "Optimization of control parameters for genetic algorithms", *IEEE Transaction on Systems, Man and Cybernetics*, vol. 16, no. 1, pp. 122–128, 1986.

[GUI 99] GUIGUE A., OUSSEDIK S., DELAHAYE D., "Sequencing aircraft landing by genetic algorithms", *Proceedings of the 1999 Genetic and Evolutionary Computation Conference*, AAAI, Orlando, Florida, USA, 1999.

[GUM 58] GUMBELL E.J., *Statistics of Extremes*, Columbia University Press, 1958.

[HAA 70] HAAN D., *On Regular Variation and its Application to Weak Convergence of Sample Extremes*, Mathematisch Centrum, North Holland, 1970.

[HAN 86] HANSEN P., "The steepest ascent mildest descent heuristic for combinatorial programming", *Congress on Numerical Methods in Combinatorial Programming*, 1986.

[HAR 66] HARTMAN G.J., STAMPACCHIA G., "On some nonlinear elliptic differential equations", *Acta Mathematica*, no. 115, pp. 271–310, 1966.

[HEA 84] HEARN D.W., LAWPHONGPANICH S., NGUYEN S., "Convex programming formulations of the asymmetric traffic assignment problem", *Transportation Research B*, vol. 18B, pp. 357–365, 1984.

[HEA 86] HEARN D.W., LAWPHONGPANISH S., VENTURA J.A., "Optimization algorithms for congested network models", *Proceedings of the NATO Advanced Research Workshop on Flow Control of Congested Network*, NATO, Capri, Italy, 1986.

[HEA 90] HEARN D.W., "A dual ascent algorithm for traffic assignment problems", *Transportation Research B*, vol. 24B, no. 6, pp. 423–430, 1990.

[HEL 92] HELME M.P., *Proceeding of the 1992 IEEE Conference on System*, Man and Cybernetics, McLean, VA, USA, 1992.

[HEN 81] HENDRICKSON C., KOGUR G., "Schedule delay and departure time decisions in a deterministic model", *Transportation Science*, vol. 15, no. 1, pp. 62–77, 1981.

[HEN 95] HENDRICKSON B., LELAND R., "An improved spectral graph partitioning algorithm for algorithm for mapping parallel computations", *SIAM Journal on Scientific Computing*, vol. 16, pp. 452–469, 1995.

[HER 87] HERTZ A., DE WERRA D., "Using tabu search techniques for graph coloring", *Computing*, vol. 29, pp. 345–351, 1987.

[HO 90] HO J.K., "Solving the dynamic traffic assignment problem on a hypercube multicomputer", *Transportation Research*, vol. 24B, no. 6, pp. 443–451, 1990.

[HOF 90] HOFFMEISTER F., BACK T., Genetic algorithms and evolution strategies: similarities and differences, Report Grunereihe 365, Department of Computer Science, University of Dortmund, November 1990.

[HOL 75] HOLLAND J.H., *Adaptation in Natural and Artificial Systems*, University of Michigan Press, 1975.

[HOM 93] HOMAIFAR A., SHANGUCHUAN G., LIEPINS G.A., "A new approach on the traveling salesman problem by genetic algorithms", *Proceedings of the 5th International Conference on Genetic Algorithm*, ICGA, Urbana-Champaign, IL, USA, 1993.

[HOO 61] HOOKE R., JEEVES T.A., "Direct search solution of numerical and statistical problems", *Journal of the Association for Computing Machinery*, vol. 8, no. 2, pp. 212–229, 1961.

[HOR 93] HORN J., NAFPLIOTIS N., Multiobjective and stochastic optimization based on parametric optimization, Report 93005, University of Illinois, 1993.

[HOR 94] HORN J., NAFPLIOTIS N., GOLDBERG D.E., "A niched pareto genetic algorithm for multiobjective optimization", *Proceedings of the 1st IEEE Conference on Evolutionary Computation*, ICGA, Orlando, Florida, 1994.

[ING 89] INGBER L., "Very fast simulated annealing", *Journal of Mathematics Computing and Modeling*, vol. 12, no. 8, pp. 967–973, 1989.

[ING 92] INGBER L., ROSEN B., "Genetic algorithms and very fast simulated re-annealing", *Mathematical Computer Modeling*, vol. 16, no. 11, pp. 87–100, 1992.

[ING 96] INGBER L., "Adaptive simulated annealing (ASA): lessons learned", *Control and Cybernetics*, vol. 25, no. 1, pp. 33–54, 1996.

[JAN 91] JANIC M., TOSIC V., "En route sector capacity model", *Transportation Science*, vol. 25, no. 4, 1991.

[JAN 93] JANSON B.N., ROBLES J., "Dynamic traffic assignment with arrival time cost", *Transportation and Traffic Theory*, Transportation Research, vol. 29B, no. 3, pp. 155–170 1993.

[JAU 88] JAULIN L., KIEFFER M., DIDRIT M., *et al.*, *Applied Interval Analysis*, Wiley Interscience, 1988.

[JAY 95] JAYAKRISHNAN R., TSAI K.W.K., CHEN A., "A dynamic traffic assignment model with traffic-flow relationship", *Transportation Research*, vol. 3C, no. 1, pp. 51–72, 1995.

[JOU 93] JOU R.C., MAHMASSANI H.S., "Comparability and transferability of commuter behavior characteristics between cities: departure time and route switching decisions", *73 Annual Meeting of the Transportation Research Record*, Washington, DC, USA, 1993.

[KAR 84] KARMARKAR N., "A new polynomial time algorithm for linear programming", *Combinatorica*, vol. 4, no. 4, pp. 373–395, 1984.

[KAR 07] KARASOZEN B., "Survey of derivative free optimization methods based on interpolation", *Journal of Industrial and Management Optimization*, vol. 3, no. 2, pp. 321–334, 2007.

[KAU 92] KAUFMAN D.E., NONIS J., SMITH R.L., *Proceeding of the 1992 IEEE Conference on System, Man and Cybernetics*, McLean, VA, USA, 1992.

[KEA 01] KEARFO D., NEMHAUSER G., *Applications of Interval Computations*, Springer, 2001.

[KEE 76] KEENEY R., RAIFFA H., *Decisions with Multiple Objectives*, Wiley, New York, NY, 1976.

[KHU 94] KHURI S., BACK T., HEITKOTER J., "The zero/one multiple knapsack problem and genetic algorithm", *Proceedings of the Symposium of Applied Computation*, *ACM*, Phoenix, AZ, USA, 1994.

[KIR 83] KIRKPATRICK S., GELATT C.D., VECCHI M.P., "Optimization by simulated annealing", *Science*, vol. 220, pp. 671–680, 1983.

[KOZ 92] KOZA J.R., *Genetic Programming*, MIT Press, 1992.

[KUO 93] KUO T., HWANG S.Y., "A genetic algorithm with disruptive selection", *Proceedings of the 5th International Conference on Genetic Algorithms*, *ICGA*, Urbana-Champaign, IL, USA, 1993.

[LAF 93] LAFORTUNE S., SENGUPTA R., KAUFMAN D.E., *et al.*, "Dynamic system-optimal traffic assignment using a state space model", *Transportation Research B*, vol. 27B, no. 6, pp. 451–472, 1993.

[LAN 60] LAND A.H., DOIG A.G., "An automatic method of solving discrete programming problems", *Econometrica*, vol. 28, no. 3, pp. 497–520, 1960.

[LAR 99] LARRANAGA P., KUIJPERS C.M.H., MURGA R.H., *et al.*, "Genetic algorithms for the travelling salesman problem: a review of representations and operators", *Artificial Intelligence Review*, vol. 13, pp. 129–170, 1999.

[LAU 98] LAUDEMAN I.V., SHELDEN S.G., BRANSTROM R., *et al.*, Dynamic density: an air traffic management metric, Technical report TM-1998-112226, NASA, 1998.

[LAW 83] LAWPHONGPANICH S., HEARN D.W., "Simplicial decomposition of the asymmetric traffic assignment problem", *Transportation Research B*, vol. 18B, no. 2, pp. 123–133, 1983.

[LAW 84] LAWPHONGPANICH S., HEARN D.W., "Simplicial decomposition of the assignment problem", *Transportation Research B*, vol. 18B, no. 2, pp. 123–133, 1984.

[LEB 75] LEBLANC L.J., MORLOK E.K., PIERSKALLA W.P., "An efficient approach to solving the road network equilibrium traffic assignment problem", *Transportation Research*, vol. 9, pp. 309–318, 1975.

[LEB 84] LEBLANC L.J., ABDULAAL M., "A comparison of user-optimum versus system-optimum traffic assignment in transportation networks", *Transportation Research B*, vol. 18B, no. 2, pp. 115–121, 1984.

[LEB 85] LEBLANC L.J., HELGASON R.V., BOYCE D.E., "Improved efficiency of the Frank-Wolfe algorithm for convex network programs", *Transportation Science*, vol. 19, no. 4, pp. 445–462, 1985.

[LEB 92] LEBLANC L.J., RAN B., BOYCE D.E., *Proceeding of the 1992 IEEE Conference on System, Man and Cybernetics*, McLean, VA, USA, 1992.

[LEE 07] LEE K., FERON A., PRICHETT E., "Air traffic complexity: an input-output approach", *Proceedings of the US Europe ATM Seminar*, Eurocontrol-FAA, Barcelona, Spain, 2007.

[LEV 73] LEVENTHAL T., NEMHAUSER G., TROTER L., "A column generation algorithm for optimal traffic assignment", *Transportation Science*, vol. 7, pp. 168–176, 1973.

[LEV 85] LEVY A.V., MONTALVO A., "The tunneling algorithm for the global minimization of functions", *SIAM Journal on Scientific and Statistical Computing*, vol. 6, pp. 15–29, 1985.

[LIN 91] LIN F.T., KAO L.Y., HSU C.C., "Incorporating genetic algorithms into simulated annealing", *Proceedings of the 4th International Symposium on Artificial Intelligence*, Cancun, Mexico, 1991.

[MAH 91a] MAHFOUD S.W., An analysis of boltzmann tournament selection, Report 92007, Illinois Genetic Algorithms Laboratory, 1991.

[MAH 92a] MAHFOUD S.W., GOLDBERG D.E., Parallel recombinative simulated annealing: a genetic algorithm, Report 92002, University of Illinois at Urbana-Champaign, 1992.

[MAH 93a] MAHFOUD S.W., Crowding and preselection revisited, Report 92004, University of Illinois at Urbana-Champaign, 1993.

[MAH 93b] MAHFOUD S.W., Simple analytical models of genetic algorithms for multimodal function optimization, Report 93001, University of Illinois at Urbana-Champaign, 1993.

[MAH 94] MAHFOUD S.W., Population sizing for sharing methods, Report 94005, University of Illinois at Urbana-Champaign, 1994.

[MAH 84] MAHMASSANI H.S., HERMAN R., "Dynamic user equilibrium departure time and route choice on idealized traffic arterials", *Transportation Science*, vol. 18, no. 4, pp. 362–384, 1984.

[MAH 86] MAHMASSANI H.S., CHANG G.L., "Experiments with departure time choice dynamics of urban commuters", *Transportation Research*, vol. 20B, no. 4, pp. 297–320, 1986.

[MAH 91b] MAHMASSANI H.S., JAYAKRISHNAN R., "System performance and user response under real-time information in a congested traffic corridor", *Transportation Research*, vol. 25A, no. 5, pp. 293–307, 1991.

[MAH 92b] MAHMASSANI H.S., PEETA S., "System optimal dynamic assignment for electronic route guidance in a congested traffic network", *Proceedings of the 2nd International Capri Seminar on Urban Traffic Networks*, 1992.

[MAI 91] MAIGNAN G., *Le Contrôle de la Circulation Aérienne*, Presses Universitaires de France, 1991.

[MAN 90] MANNERING F.L., ABU-EISHEH S.A., ARNADOTTIR A.T., "Dynamic traffic equilibrium with discrete/continuous econometric models", *Transportation Science*, vol. 24, no. 2, pp. 105–116, 1990.

[MAR 65] MARTIN B.V., MANHEIM M.L., A research program for comparison of traffic assignment techniques, Technical report 88, Highway Research Records, 1965.

[MAR 83] MARCOTTE P., "Network optimization with continuous control science", *Transportation Science*, vol. 17, no. 21, pp. 181–197, 1983.

[MAR 85] MARCOTTE P., "A new algorithm for solving variational inequalities with application to the traffic assignment problem", *Mathematical Programming*, vol. 33, pp. 339–351, 1985.

[MAU 96] MAUGIS L., "Mathematical programming for the air traffic flow management problem with en-route capacities", *IFORS: International Federation of Operational Researchs Societies*, 1996.

[MAU 97] MAUGIS L., GOTTELAND J.B., Techniques de détermination de la capacité des secteurs de contrôle de l'espace aérien: statistiques et simulations, Technical report, Centre d'études de la navigation aérienne, 1997.

[MCQ 67] MCQUEEN J., "Some methods for classification and analysis of multivariate observations", *Proceedings of the 5th Berkeley Symposium Probability and Statistics*, University of California Press, pp. 281–297, 1967.

[MER 71] MERTZ W.L., "Review and evaluation of electronic computer traffic assignment programs", *Highways Research Board*, vol. 297, pp. 94–105, 1971.

[MER 78a] MERCHANT D.K., NEMHAUSER G.L., "A model and an algorithm for the dynamic traffic assignment problems", *Transportation Science*, vol. 12, no. 3, pp. 183–199, 1978.

[MER 78b] MERCHANT D.K., NEMHAUSER G.L., "Optimality conditions for a dynamic traffic assignment model", *Transportation Science*, vol. 12, no. 3, pp. 200–207, 1978.

[MET 53] METROPOLIS N., ROSENBLUTH A., ROSENBLUTH M., *et al.*, "Equation of chemical physics", *Journal of Mathematics Computing and Modeling*, vol. 21, pp. 1087–1092, 1953.

[MIC 91a] MICHALEWICZ Z., *Genetic Algorithms + Data Structures = Evolution Programs*, Springer-Verlag, 1992.

[MIC 91b] MICHALEWICZ Z., JANIKOV C.Z., "Handling constraints in genetic algorithms", *Proceedings of the 4th International Conference on Genetic Algorithm*, ICGA, San Diego, CA, USA, 1991.

[MIR 87] MIRCHANDANI P., SOROUCH H., "Generalized traffic equilibrium with probabilistic travel times and perception", *Transportation Science*, vol. 21, no. 7, 1987.

[MOS 89] MOSCATO P., On evolution, search, optimization, genetic algorithms and martial arts: towards memetic algorithms, Report C3P-829, Caltech Concurrent Computation Program, Caltech, 1989.

[MOS 03] MOSCATO P., COTTA C., *A Gentle Introduction to Memetic Algorithms*, Kluwer Academic, 2003.

[MUH 89] MUHLENBEIN H., "Parallel genetic algorithms, population genetics and combinatorial optimization", *Proceedings of the 3rd International Conference on Genetic Algorithms*, ICGA, Fairfax, Virginia, USA, 1989.

[NAG 84] NAGURNEY A., "Comparative tests of multimodal traffic equilibrium method", *Transportation Research B*, vol. 18B, no. 6, pp. 469–485, 1984.

[NAG 86] NAGURNEY A., "Computational comparisons of algorithms for general asymmetric traffic equilibrium problems with fixed and elastic demands", *Transportation Research B*, vol. 20, pp. 78–84, 1986.

[NAS 51] NASH J., "Non-cooperative games", *The Annals of Mathematics*, vol. 54, no. 2, pp. 286–295, 1951.

[NEL 65] NELDER J., MEAD R., "A simplex method for function minimization", *Computer Journal*, vol. 7, no. 4, pp. 308–313, 1965.

[NET 70] NETTER N., SENDER J.G., Équilibre offre-demande et tarification sur un réseau de transport, Technical report, National Institute of Transport Research, Arcueil, France, 1970.

[NGU 76] NGUYEN S., *Traffic Equilibrium Methods (A Unified Approach to Equilibrium Methods for Traffic Assignment)*, Springer, Berlin, 1976.

[NIL 80] NILSSON N.J., *Principles of Artificial Intelligence*, Tioga Publishing Company, 1980.

[NOC 80] NOCEDAL J., "Updating quasi-Newton matrices with limited storage", *Mathematics of Computation*, vol. 35, pp. 773–782, 1980.

[NOC 06] NOCEDAL J., WRIGHT S., *Numerical Optimization*, Springer, 2006.

[ODO 87] ODONI A.R., "The flow management problem in air traffic control", in ODONI A.R. *et al.* (eds), *Flow Control of Congested Networks*, ASI Series, vol. F38, NATO, pp. 269–288, 1987.

[OEI 91] OEI C.K., GOLBERG D.E., CHANG S.J., Tournament selection, niching, and the preservation of diversity, Report 91011, Illinois Genetic Algorithms Laboratory, 1991.

[OUS 99] OUSSEDIK S., DELAHAYE D., SCHOENAUER M., "Dynamic air traffic planning by genetic algorithms", *Proceedings of the 1999 International Conference on Evolutionary Computation*, Natural Selection, Inc., 1999.

[OUS 00a] OUSSEDIK S., Affectation de trafic par Algorithmes Génétiques, PhD Thesis, Centre de Mathématiques Appliquées de l'Ecole Polytechnique, 2000.

[OUS 00b] OUSSEDIK S., DELAHAYE D., SCHOENAUER M., "Flight alternative routes generator by genetic algorithms", *Proceedings of the 2000 Congress on Evolutionary Computation*, IEEE, La Jolla, California, USA, 2000.

[PAP 90] PAPAGEORGIOU M., "Dynamic modeling, assignment, and route guidance in traffic networks", *Transportation Research*, vol. 24B, no. 6, pp. 471–495, 1990.

[PET 87] PETTEY C., LEUZE M., GREFENSTETTE J., "A parallel genetic algorithm", *Proceedings of the Second International Conference on Genetic Algorithms, ICGA*, Cambridge, MA, USA, 1987.

[POW 82] POWELL W.B., SHEFFI Y., "The convergence of equilibrium algorithms with predetermined step size", *Transportation Science*, vol. 16, no. 1, pp. 45–55, 1982.

[PRA 54] PRAGER W., "Problems of traffic and transportation", *Proceedings of Symposium on Operation Research*, Kansas City, MO, USA, 1954.

[PRE 85] PREPARATA F.R., SHAMOS M.I., *Computational Geometry: An Introduction*, Springer-Verlag, 1985.

[QI 93] QI X., PALMIERI F., "The diversification role of crossover in the genetic algorithm", *Proceedings of the 5th International Conference on Genetic Algorithms, ICGA*, Urbana-Champaign, IL, USA, 1993.

[RAN 93] RAN B., BOYCE D.E., LEBLANC L.J., "A new class of instantaneous dynamic user-optimal traffic assignment models", *Operations Research*, vol. 41, no. 1, pp. 192–202, 1993.

[REE 95] REEVES C.R., *Modern Heuristic Techniques for Combinatorial Problems*, Advanced Topics in Computer Science, Chapter 4, McGraw-Hill, 1995.

[REI 89] REISS R.D., *Approximate Distributions of Order Statistics*, Springer-Verlag, 1989.

[RIC 93] RICHETTA O., ODONI A.R., "Solving optimally the static ground holding policy problem in air traffic control", *Transportation Science*, vol. 27, no. 3, pp. 228–238, 1993.

[RIC 94] RICHETTA O., ODONI A.R., "Dynamic solution to the ground-holding problem in air traffic control", *Transportation Research*, vol. 28A, no. 3, pp. 167–185, 1994.

[ROU 08] ROUSSOS G., CHALOULOS G., KYRIAKOPOULOS K., *et al.*, "Control of multiple non-holonomic air vehicles under wind uncertainty using model predictive control and decentralized navigation function", *IEEE Conference on Decision and Control*, IEEE, Cancun, Mexico, 2008.

[SAW 85] SAWARAGI Y., NAKAYAMA H., TAMINO T., *Theory of Multiobjective Optimization* (in Mathematics in Science and Engineering), Academic Press, 1985.

[SCH 78] SCHMIDT D., "A queueing analysis on the air traffic controller's workload", *IEEE Transactions on Systems, Man, and Cybernetics*, vol. 8, pp. 492–498, 1978.

[SCH 93a] SCHAFFER J.D., ESHELMAN J.E., "Designing multiplierless digital filter using genetic algorithms", *Proceedings of the 5th International Conference on Genetic Algorithm, ICGA*, Urbana-Champaign, IL, USA, 1993.

[SCH 93b] SCHOENAUER M., RONALD E., DAMOUR S., "Evolving nets for control", *Proceedings of the 6th International Conference on Neural Networks and their Industrial and Cognitive Applications*, AFIA, Nîmes, France, 1993.

[SCH 95] SCHWEFEL H.P., *Evolution and Optimum Seeking*, Wiley, New York, 1995.

[SEB 94] SEBAG M., SCHOENAUER M., RAVISÉ C., "Evolution Darwinienne ou évolution civilisée", *Journées évolution artificielle*, Ecole nationale de l'aviation civile, Toulouse, France, 1994.

[SHA 70] SHANNO D.F., "Conditioning of quasi-Newton methods for function minimization", *Mathematics of Computation*, vol. 24, pp. 647–656, 1970.

[SHA 85] SHAFFER J.D., "Multiple objective optimization with vector evaluated genetic algorithms", *Proceedings of an International Conference on Genetic Algorithm*, Pittsburgh, PA, USA, 1985.

[SHA 94] SHAFAREVICH I.R., *Basic Algebraic Geometry*, Springer-Verlag, 1994.

[SHE 82] SHEFFI Y., HALL R., DAGANZO C., "On the estimation of the multinomial probit model", *Transportation Research A*, vol. 16A, no. 5, pp. 447–456, 1982.

[SHE 85] SHEFFI Y., *Urban Transportation Networks*, Prentice Hall, 1985.

[SIR 87] SIRAG D.J., WEISSER P.T., "Towards a unified thermodynamic genetic operator", *Proceedings of the 2nd International Conference on Genetic Algorithm*, ICGA, Cambridge, MA, USA, 1987.

[SKO 90] SKORIN-KAPOV J., "Tabu search applied to the quadratic assignment problem", *ORSA Journal on Computing*, vol. 2, pp. 3–45, 1990.

[SMA 82] SMALL K., "The scheduling of consumer activities work trips", *American Economic Review*, vol. 72, pp. 467–479, 1982.

[SMI 79] SMITH M.J., "The existence, uniqueness and stability of traffic equilibria", *Transportation Research B*, vol. 13B, pp. 295–304, 1979.

[SMI 81] SMITH M.J., "The existence of an equilibrium solution to the traffic assignment problem when there junction interactions", *Transportation Research B*, vol. 15B, no. 6, pp. 443–451, 1981.

[SMI 83] SMITH M.J., "An algorithm for solving asymmetric equilibrium problems with a cost-flow function", *Transportation Research B*, vol. 17B, no. 5, pp. 365–371, 1983.

[SMI 93a] SMITH M.J., "A new dynamic traffic model and the existence and calculation of dynamic user equilibria on congested capacity-constrained road networks", *Transportation Research B*, vol. 27B, no. 1, pp. 49–63, 1993.

[SMI 93b] SMITH R.E., PERELSON A.S., FORREST S., "Searching for diverse, cooperative populations with genetic algorithms", *Evolutionary Computation*, vol. 1, no. 2, pp. 127–149, 1993.

[SOR 85] SOROUSH H., MIRCHANDANI P.B., Traffic equilibrium in a stochastic network, Technical report TRS 8402, Laboratory of Large Scale System, Electrical, Computer and Systems Engineering, Rensselaer Polytechnic Institute, Troy, NY, 1985.

[SOR 90] SOROUSH H., MIRCHANDANI P.B., "The stochastic multicommodity flow problem", *Networks*, vol. 20, pp. 121–155, 1990.

[SRI 95] SRINIVAS N., DEB K., "Multi-objective function optimization using non-dominated sorting genetic algorithms", *Evolutionary Computation*, vol. 2, no. 3, pp. 221–248, 1995.

[SRI 01] SRIDHAR B., SETH K.S., GRABBE S., "Airspace complexity and its application in air traffic management", *Proceedings of the 2nd USA/EUROPE ATM R&D Seminar*, Eurocontrol/FAA, Santa Fe, NM, USA, 2001.

[SYS 89] SYSWERDA G., "Uniform crossover in genetic algorithms", *Proceedings of the 3rd International Conference on Genetic Algorithms*, ICGA, Fairfax, Virginia, USA, 1989.

[TAT 93] TATE D.M., SMITH A.E., "Expected allele coverage and the role of mutation in genetic algorithms", *Proceedings of the 5th International Conference on Genetic Algorithms*, ICGA, Urbana-Champaign, IL, USA, 1993.

[TER 93] TERRAB M., ODONI A.R., "Strategic flow management for air traffic control", *Operations Research*, vol. 41, no. 1, pp. 138–152, 1993.

[TOS 97] TOSIC V., BABIC O., CANGALOVIC M., *et al.*, "Some model algorithms for en-route air traffic flow management faculty transport", *Proceedings of the US Europe ATM Seminar*, Eurocontrol-FAA, Saclay, France, 1997.

[TSI 86] TSITSIKLIS J., BERTSEKAS D.P., "Distributed asynchronous optimal routing in data networks", *IEEE Transactions on Automatic Control*, vol. 38, 1987, pp. 215–222, 1986.

[TUA 76] TUAN P.L., PROCTER H.S., COULURIS G.J., Advanced productivity analysis methods for air traffic control operation, Technical report, Stanford Research Institute, Menlo Park, CA, December 1976.

[UNG 93] UNGER R., MOULT J., "A genetic algorithm for 3D protein folding simulations", *Proceedings of the 5th International Conference on Genetic Algorithm*, *ICGA*, Urbana-Champaign, IL, USA, 1993.

[VAN 79] VAN VLIET D., DOW P.D.C., "Capacity-restrained road assignment", *Traffic Engineering and Control*, vol. 20, no. 6, pp. 296–305, 1979.

[VAN 87] VAN VLIET D., "The Frank-Wolfe algorithm for equilibrium traffic assignment viewed as a variational inequality", *Transportation Research*, vol. 21, no. 1, pp. 87–89, 1987.

[VIL 84] VILLIERS J., Contribution à une théorie du système de controle en route et ses perspectives d'évolution, Technical report, French Civil Aviation Authority, Paris, France, August 1984.

[VON 66] VON FALKENHAUSEN H., "Traffic assignment by a stochastic model", *Proceedings of the 4th International Conference on Operational Research*, MIT, Cambridge, MA, USA, 1966.

[VRA 94a] VRANAS P.B.M., BERTSIMAS D., ODONI A.R., "The multi-airport ground-holding problem in air traffic control", *Operations Research*, vol. 42, no. 2, pp. 249–261, 1994.

[VRA 94b] VRANAS P.B.M., BERTSIMAS D., ODONI A.R., "Dynamic ground-holding policies for a network of airports", *Transportation Science*, vol. 28, no. 4, pp. 275–291, 1994.

[VYT 90a] VYTHOULKAS P.C., "A dynamic stochastic assignment model for the analysis of general networks", *Transportation Research*, vol. 24B, no. 6, pp. 453–469, 1990.

[VYT 90b] VYTHOULKAS P.C., Two models for predicting dynamic stochastic equilibria in urban transportation networks, Technical report TSU/REF 532, National Technical Information Service, Springfield, VA, 1990.

[WAR 52] WARDROP J.C., "Some theoretical aspects of road traffic research", *Proceedings of the Institution of Civil Engineers*, vol. 2, no. 1, pp. 325–378, 1952.

[WAT 93] WATABE H., OKINO N., "A study on genetic shape design", *Proceedings of the 5th International Conference on Genetic Algorithm, ICGA*, Urbana-Champaign, IL, USA, 1993.

[WID 89] WIDMER M., HERTZ A., "A new method for the flow sequencing problem", *European Journal of Operations Research*, vol. 41, pp. 186–193, 1989.

[WIE 90] WIE B.W., FRIESZ T.L., TOBIN R.L., "Dynamic user optimal traffic assignment on congested multi-destination networks", *Transportation Research*, vol. 24B, no. 6, pp. 431–442, 1990.

[WIE 94] WIE B.W., TOBIN R.L., FRIESZ T.L., "The augmented Lagrangian method for solving dynamic network traffic assignment models in discrete time", *Transportation Science*, vol. 28, no. 3, pp. 204–220, 1994.

[WIE 95] WIE B.W., TOBIN R.L., FRIESZ T.L., *et al.*, "A discrete time, nested cost operator approach to the dynamic network user equilibrium problem", *Transportation Science*, vol. 29, no. 1, pp. 79–92, 1995.

[WRI 91a] WRIGHT A.H., "Genetic algorithms for real parameter optimization", *Proceedings of the Foundation of Genetic Algorithms, FOGA*, Bloomington, Indiana, USA, 1991.

[YIN 91] YIN X., GERMAY N., "Investigations on solving the load flow problem by genetic algorithms", *Electric Power Systems Research*, vol. 22, pp. 151–163, 1991.

[YIN 93] YIN X., GERMAY N., "A fast genetic algorithm with sharing scheme using cluster analysis methods in multimodal function optimization", *Proceedings of the Artificial Neural Nets and Genetic Algorithms*, Innsbruck, Austria, 1993.

[ZAN 94] ZANNI R., A methodology for airspace organization, Technical report, Air Navigation Research Center, Toulouse France, April 1994.

[ZAW 87] ZAWACK D.J., THOMPSON G.L., "A dynamic space-time network flow model for city traffic congestion", *Transportation Science*, vol. 21, no. 3, pp. 153–162, 1987.

[ZEN 91] ZENIOS S.A., "Network based models for air traffic control", *European Journal of Operational Research*, vol. 50, pp. 166–178, 1991.

[ZHI 91] ZHIGLJAVSKY A.A., *Theory of Global Random Search*, Kluwer Academic Publishers, 1991.

[ZIT 99] ZITZLER E., THIELE L., "Multi-objective evolutionary algorithms: a comparative case study and the strength pareto approach", *IEEE Transaction on Evolutionary Computation*, vol. 3, no. 4, pp. 257–271, 1999.

Index